SECOND ED.

WORDS

YOU NEED TO KNOW

&

FACTS

**You're Embarrassed
Not to Know**

Over **5,000** Entries

By

Lee G. Lovett
&
Lee G. Lovett III

TABLE OF CONTENTS

DEDICATION

To my grandchildren (one of whom, Lee III, joins me as co-author of the 2nd Edition) and one great-grandchild, shown (left-to-right) from oldest to youngest:

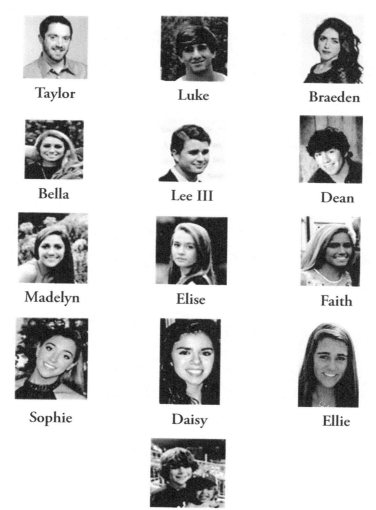

Taylor   Luke   Braeden

Bella   Lee III   Dean

Madelyn   Elise   Faith

Sophie   Daisy   Ellie

Cal & Moore

WORDS YOU NEED TO KNOW
And FACTS You're Embarrassed Not to Know

FOREWORD

Why Read (and Master) This Book?

The author (an indefatigable reader, a long-retired attorney and co-founder of roughly 100 still-operating companies and author of seven books (www.leeglovett.com) created this book over a span of 50+ years, extracting words from reading a book or so a week, often classics. There is a surprising amount of overlap among the words that are so artfully employed by The Great Writers. You might say that these are "the elevated words most commonly used by the educated", perhaps because they read each other's work. *Yet, most of us won't know, much less learn, these "words of the educated", not unless we make an overt effort to **find** them and **learn** them.* In addition, sensing his own inadequacies, the author added "facts that are embarrassing not to now". So, there are seven reasons to read and master this book:

(1) Better vocabularies are widely equated with more intelligence; yet, *few of us do anything much to augment or distinguish our vocabularies.*

(2) Dictionaries are too big to memorize, and *we have no idea which words to learn.* (All dictionaries are not equal, and definitions offer

vary disturbingly. Online searches often pull up weak or even misleading definitions. The author prefers the widely acclaimed Merriam Webster's Collegiate Dictionary and the Oxford Unabridged [20 volume] Dictionary.)

(3) Most vocabulary books contain *words that are too simple* and they generally offer a *only a few hundred to 1,000 or so words* versus the 5,000 entries that are offered in this book.

(4) The *words herein are those used by some of history's greatest classical and contemporary writers.* (However, some VERY SIMPLE words are included, too, for various reasons: As signposts to direct the reader to elevated synonyms, antonyms, confusingly similar words and/or to highlight the correct pronunciation; a classic example of common miss-pronunciation is "divisive". It is NOT "dih-VIE-sive", but, rather, "dih-VIH-sive". The mistake is becoming so prevalent, that common usage may eventually force the inclusion of both pronunciations even in higher caliber dictionaries, but, until then, let's pronounce it correctly.)

(5) The definitions herein present "families" of words with *elevated synonyms, antonyms and distinguish confusingly similar words –* going far beyond the helpful but simplistic offerings so often produced by Google searches.

(6) This book offers many *KEY FACTS that most of us are embarrassed not to know*, but do not know. These facts are a joy to learn and are fun to use as party games, being far more academic than the run-of-the-mill Trivial Pursuits questions. Our children and grandchildren need to know this data; and we-parents need it for career advancement and, most importantly, for self-respect –

plus, it's flat-fun to learn such facts. Why these rudimentary and fascinating facts aren't taught in school is beyond this writer's ken.

(7) Finally, as early as age thirty, we need to begin to *expand our learning skills* (as they wane fast, once we leave school); even that early, we need to begin to *fight memory loss*. This book offers *a life-long memory exercise program*. In paperback, this book is approximately 350 pages, about 300 pages of which is comprised of word-definitions and key facts. The author recommends that, after making a solid effort to memorize all of the entries once, the book be reviewed at the rate of 1/50th (about six pages) per week, indefinitely. Once the reader has learned each page once, the review should take only 15 minutes or so per page. This can make a rewarding, brief memory exercise right before the night's sleep. Indeed, if we would fight memory loss, dementia, Alzheimer's and other mind-related aging problems, *we need to exercise our mind-muscles every day*, and memorization, and active use of what we learn, are marvelously healing methods of "feeding our minds" and delaying and even mitigating the issues of senescence. Instead of acquiescing to the ongoing literal shrinking of our brain-mass (a medical fact) and the brain cells responsible for memory, why not FIGHT these attritions? Rather than retreat, retreat, retreat, as is the wont of age, let us charge, charge and, then, charge some more. You may remember the beloved poet, song-writer Bob Dylan ("The answer my friend is blowin' in the wind"), who sagaciously admonished, "Rage, rage, rage, against the dying of the light." Now, let us learn, learn and LEARN some more – and smile as we *feed our minds with nourishing and valuable data*.

Some Basics About Words

How many words are there in the English language? No one claims to know the number of words in any language. There are only guesstimates. The English language, more than any other, is a *hybrid of many languages*, and, predictably, has the most words (about 300,000 words in the Oxford Unabridged 20-Volume Dictionary but some scholars assert as many as one million counting variations, which is roughly *twice as many words as guesstimates for Chinese and four times as many as Japanese, Italian, Spanish, French, Russian, the Slavic tongues, etc.).* The average person can only comfortably use about 100,000 words, and probably around 10,000 on a day-to-day basis, a fraction of those available, and most of our work-a-day words are embarrassingly pedestrian – and boring. This book of "Words You Need to Know" includes about 5,000 entries-worth-knowing (words and facts) that the author finds embarrassing not to know, the preponderance of which, as above noted, stem from a long lifetime of reading classic literature, philosophy and financial-related texts.

Words, like people and countries, have histories and growth cycles. They evolve over time; *meanings often overlap and change; and, dictionaries often disagree.* Various editions of *Webster's Unabridged Dictionary, Merriam-Webster's Collegiate Dictionary,* and *Oxford Unabridged 20 Volumes* have been the main sources for this book. Google now offers definitions from multiple sources, just one click away, but Google's offerings (although very helpful for speedy reference) lean in the direction of slang and some of its sources opt for *misleadingly* broad, or even erroneous, "synonyms". This author prefers the more traditional Webster's' Unabridged, Merriam Webster's Collegiate and Oxford Dictionaries. Over time, usage alters definitions, and this list was *50 years in the making*, but, for the most part, the definitions herein will remain valid for eons to come. Definitions of broader terms (e.g., existentialism, yoga, zen, stoic, spacetime) reflect composites from myriad sources far beyond dictionaries.

This book avoids words that are not useful in routine conversations. Even though this book offers sophisticated words, it eschews words that can't be easily used in day-to-day communications, and which, therefore, won't enhance the speaker-writer's ability to communicate with more precision, variety and elegance — for those are the goals of this book, all of which will enhance one's self-respect. After mastering this book, the reader can keep this list alive and fresh by keeping it alongside whatever books he/she is reading, *adding his/ her own appendix of new words or sharpening definitions.* As above noted, this book also contains some very simple words, which you already know, but they are there to steer you (and especially younger readers) to more elevated words that are closely related to the simple words that are included.

What is the best and fastest way to learn the words in this book? *Learn to identify the words from the definitions.* This has proved to be the *best method of memorizing and remembering — and, hence, of stimulating use of the words.*

Synonyms and related words here abound. Much more than a typical dictionary, this Word list offers synonyms and related words, including homonyms (those that sound-alike or are spelled alike but which have different meanings). So, when you learn a word here, you'll learn many of its "cousins", hence "families" of words, which will *enable you to express the same thoughts with a variety of similar words, which will* *make your communications more varied and interesting to other*s (and to yourself). The abbreviation **"cp", meaning "compare", is, thus, the most important abbreviation in this book. See the abbreviations** as described below. Don't mistake "cp" for "syn" (synonym) or "ant" (antonym), lest you teach yourself the wrong definitions.

Roots are essential. No one can learn "all" the words. The greatest weakness in most people's vocabularies is the relative paucity roots. Knowing prefixes, suffixes and other roots of words (most of which come from Greek and Latin) enables one to decipher many words not previously encountered. *Roots can have multiple, sometimes disparate meanings, because they may come from multiple languages and are used differently in each.* Roots also define the origins/histories of words, which is interesting and helps one remember the words. Thus, *to know origins/histories, roots, prefixes and suffixes is to know (and grow to love) words.* It took me years to appreciate this fact and to begin to include them in my list, which has become this word book.

Words expand the mind, as tools and materials enable a builder to construct a better building. That is, the more words that we know, the better and more precisely we can *think*. Words, then, expand our intelligence. Thus, *words not only elevate our communication-skills, they add vital additional tools of the mind, thus expanding our ability to think more clearly.* The less words that we know, the more primitive our thoughts, actions and personas. So, *words not only imply erudition, and possibly intelligence, words are likely synonymous with erudition and intelligence.* So, dear reader, if you would garner respect from your peers, co-workers, bosses, underlings, children, friends and the world, and enhance your personal lexicon: Learn exciting new words and begin using them ASAP.

Words are fun – and lovable. Knowing words is simply fun, and the more words you learn and use and review and continue to use more and more, the more you will grow to love words. Learning roots and word-histories personalizes words and makes them your friends. You can know and enjoy little secrets about words, secrets unknown by most of your friends. You'll join The Word Society; that is, you'll become a lay etymologist, joining other lovers of words. It's a wonderfully elite, if informal, group.

Learning and using the words. It may take you, perhaps, a few hundred hours to go through this book once and learn its very approximate 5,000 entries, which allows a few minutes minutes per entry, but, when you finish, you're going to feel so much better educated.

Testing Yourself. When you've finished learning one page, test yourself two ways: First, cover the definitions and just look at the words and define them. Second, and much more important, then cover the words and just look at the definitions and name the words. The latter method is the best way to make sure that you will actually USE the words. *If you can't name the words BY THEIR DEFINITIONS, you won't use the words*, period.

Reviewing the words. Going through this book one time, and learning the words and factual-entries ONE TIME, won't cut it. I review all the words in this book once a year. I review roughly 1/50th of it every week. It will not take as long to review as it did to learn. Each review will go faster. A couple hours per week should do it very nicely – and remember, it's FUN, fun to learn, fun to know, fun to use, fun to be different, fun to be "smarter" (at least than you were); it just makes your life more fun!

Remember Your Secondary Goal: To Improve Your Memory, Exercise Your Memory, and Keep It Sharp. This book is a fantastic tool to improve your memory and fight memory loss. *Medical doctors say, "Learn another language to improve your memory." **Here's a better alternative**:*

LEARN YOUR OWN LANGUAGE

WHILE IMPROVING:

your memory,

your intellect,

your peers' opinion of you,

and

your self-resect.

L et's now turn to abbreviations and other essential tools and methods that you need to know to jump-start the elevation of your vocabulary.

GUIDELINES FOR USE

ABBREVIATIONS
used throughout to save space and your valuable time

This book teaches words IN GROUPS or "families". We want you to learn word-concepts and roots, and many *words will suddenly be burned into your mind in families*, and your mind will begin to draw more exacting and more interesting words from your memory bank, and they'll begin to fall off your tongue effortlessly. To do this, we must use many abbreviations within our definitions.

The author has done his best to minimize the abbreviations (or coding), BUT be on notice: ***IF you don't learn these abbreviations, you're going to be lost in this book.*** You'll confuse synonyms with sound-alikes and antonyms and related words. You don't do "an assignment" without reading the instructions, and the abbreviations are your instructions here. LEARN THE ABBREVIATIONS and refer back to them until you know them. Some of these are painfully obvious. The author does not wish to insult anyone's intelligence, but, rather, simply and kindly to avoid misunderstandings and misguidance.

"a": Refers to adverbs AND adjectives, because all adverbs end in "ly" and are, thus, easy to identify; all the others, obviously, are adjectives.

"abbrv." for abbreviation

"aka" for "also known as", which is another way of saying "synonym"

"A.D. and C.E. refers to Anno Domini (Year of Our Lord or Christ's birth); CE stand for Common Era and means the same thing; some scholars us A.D., but, increasingly, the "politically correct" term is "C.E."; depending on the source quoted, this book uses both.

"ant" for antonym

"Arch" for archaic

"BYA" means billion years ago; **"YA"** means years ago

"B.C. or B.C.E" mean before Christ and before Common Era;

"c." means "circa", which is Lat. for "approximately"

"CE", again, means Common Era, which dates from Christ's birth

"cp" for compare (*by far the most frequently used abbreviation*)

"i.e." for "that is"

"e.g." and "ex." for "for example"

"esp" for especially

"KYA" means thousand years ago

"Leg." means definition as used in law

"Med." means definition as used in medicine

"MYA" means million years ago

"n" for noun

"syn" for synonym; "c." for circa/approximately;

in that "family" without searching for them elsewhere in the book (or beyond the book).

Examples of the usage of words *are only given where they seem to be needed.* The goal is not to write a large book or to insert unnecessary clutter; it is to identify and define elevated words and the family of words associated with them, and to get you where you want to go ASAP.

Tests. *There are no tests in this book.* The author assumes that the reader is student, of any age, but one who has developed his/her own methods of memorizing and of testing his memory. As such, no space will be wasted on tests.

Simple Words Sometimes Inserted to Point to More Sophisticated Words. For example, the words "abjure, foreswear, gainsay, repudiate," generally mean "deny"; each is listed individually, and even "deny" is listed individually, as the less learned user might look for it first. *The point is to try to make it easy for users learn and include more interesting words, which have very similar meanings.* When the author began to ask his grandchildren to learn this book, he found it helpful to insert some simpler words to expedited the learning of their more interesting "cousins".

Repetition: There is a lot of repetition, and it is *intentional*; it is part of the learning process, as the author sees it. Also, some words need to be continuously associated with another, as this tends to cement them into the mind, and it also facilitates finding "the right word". Example from the book:

> **descant/discant** -n- <u>Music</u>: a counterpoint or highest part sung above the melody; <u>Other</u>: *tedious & protracted talk;*

Lat. investigation; cp. disquisition (a *formal* discourse, often written / colloquy / dissertation); dialectics (reasoning); banter / badinage / doggerel (comic talk); natter / chatter / palaver / prattle (idle or silly talk); persiflage (flippant conversation); polemics (debate).

Every one of the words in the list under "descant" should be separately listed. They probably aren't, but most likely are. Again, such repetition helps one learn, remember and find the best words. So, don't let the repetition bother you; be grateful for it and capitalize on it.

Not a Dictionary. This book makes no attempt to be a dictionary. It is an effort to help the reader find more and better words to substitute for the simpler ones that most use. This books makes the decision for you: Which words, from massive dictionaries, will I find most useful to learn and use? Of course, this book must exclude most of the thousands of options, but, if you will learn the words AND ROOTS of the words here selected for you, it is respectfully submitted that you will be WELL on your way to understanding a VERY high percentage of the words that you encounter for the first time in reading the most elevated (non-scientific) texts.

So, now, you have mastered the abbreviations and guidelines above, and you're ready to begin.

Prefixes

There are countless prefixes, suffixes and roots worthy of knowing. The list of Prefixes that follows provides some of those most commonly used.

"a" -prefix[1]- "without" or "to".

ab -prefix- from; away; off.

ac/ad/af/ag/al/ap/as -prefixes- meanings: to; before; near ; see "al" as a suffix.

acr/acer -prefixes- Meaning "sharp", from Lat.

ad -prefix- to or toward or in the direction of.

al -prefix/suffix- as a prefix means "the"; when used as a *suffix* means "relating to"; ex. functional; see ax / ad.

ambi -prefix- Lat. for "on both sides"; e.g. ambidextrous (right and left handed).

an/ap -prefix- Lat. to or by; cp. prefix "a".

ana -prefix- Gk. up, on, toward, part; cp. an/ano (back, against); see anagram, anonym.

andro -prefix- Gr. male; ant. meno (prefix for female).

ante [ant-tee] -prefix- before; e.g. antebellum; cp. prefix-anti (against).

apo -prefix- from.

---

1 **Prefixes, suffixes and roots** enable us to understand many words that we have not seen or heard. While roots are sometimes misleading, on balance, they will expand one's ability to decipher unfamiliar words exponentially.

---

arch -prefix- ancient.

aud -prefix- Lat. to hear; e.g., audible; audition.

aut/auto -prefix- meaning "self" or "same".

bene -prefix- Lat. for "good" or "well".

bi -prefix- two (examples; biceps; bicameral; bicuspid; biennial; bifocals; bitheism.

caco -prefix- Gk. bad.

cant -prefix- Lat. from verb cantare, to sing.

carn -prefix- Lat. for flesh or meat.

cata -prefix- Gk. "down".

ced -prefix- Lat. from v. cedere, meaning to yield.

com/ con -prefix- with, together, joined, joint (Lat. OFr, ME).

con -prefix- a variant of "com"; with, together, join; a/k/a "sym".

cur -prefix- Lat. care for; e.g. procure (obtain); secure (make safe); curator (one who cares for things like museums, zoos, churches).

de -prefix- root for "away", "down", from, of, remove, reduce; e.g. deactivate.

dec / deca -prefix- ten; Exs. decathalon; decade; Decalogue.

dia -prefix- through; across.

dis -prefix- opposite; apart; not; e.g., dissimilar.

dys/dis -prefix- Gk. "bad"/difficult; see dystopia; dyspeptic; dysfunctional.

"e" -prefix- missing; absent.

en or em -prefix- to put into or onto.

epi -prefix- on/upon/after/*the last/final*; see epicenter; epilogue; epitaph.

---

equ -prefix- Lat. equal; exs. equable; equinox.

eu -prefix- Gk. well/good/true; see eugenics, euphemism, euphoria, eulogy.

ex -prefix- *out*; from; away; not; former/previous; Lat.

homeo -prefix- like; similar.

hos -prefix- Lat. for host; cp. hospital, hospice, hostel, hoteliers, house.

hyper -prefix- above; cp. hypo / sub (below).

hypo -prefix- below or *under* / sub; e.g. hypodermis/under the skin.

icon -prefix- Gk. for "image"; e.g. icon (religious *idol*, emblem, symbol or someone held in the highest esteem); iconic (anything relating to an icon).

idio -prefix- Lat. peculiar, hence personal

im -prefix- "without"; beyond; syn. prefix "a"; confusingly, "im" may mean "not" or "in" (e.g. import).

in/un (root) -prefix- "not"; sometimes "without"; syn. for "im".

inter -prefix- between; *among*.

kilo -prefix- means 1,000; e.g. kilobyte (1,024 bytes).

mal -prefix- Lat. bad; see malevolent; malicious (intending to cause pain or great injury).

mis -prefix- means hate or bad.

mon -prefix- British variant of man.

mono -prefix- "one"; ex. monocle (one lens); monogamy (one marriage); monologue (speech by one), etc.

ne/neo -prefix- Gr. new.

ob -prefix- in the way, against, toward; ex. obnoxious (toward noxa-harm = offensive)

---

oli -prefix- means "few"; cp. poly (many).

om -prefix- about [remember that different languages often give varied meanings to roots].

on -prefix- subatomic particle, basic component of life; this root has many less-used meanings.

ortho -prefix- Gk. straight.

osteo -prefix- bone.

pac -prefix- Lat. for agree or peace; e.g. pact (agreement).

pan -prefix- Gr. for "all"; syn. omni; e.g. __demic; __oply; __acea; __gea.

para -prefix- *beside*; alongside; e.g. paralegal, paramedic, paradigm; parallel.

phil/philo -prefix- Gr. loving; love.

port -prefix- from Lat. verb, to <u>carry</u>; e.g. portable, porter; deport.

prim -prefix- first; e.g. primate; primal; primer.

pro -prefix- for, forward, first.

prop -prefix- Lat. "own"; e.g. proprietary (ownership); propriety (being proper).

psyche -prefix- the mind; e.g., psychiatrist (mind doctor).

psych/o -prefix- Gr. breath, life, soul, mind, mental processes.

re -prefix- *again*; backwards; back.

retro -prefix- La. "back"; e.g. retroactive (take effect in past); retrofit (to fix, update something).

strat -prefix- Lat. for "spread"; e.g. stratum (layer); strategize (stretch thought).

sub (root) -prefix- Lat. below, beneath, under; *this root can be misleading* (e.g. sublimate).

sym or syn -prefix- along with; together; at the same time; see synthesize (combine).

tri/tres -prefix- three; e.g. triad (group of three); trilogy (three stories); triangle, trio, tripod.

un/in -prefix- not.

uni -prefix- one; e.g. uniform; unify (bring to one); unicycle (one wheel); union (joining two parties); unilateral (one sided); unique (the only one); unison (together).

ur -prefix- Gr. thoroughly.

urb -prefix- Lat. "city".

viv -prefix- Lat. to live or be alive; e.g. vivacious (positive exuberance).

Part I

WORDS
YOU NEED TO KNOW

"A"

abash/ed [ah-<u>bashed</u>] -v- to *embarrass*, humiliate, disconcert; to + bash; to be so; cp. denigrate; ant. unabashed; Ex. He was abashed to admit his oversight.

abase [ah-<u>base</u>] -v- to lower in *rank or esteem*; Lat. low; M.E.; cp. debase (lower in character); efface (erase). Ex. Her comment abased his work.

abdicate [ab-dick-cate] -v- to *relinquish power* formally; ab-away + dicare = proclaim.

aberration/ant [ab-bur-a-tion/ahnt] -n/a- a *deviation from the norm* or expected course; cp. anomaly (irregular). Ex. Trump was an aberration among politicians.

ab inito [ab-in-<u>ee</u>-toe] -Lat. phrase- from the beginning ; from + beginning; Ex. He read the text, ab initio; cp. initial (first); initiate (begin); initiative (stimulus).

abject -a- sunk to the bottom; off + throw; Ex. He lived in abject poverty.

abjure/**abjuration** -v/n- to *retract / disavow /* foreswear / *renounce /* recant, esp. *under oath*; cp. gainsay (deny or contradict but not under oath); rescind (formal cancellation); repudiate (challenge or rebut); ant. adjure / avow / swear under oath; Ex. He took the oath and abjured as follows . . ."

abort/ive [ah-<u>bort</u>]² -v/a- to abandon. Ex. They aborted ship.

---

2 **Pronunciation** Guide: Words in brackets [ ] provide phonetic pronunciation; syllables deserving emphasis are in **bold**, both are primarily for the benefit of others who have expressed an interest in my etymological affinities and idiosyncrasies.

abhor/ent [ab-hoar-ent] -v/n- curse, damn; cp.[3] rue (regret or find repugnant / extremely distasteful); animus (hatred) / execrate & imprecate (hate); deprecate (disapprove). Ex. She abhorred the day that she met him.

ablution [ab-blue-tion] -n- washing of one's body; from + wash. Ex. He completed his ablutions.

abnegation [ab-neg-gay-tion] -n- *self-denial; from + negate; abstinence;* Jainism; Lat. to negate; cp. abstemious (temperate in eating/drink-ing); asceticism (self-*control*); stoicism (indifference to pain/pleasure; see Serenity Prayer). Ex. He lived in abnegation of his deficiencies.

abolition/ism [ah-<u>bol</u>-lih-shun] -n- act of *abolishing* something; the anti-slavery movement.

abominable -a- deserving hatred / execrable / enmity; cp. imprecate (to hate); odious (causing hatred); invidious (envy). Ex. The abominable snowman tortured the civilians.

abrade/abrasive -v/a- to rub away; erode; wear down; irritate; Lat. to scrape away by friction; cp. expunge (erase).

abridge [ah-<u>bridge</u>] -v- abbreviate / apostrophize / condense / shorten / truncate. Ex. The book is abridged.

abstemious [ab-<u>stem</u>-ee-us] -a/n- *abstaining; temperate* in eating / drinking; not self-indulgent; cp. abnegation (self-denial); asceticism (self-control); stoicism (indifference to pain or pleasure); Jainism (a nontheistic belief system embodying all of the foregoing); Ex. He was abstemious, ascetic and stoic.

---

3 "cp", again, is the most frequently used and is an abbreviation for "compare". Do not confuse it with syn for synonym.

abstruse [ab-strooce] -a- difficult to comprehend; obscure / Delphic; recondite; inscrutable (unfathomable); cp. ambiguous (indefinite/ vague); arcane (understood by a few); esoteric (understood by specially trained); enigmatic (puzzling); ineffable (indescribable).

abundance -n- an *ample* amount; a copious quantity; syns. plentitude / profusion / repletion; cp. plethora / superfluity / surfeit (excess).

abyss [ah-biss] -n- deep chasm; M.E. w/o + bottom.

a cappella [ah-kah-pell-ah] -n- *without music*; root: "to + the church".

accede [ack-seed] -v- yield to a request; cp. capitulate.

accolade [ak-co-lade] -n- expression of approval; approbation / plaudits (formal praise).

accord [ak-cord] -n/v/a- an agreement or harmony between people; to agree; to be in agreement with someone or thing; syn. concord.

accost [ah-cost] -v- to greet, approach, or speak to.

accoutrement [ah-coot-trah-mant] -n- additional items of dress or equipment.

acerbic [ah-sir-bic] -a- *sour or bitter* in *taste, mood or expression*; syn. acrid / acidic / caustic / vitriolic.

acme -n- Gr. the point of utmost attainment; apex; / apotheosis / capstone; epitome / pinnacle / Horeb height / vertex / zenith; cp. apogee (most distant); solstice (sun's or any highest point).

acolyte [ack-oh-light] -n- an attendant or follower, esp. to a priest; cp. servitor; valet; varlet.

acrid/acrimony/ious -n/a- *bitterness*; acerbic / acidic / caustic / vitriolic (usually used re a scathing rebuke).

acronym [ack-crow-nim] -n- a word formed with the initials of a name; e.g. WAC, WOP; cp.

---

acrostic [ah-<u>cross</u>-tic] (word formed by 1ˢᵗ letters of each line of verse of poetry, slogan, etc) ; **anagram** (rearranged letters to form new word: pea to ape, god to dog); **anonym** (name written backwards, ttevol for Lovett, dog for God); **eponym** (name based on a place: Romulus / Tex); **homonym** (words that *sound* alike OR *mean* the same thing and/or may be spelled the same or differently, e.g., but//butt//butt); **pseudonym** (a false name, such as a nom de plume, an assumed name for authors or actors).

acrophobia [ak-crow-<u>phobe</u>- ee-ah] -n- fear of heights; root: high + fear; see phobe.

actuate -v- to cause something to operate; hence to *stimulate to action.*

adage [add-edge] -n- a short ***RULE***: aphorism, apothegm, maxim, tenet (of an org), e.g. "Neither a lender nor a borrower be." Cp. a ***TRUTH***: axiom; epigram; proverb; ("A stitch in time saves nine."); epigram (short, witty and often *paradoxical truth*, "Too soon old, too late smart"); trope (figure of speech or cliché, e.g., "Time is money").

addle/d -a/v- *confused*; rotten; root-filth; Ex. His ideas are addled.

adduce -v- to *cite as an <u>example</u> or proof* in support of an argument; cp. *deduce* (to conclude as result of argument).

adept -a- *skilled*; adroit / deft / expert / proficient; cp. dexterous (skilled esp. with hands).

adjudicate -v- to settle a case by judicial procedure; Lat. to + court.

adjure/ation -v/n- solemn oath; swear under oath / **avow**; ant. abjure (recant / foreswear / gainsay)

adherent -n- one who supports a particular party, person or set of ideas; near syns. advocate, apostle, disciple, devotee, partisan, votary; cp. proponent / protagonist (one who advances same);

ad hoc -Lat. term- to this [case or situation]; esp., case-by-case; ex. "Make _____ judgments."

ad hominem -a- Lat. "to the man"; appealing to *personal* interests or emotions or prejudices, as in "an ad hominine argument"; tendentious (promoting a cause or tendency).

admonish [add-mon-ish] -v- to *advise OR reprove mildly* or kindly but seriously; Lat. to warn; exhort; cp. entreat, beseech (urge) and importune (beg).

ad nauseam -Lat. term- to the point of nausea; cp. emetic (causing vomiting).

adonis [ah-<u>don</u>-iss] -n- one who is *handsome*, like a mythological Greek god.

adulterous -a- breach of marital vows; infidelity; cp. perfidy (breach of trust); cuckold.

adumbrate [ah-<u>dum</u>-brate] -v- to give a *sketchy outline; foreshadow.*

adroit/ly [ah-droit] -a- adept / deft; skilled; cp. dexterous (with hands or mind).

advent [add-vent] -n- the *arrival* of an important person or a *turning point*; Ex. Now is the advent of our new government; cp. event.

advert/isement -v/n- to *call to attention*; to refer to; Lat. to turn towards; cp. revert (return to).

aegis [aa-<u>ee</u>-gis] -n- the *shield* of Zeus; *protection*; cp. patronage; sponsorship.

aeronautic/al -a- relating to aircraft; root: flight + navigation.

aesthete/esthete [<u>ess</u>-theet] -n- one who loves the arts (music, poetry, painting, etc.).

affable [<u>aff</u>-able] -a- agreeable / amiable / congenial / cordial / friendly.

affect [ah-<u>fect</u>] -v- to put on a *pretense* of; to feign or *pretend*; cp. effect (cause a result); Ex. He affects great knowledge.

affiliate/tion -n/v- one who is *connected* to another; one who does so; an *alliance.*

aficionado [ah-<u>fee</u>-shun-ah/\-do] -n- one devoted to pursuit of something (esp, art); syn. devotee.

affix [ah-fix] -n/v- an attachment; to + attach; cp. prefix (attachment at beginning); suffix (same at end).

agape [ah-gape] -a/n- *wide open*; cp. aperture (an opening).

agate [<u>ah</u>-git] -n- a child's marble with irregular clouding; a tool made of same.

agnostic [ag-noss-tic] -n- one who does not know; Gr. a = without + gnosis = knowledge.

agog [ah-gogue] -a- a state of keen *anticipation, excitement;* cp. agape (open); angst (anxiety).

agoraphobia -n- abnormal fear of *open spaces*; Gr. space + fear; see phobe.

ague [<u>ah</u>-goo] -n- sharp fever, shivering (e.g. malaria); Lat. fever.

ailurophobia [ail-er-oh-<u>phobe</u>-ee-ah] -n- morbid fear of *cats*; Gr. cats + fear.

air -n- the mixture of invisible, odorless, tasteless *gases* that we breathe. See hydrogen, nitrogen, photon and "elements". *Earth's atmosphere is 80% nitrogen and 20% oxygen; the universe is largely a vacuum, but, where not, the universe is 92% hydrogen.* Oxygen is created by plants; without plants, we don't breathe.

akin [ah-kin] -a- related; to + kin.

---

akinesia -n- loss or impaired physical movement; Lat. w/o + movement.

alacrity [ah-**lack**-kri-ty] -n- brisk; quick; ready; ex. She did it with _____.

alchemy -n- a Medieval, *seemingly magical power* of elixirs and panaceas; to + chemistry; today, also means *any bogus solution* to a problem.

algorism -n- the *Arabic decimal system* of numeration; Arabic root.

algorithm -n- a set of instructions to help solve a numerical problem, especially on a computer; these are usually mechanical or *recursive* (running backward) *computational procedure.*

allay [ah-**lay**] -v- to reduce intensity; alleviate (lessen); see ameliorate.

allege/d/gation -v/n- to accuse; an accusation before proof.

allegory -n- a literary work in which *characters* symbolize *ideas* or *principles.*

alligator -n- a large, ferocious, predatory reptile, similar to a crocodile, but with a broader, shorter snout, native to the Americas and China; cp. crocodiles have salt glands in their tongues and, therefore, adapt easily to salt water as well.

alluvial/ium -a/n- sediments deposited by *flowing* water; cp. diluvial (fm a flood); placer (a mineral deposit in water).

alpha -n- the *first* of anything; 1st letter of Gr. alphabet; the *brightest* star in a constellation

"'I am the alpha and omega,' saith the Lord" (Rev 1:8) - the first and last.

altruist/ism -n- devotion to interests of others; ant. egoism / selfishness; Lat. to + this other.

---

amaneus [am-an-a-us] -n- an assistant, esp. who takes dictation or copies manuscripts; Lat. manu (slave); ensis (belonging to); cp. minion/servitor (servile dependent or underling).

amative [ah-mah-tive] -a- amorous.

amazon -n- a large, strong, masculine woman / virago; cp. circe (domineering woman); cp. shrew (a nagging woman or a mammal with a pointed nose); virago/aginous [veer-ah-go] (a large, domineering woman; Lat. vir = man); amazon; cp. termagant (overbearing woman); circe (a woman who destroys men); vixen (ill-tempered woman).

ambiance/ent -n/a- the special *atmosphere* or *mood* of an environment; milieu (environment).

ambiguity/ous [am-bih-**gue**-ity] -a- that which is *indefinite, vague*; see abstruse / obscure.

ambivalence [am-**biv**-el-lence] -n- *simultaneous attraction and repulsion* to and from a person or thing.

ambivert -n- neither an introvert nor an extrovert; a blend of both; two + poles.

ambrosia [am-brose-ya] -n- the food of the gods; *whatever tastes or smells divine*; Gk. Immortal.

ameliorate -v- *reduce* problems; allay / appease / assuage / conciliate / pacify / palliate / placate / propitiate.

ambulant/ory/ance -a/n- something or person who is mobile; not confined to bed; Lat. to walk.

amity -n- a friendly relationship; goodwill; Lat. amicas-friend; Ex. international amity; cp. Amish (peaceful Christian religious sect, aka "Pennsylvanika Dutch", of German roots, similar to the Menonnonites).

---

amnesia -n- loss of memory; Gr. without + memory.

amoeba [ah-meeba] -n- any of various *protozoans* (**single**-celled, microscopic organisms); of indefinite and *changeable* forms.

amore/ous -n/a- love; feeling loving; amative.

amorphous -a- having no determinative form; *shapeless;* to + change; cp. amoeba.

amphibious/ian -a/n- able to function on land and water.

amulet -n- an object usually *worn around the neck* to ward off evil; talisman (anything with *magical* power to protect).

anachronism/istic -n- an error in time or chronology (the science of measuring time).

anagram -n- *a word/phrase formed by reordering another word/phrase*: e.g. God/dog; pea/ape; cp. acronym (WAC, WOP, COP, IRS); acrostic; anonym(name backwards); epigram (axiom, esp. in 2 line couplet); homonym (look or sound alike but different meanings); pseudonym (false name, esp. pen name).

analects -n- a collection of works; anthology (collection of *literary* works); omnibus (one person's works).

analgesia/ic -n/a- the inability to feel pain / anodyne; Gr. not + pain; adj., - anything that relieves pain; cp. anesthesia (a drug to prevent feeling pain); stoic (indifferent to pain or pleasure).

analogue -n- something that bears an *analogy (a likeness)* to something else; cp. ecologue. (a poem in the form of a dialogue); epilogue (writing at the end of a work); prologue (at beginning); monologue (one speaker).

anarchy -n- a state *without government* or political order; cp. anomie (collapse of society); ochlocracy (mob rule).

anathema [an-ath-ah-ma] -n- hated thing or person; animosity / enmity / execrate / imprecate; abhorrent (repugnant).

androgynous -a- having male & female *characteristics*; unisex; Gr. man + woman; cp. hermaphrodite (m/f organs).

andropause -n- male menopause.

anema [ah-nay-ma] -a- Italian word for *soul* or spirit; "Anema Cuore" (Soul + Heart); nightclub in Capri.

anemic [ah-nee-mick] -a- Gr. lack of blood.

anesthesia/iologist -n- Gr. without + sensation; drug that puts you to sleep; doctor who does so; cp. bromide; sedative.

angel -n- a spiritual being, appearing in human form and/or with wings in a long robe, acting as God's messenger; a messenger; today: one of exemplary conduct.

Anglophobe -n- one who hates the English; Lat. English + fear; Gk. English + phobia, i.e., repugnance; cp. ant. anglophile (lover of the English).

angst [ank-st] -n- a feeling of anxiety.

anima -n- the true *inner self-soul-spirit*; a term of Carl Jung (Swiss psychiatrist).

animate [an-ih-mate] -v- to *breathe life into; full of life;* from + mate.

animate [an-ih-mut] -a- having life; ant. inanimate.

animus/animosity -n- a feeling of hatred / odious / execrable; cp. abhorrent; antipathy.

anodyne [an-o-dine] **-Adj-** not contentious; **-Noun-** pain-killing drug; analgesia; Gk. to + pain.

anomalous [ah-nom-ah-lous] -a- see next definition.

---

anomaly -n- that which deviates; something peculiar, irregular, abnormal; aberration.

anomie or **anomy** -n- a *collapse* of societies social structure; the resultant state of alienation; Gr. Lawless; cp. anarchy.

annihilate -v- to destroy completely; Lat: to + nothing; syns. obliterate / eradicate; cp. efface / expunge (erase); deface (disfigure).

annuity -n- any investment, such as an ordinary life insurance policy, that pays a sum of money annually or at regular intervals and usually for life.

anon -a- O.E., archaic: *soon* or *later*; cp. erstwhile (former); ergo (therefore).

anonym -n- a *pseudonym* consisting of the real name written *backwards* (e.g. eel ttevol); cp. chiasmus (a statement reversing words: "Never let a fool kiss you or be fooled by a kiss"); acronym (WAC, WOP); anagram (word with rearranged letters, e.g., pea/ape, god/dog); eponym (named after a place, e.g., Tex, Romulus); homonym (sound or look alike but different meanings).

anonymous -a- without a name.

anorexia [an-or-**X**-e-ah] -n- obsessive desire to lose weight by not eating; Gk an/to/by + orexis/appetite; cp. bulimia (obsessive overeating for short periods, followed by guilt, self-induced vomiting, fasting and depression (Gk. bous/out+limos/hunger).

antebellum -a- before + war; generally used to refer to the pre-American Civil War era.

antecedent -n- that which precedes something; Lat. before + to go.

antediluvian -n- occurring before the Biblical flood that Noah survived; see Noah.

anterior -n- hear the front; Lat. ante-before; cp. interior (inside); posterior (after).

anthology -n- a collection of *literary* works; Gr. flower gathering; cp. analects (selected works); omnibus (analects of *one* author's works).

anthropic -a- of or related to human beings and/or their existence on earth.

anthropocentric -a- assuming *man* is the *center* of all things; homo sapiens + centered.

anthropoid/ology -n- *resembling man*, e.g., apes; the study of; man + like/study of.

anthropology -n- study or knowledge of mankind; cp. arthropod (animals with jointed legs and segmented bodies, like insects and crustaceans, of which there are more species than any other animals).

anthropomorphous/ic -n/a- having or suggesting the human form.

anticlimax/mactic -n- a less important climax.

antipathy/ic/thetical -n/a- aversion; *dislike*; antipathy; against + path; cp. abhorrent (repugnant); animosity (hatred).

antipode/al -n/a- *diametrical* opposites, usually parts of the globe; anti = against; pode = foot; having feet in opposite places, hence poles; cp. antithetical (against beliefs).

Antipodes -n- when spelled with a capital "A", refers to Australia & New Zealand.

antiquity -n- the quality of being old or ancient; considerable age; originally, that which preceded the Middle Ages.

ataxia [ah-tax-ee-ah] -n- w/o "taxis" (Gr. for control); loss of control of body; aka: cerebral ataxia.

atheism/ist/ic -a/n- a=without + theo=god; cp. agnosticism; deism; humanism; theism.

atomic bomb -n- when the subatomic particles are broken apart, a massive amount of energy is released; see Big Bang.

atone/ment -v/n- to give payment//*reparation for an injury* or wrong; syn. *expiate/expiation/penitence/recompense;* cp. *contrition* /contrite/ *repentant (expressing sorrow for error);* to be at-one-with the injured party.

atoll [ah-tall] -n- *a ring-shaped reef, island or chain* of islands, usually of coral.

atomist -n- one who believes that all matter is comprised of randomly formed atoms, accidents of nature and not divinely orchestrated, hence a pantheist and atheist.

atrabilious [at-trah-bill-eeous] -a- melancholy or ill-tempered; Lat. from bile; Gk from melancholy.

atrophy [**at**-tro-*fee*] -noun- a *wasting away*, deterioration, *withering.*; wizened; Gr. without food; cp. sere;. ossify (turn to bone); petrify (turn to stone/frighten).

atrophy [at-tro-***phi***] -verb- to waste away, deteriorate, wither//wizen.

au contraire -Fr. term- to the contrary.

audacious/ty -a/n- *fearlessly daring;* unrestrained by convention; Lat. to dare; cp. effrontery (same but insulting); bodacious (arrant, bold+audacious).

augur/augury -v/n- foretell / predict / presage (prophetic sign) / auspice; seer or prophet; a soothsayer/prediction; cp. auspice (favorable sign); portent (usually an unfavorable sign); cp. medium.

---

august [awe-**gust**] -a- of *majestic* dignity; regal; stately; *exalted*; Gr. based on Augustus Caeser.

aura -n- *distinctive atmosphere* of a place (**ambience**) or person; near syn. **cachet** (individualistic. characteristics); **karma** (essence of a person); cp. **élan** (*style*; flair; enthusiastic vigor); **ethos** (distinguishing aspect of a person/thing, a near syn. of karma); **panache** (flamboyance).

aural/auditory -n- that which is *perceived* by the **ear**; cp. oral = spoken, not written.

Aureole -n- a bright aura of *light surrounding someone* such as a holy person / *halo*; cp. corona (a gaseous ring or circle around an object such as the moon).

aurora [ah-<u>roar</u>-ah] -n- the *rising light of dawn* (often a rich orange).

Aurora borealis -n- the poet's term for dawn's light emanating *from the* **north.**

auscultate -v- to *listen to the heart or other human organs* as with a *stethoscope*; cp. vet (critically examine).

auspice/auspicious -n/a- a *favorable*, *prophetic sign*/affording a favorable sign; cp. portent, augury.

autism -n- a human mind that *cannot conceive of other minds* and, so, can't form social relationships; *avoids eye contact*; usually develops by age three; often hyper-sensitive to sound and touch and are easily overloaded by stimulation; many have *epilepsy*; most have *IQ's under 70* but some have savant abilities in limited areas.

autonomic -a- involuntary or unconscious; relating to the nervous system.

autoclave -n- *an area or device for cleansing*, sterilizing, as in a hospital; self + clean.

autocracy [awe-**tock**-ra-cy] -n- government by a *single* person having unlimited power; Gr. self + rule; syn. dictatorship; monarchy; CP. despotism; aristocracy (rule by the "best"); democracy(by majority); gerontocracy (by seniors); kakistocracy (rule by the worst); ochlocracy(mob); oligarchy (by few); plutocracy(by rich); tyranny.

avaricious/avarice -a- *excessive* greed; cp. acquisitive (likes to acquire).

avatar -n- *one who personifies a given abstract idea; a divine incarnation* (esp. a person). extensive usage and misusage is rapidly changing the meaning of this word; cp. allegory (a story where the characters represent qualities); apparition (ghost); epiphany (to witness divine incarnation); see "Second Life" Online.

aviary -n- where birds are kept. Fr. avian = bird; cp. rookery (a nesting place for birds).

avidity/avid [ah-**vid**-ity] -n- eager pursuit; *enthusiasm*; state of *craving*.

avow -v- to confess, assert, swear under oath; syn. adjure / attest.

avuncular [ah-**vun**-cu-lar] -a- of or pertaining to an *uncle*; so, benevolent; cp. atavistic (ancestor).

axiom -n- a self-evident or universally recognized ***truth***; syn., proverb; epigram; cp. adage (a rule/aphorism/apothegm/maxim/tenet).

azure -a- the color of the sky.

"B"

bacchanal [bac-kan-al] -n- an occasion of drunken revelry; one who is (from Baccus-wine god).

badinage [bah-din-ahhge] -n- Fr. to joke; *humorous*/witty conversation/ banter/repartee; cp. doggerel (comic *verse*); cp. persiflage (flippant); chatter/natter/palaver/prattle (silly conversation); rigmarole (confused talk).

bagatelle -n- an *unimportant thing*, trifle; game with a cue/balls on oblong table; cp. peccadillo (small fault).

baleful -a- *intending harm*/malevolent; e.g., "a _____ smile; cp. malignant (causing great harm).

ballast -n- heavy material that stabilizes a ship, balloon, etc.; cp. balustrade.

balustrade [ball-ah-strad] -n- a rail and its supporting posts, as along the edge of a staircase.

banal [**bain**-al] -a- *commonplace*//flat//mundane//pedestrian//pro-saic//prosy; plebian; cp. quotidian (daily/commonplace); trite (over-used); plebian (low rank).

bane -n- deadly; *ruinous*; e.g., "the ___ of my existence"; cp. lethal// pernicious//truculent, cp. virulent (poisonous).

banter -v/n- to speak in *humorous* way; root unknown/badinage/ repartee; cp. doggerel (comic verse); chatter//natter//palaver/ (to *talk idly*); colloquy (formal conversation); persiflage (flippant colloquy); claptrap/prate/prattle (talk foolishly, nonsensically or tediously); rigmarole (confused talk). prosaic/prosy (banal speech or writing); cp. malapropism (humorous misuse of words)

baptism/ize -n/v- Gr. for immersion (in water); the Christian rite of sprinkling water as symbol of purification (*to cleanse Adam's/Eve's allegorical "original sin"*).

baroque [bah-**roke**] -n- pertaining to 1500-1700 AD architecture/music/furniture; with scrolls, curves; ornate twists.

base -n/a- the *bottom* of anything; adj: *immoral*; dissolute/licentious/a libertine/a reprobate; see/cp. lascivious.

basilica [bah-**sil**-ica] -n- an oblong building with an apse (a semicircular alter) at one end, usually used as a church or meeting hall.

bathos [bath-ose]/**bathetic** -n/a- excessively sentimental or anti-climactic; Gk. depth; cp. near syns. cloying (disgustingly sentimental); maudlin (self-pitying or tearfully sentimental).

battlement -n- a parapet (a low protective wall) at the top of a building, usually of a fort or castle that has regularly spaced openings through which one can shoot.

baud -n- *a unit of speed in data transmission*; one baud = one bit/letter per second; see bit for details; Fr, J.M.E. Baudot inventor (1931).

bawd/bawdy -n/a- a "madam"; one who keeps a house of prostitution; adj. whore-like.

bay/ed -n/v- a body of water; a part of building; a reddish-brown animal; a deep prolonged bark, as of hounds, or the act of doing so; a crown of leaves.

beatitude -n- a feeling of utmost bliss; ecstasy//euphoria/felicity; cp. Elysian; utopic

Beck -n- Ger. a stream or brook, esp. with a stony bottom; syn. rivulet.

Bedoin -n- one who lives in the desert, usually an Arab. Arabic: desert.

beenz [beans] -n- a c. 2010 universal form of *credit* on the Internet.

beggar -n/v- mendicant; one who begs; v: to reduce to poverty or a low position.

begrime(d) -v- to blacken with ingrained dirt.

beguile [bee-**geye-ul**] -v- to trick; to cheat, charm or amuse; root: deception.

behemoth [be-**hee**-moth] -n- an enormous bull (Jewish mythology)// elephantine//gargantuan//Gothic//titan.

belfry [bell-free] -n- bell tower; siege tower; M.E.; slang for "the mind"; e.g. bats in your __.

belittle -v- approx. syns: abash; asperse; calumniate; decry; defame; denigrate; derogate; disparage; malign; cp. deprecate (disapprove).

bellicose -a- belligerent//militant//pugilistic//pugnacious; jingoistic (re country); Lat. "of war".

bemuse -v- to confuse: bewilder, befuddle, puzzle, disorient, disconcert.

benediction -n- a blessing or *grace* often before an event; good + diction.

benefaction/or/ficent -n/a- the act of *conferring a benefit*/gift/one who does; benevolent; munificent (generous).

benighted -a- a state of *intellectual or moral ignorance*; O.E.; benight (cover in darkness/obscure).

benign -a- kindly; *mild*; gentle; cp. pacific//placid (peaceful); ant. malignant.

benignant [be-nig-nant] -a- kindly; benevolent; having a good effect; cp. benign.

bereft/reaved [be-**reft**] -a/v- deprived of *something* (e.g. dignity); bereaved (grieve death of someone); bemoaning; soulful; mourning; lamenting.

"Bernal's Ladder" -a term- refers to John Bernal (1901-71) a renowned 20th Century British *physicist,* gave this famous, humorous explanation of the reception accorded new ideas by scientists: 1) it's **not true**; 2) it may be true but it's **not important**; 3) it may be important, but it's **not original**; 4) it may be original, but it's **what I always thought**.

beseech -v- make an *urgent request*; entreat; implore; importune (beg); cp. admonish (reprove mildly).

beset -v- surround or harass; O.E.

bespeak -v- to be evidence of something; e.g. Her jewelry bespeaks her wealth.

bespoke -a- something that is custom-made; e.g. It is a bespoke plan.

beta [**bait**-ta] -n- 2nd letter of Greek alphabet; 2nd in a series; e.g. a ____ test; cp. alpha (1st); omega (last).

bête noire -term- Fr. black beast; a *thing* widely *detested.*

bevy -n- a large group of people or things, esp. girls; M.E.

---

bewail -v- to express regret or sorrow; to *cry* about; bereave/lament/ mourn; cp. bemoan (express regret OR disapproval); commiserate (console); eulogize.

Bibliophile -n- a lover and collector of books; Gk. books + love.

bicameral -n- two chambers in a legislative body; Lat. two + rooms.

bifurcate -v- divide into two parts; to fork.

bigamy/ist [**big**-gam-ee] -n- having two marriages; one who does so.

bigot -n- one convinced of the superiority of one's own opinions and prejudices against others.

bile -n/a- *greenish fluid* excreted by liver to digest food.

bilious [**bill**-ee-ous] -a- nauseous, vomiting; ill-tempered/irascible/ choleric; cp. emetic (causes vomiting).

billet -n/v- *board and lodging* for troops; quarters; Celtic (British-Welch-Irish-Scottish).

billow -n- a large, undulating mass of something (e.g., clouds, smoke, steam).

binary -a- anything composed of *two different parts*; also a _____ digit – either 0 or 1; a *numbering system* in which all numbers are represented by 0's or 1's; attributed to Hindu scholar **Pingala** c. 500BC in a form similar to Morse Code; also the basis of prosody (the metrical structure of classic poetry).

bine -n- the *flexible stem* of any climbing plant or weed; cp. tenacle (flexible limb); tendril (stem/extension); pith.

biomedicine/medical -n- the application of *biology and chemistry to medicine*.

biopic -n- a biographical film/picture.

biped -n- animal with two feet; cp. tetrapod (4 limbs with 5 fingers and/or 5 toes).

bipolar -n- having two poles; antipodal; *expressing contradictory ideas or characteristics*; also known as manic depressive.

bit, byte, KB, MB, GB -n- bit roughly equals one character or letter; avg. word=5 letters; eight "bits" equals one byte or 1.6 words; 1,000 bytes (not bits) = one **KB** or 1600 words or about **5 pages** with 300 words/page; 1,000 KB's = one **MB** or 1.6**M** words//5000 pages; 1,000 MB's = one GB/gigabyte or 1.6 billion words//5 million pages.

blanch -v- bleach; make white.

blandish/ment -v/n- to entice by flattery; flattery; syns. inveigle/wheedle; cp. sychophant/toady (flatterer); brandish (wave/flourish menacingly).

bleat -n- the characteristic *cry of a goat* or sheep or a similar sound, *whimper.*

blithe -a- *carefree*, cheerful; convivial; cp. insouciant (not concerned).

blog -n/v- short for "web logs" (frequently updated journals); where people talk to each other; businesses now use them extensively, even through pseudonyms, to promote products and services; blogs are about talking *with* customers rather than "to" or "at" them; people seem to want the human contact.

bloviate -v- to be verbose; to "blow" as hot air; near syns. loquacious (talkative), garrulous (too talkative), voluble (one who emits a free flow of words), verbose (too wordy).

blunderbuss -n- a short musket with a flared tip; a precursor of the shotgun.

bodacious -a- complete/thorough/arrant; also, bold + audacious = fearless; cp. apodictic (perfect).

bodkin -n- a small, sharply pointed object for making holes in leather; slang for penis; cp. bobbin (a spool or reel that holds thread or yarn while weaving).

bog -n/v- waterlogged *ground*; *marsh*; quagmire.

Boko Haram -term- "Western education is forbidden"; refers to a Nigerian-based group of 1-K to 10K killers, who claim to control 20K sq. miles of Nigeria, and who pledge alliance to ISIS.

Bolshevik -n- a member of the *Communist Party* (aka "Reds") in the Russian Revolution; hence, an *extreme liberal* or radical; cp. proletariat(labor class); bourgeoisie (middle class/average).

bombast/ic -n/a- *overdone/sometimes empty speech or writing* (Lat. cotton padding); formal speaking; cp. hyperbole (exaggerated); euphuistic (affected); prolix (verbose); fustian / orotund (pretentious wording).

bonhomie [bon-**ho**-mee] Fr. good man; cheerful; friendly; cordial/collegial.

bonny -a- attractive, healthy, a Scottish word.

boodle -n- slang for money, esp. counterfit; bucks/clams/dough/greenbacks/moola; cp. caboodle (group, bunch); loot (stolen money); lucre (a reward).

boor -n- a *rude, unmannerly* person; a peasant, yokel; Ger. farmer; cp. bore/ing.

---

boring -a- uninteresting; cp. comatose (unconscious); diffident (shy); stolid (w/o emotion); taciturn (silent); torpid (numbed); moribund (dying); non compos mentis (not control of mind).

bourgeois/sie [bour-zhwa/zee] -n- a member of the *middle class/average*; to Marx: a property owner ("kulak") and capitalist; a materialist; cp. Bolshevik (Communist, extreme liberal); proletariat (laboring class).

bovine -a- relating to cattle/cows; hence, plump; today used to refer to women's busts; long ago, it meant slow or stupid.

bowdlerize -n- expunge offensive content; syn. expurgate; origin: Dr. Bowdler who expurgated Shakespeare's works.

bower -n- General: a pleasant, shady place, Ger. On ship: the heaviest of ship's *anchors, carried at the bow.*

braggadocio -n- empty *boasting*; cp. bombast (empty words); hyperbole (exaggerations); see persiflage.

Brahmin [Brah-min] -n- a Buddhist priest; see Buddha.

brash -a- bold/brazen; cp. bodacious (arrant, fearless).

breviary -n- Lat. for a summary; esp. a priest's abridged daily prayers; cp. lawyer's brief.

brig -n- a jail; a sailing vessel with two masts; see boats.

brio -n- vigor, vitality, life force; Lat.

broker -n- a salesman, esp. of stocks, bonds, real estate and insurance.

bromide -n- Med. sedative or drug, esp. to relax; Other: a trite/unoriginal remark to soothe.

buffet [boo-fay] -n/v- large sideboard; food served on a long table.

---

buffet [<u>buff</u>-fet] -n/v- a blow; to hit; cp, butt (hit with head); cudgel (a club).

bugger -n/v- Eng. slang for a sodomite or the act of sodomizing (anal sex with humans or sex with animals); cp. faggot; as feces are full of bacteria, buggery / sodomy is said to cause or cause myriad diseases, for example, AIDS, cholera, dysentery, typhoid fever, syphilis, some cancers (colon, larynx) and virtually any disease that is triggered by excessive bacteria, in short a death wish, as well as disgusting.

bulimia [bull-**eem**-e-ah] -n- obsessive overeating for short periods, followed by guilt, self-induced vomiting, fasting and depression (Gk. bous/out+limos/hunger); **cp.** anorexia (obsessive desire to lose weight by not eating; reaching 80% of normal body weight; Gk an/without+orexis/appetite).

bullock [**bull**-luck] -n- a *castrated* bull.

burka [burr-ka] -n- a head-to-toe garment, worn by some Muslim women, which covers all but their eyes; cp. sari (garment that covers body and/or head but not face).

burnish -v- to polish, shine, publicize; Fr. to make known.

butt -v/n- to hit/buffet; the end of something; the object of ridicule; a large cask; butt/butt is a good example of a homonym.

"C"

cabal -n- *secret plot/machination*; intrigue; body of people engaged in one; machination (plot); Lat.

caboodle [cah-**boodle**] -n- your "kit and _____"; lot, group, bunch; cp. boodle (money).

cachet [cah-**shea**] -n- *a mark or quality of distinction*, individuality, authenticity; cp. élan (style); ethos (distinguishing character or spirit esp of a place); karma (essence, spirit); panache (flamboyant style); insignia (distinguishing mark).

cacophony [kah-koff-onee] -n- *jarring, discordant sounds//dissonance*; cp. din (loud and discordant).

cadavor/ous [ca-**dav**-or] -n/a- corpse; something like a corpse.

cachinnate/anation [kack-in-a-tion] -n- a loud laugh; Lat. to laugh.

cajole [cah-**joel**] -n- to *coax gently* but persistently; cp. admonish; beseech//entreat (encourage); cp. implore(urge); importune (beg); genuflect (beg on one knee).

Caleb -n- Heb. name meaning "whole-hearted."

caliph -n- Arabic for *successor to power*; refers to those who claim to be direct descendants of Mohammed and, thus, are chosen to succeed Mohammad; each Middle Eastern country or region tends to have one, e.g. Kohmeni; caliphate is the area the caliph rules; see Shiite.

calligraphy [kal-lig-graff-fee] -n- *decorative handwriting*; Gk. kallos (beauty) + graph (write).

callow -a- unsophisticated; *immature*; a youth; root is misleading; see tyro.

calumny/calumniate [**cal**-um-ny] -n/v- asperse; *slander*, making false statements; cp. *obloquy* / vilification (abusive language); decry// denigrate, deride; derogate; malign.

calvery -n- an experience of suffering.

canard -n- a false or unfounded report or *groundless rumor*; from Fr. duck; a half duck sold as whole.

canon/ize -n/v- an *ecclesiastical* (church) law; *today, any law*; when RC's declare a deceased person a saint.

capacious -a- capacity to hold a large quantity; commodious / roomy/ spacious.

caper -v/n- to skip or dance playfully; the act of doing so.

capitulate -v- surrender on agreed conditions.

capricious/price -a- *impetuous*/ impulsive/ precipitous/ unpredictable/ whimsical; willy nilly; near syns. capricious / *erratic* / *unpredictable*/ mercurial behavior / vagarious; cp. bipolar (extreme highs and lows, manic depressive); mutable (changeable).

capstone -n- cap or top stone//acme//apex//apogee (highest point in orbit); Horeb height; pinnacle; solstice (sun's highest point— when it crosses equator); vertex//zenith.

capsule/capsulate -n/v- a membrane or sac/small container; to summarize; L. box, case, cap.

captious -a- pointing *out trivial faults*; carp; cavil; a niggler; pettifogger; cp. peccadillo (small fault).

---

carapace [car-ah-pace] -n- a bony shield covering the back of an animal as a turtle or crab.

carmine -n- a vivid crimson color; cp. crimson; Arabic.

carnal -a- Lat.: relating to the desires of the flesh; i.e., sensual/sexual; see lascivious.

carnage -a- slaughter of humans; ex. the _____ of war.

carp -v/n- to find fault or *complain* constantly; M.E.; an edible freshwater fish; cp. captious/cavil (critical); remonstrate (oppose).

carpe diem [car-pay dee-um] -v/n- Lat. *seize the day*; usually meaning seize the pleasures of the day; carpe gaudium (seize the joy).

carrion -n- the decaying flesh of *dead* animals.

carte blanche [cart blahnshh] -phrase- Fr. unconditional authority; Fr. ticket + blank.

casement -n- a window that looks like a door.

Cassipeia [Cass-si-**pee**-a] -n- debris in a cloud left after a star explodes; a "W" shaped constellation, Gr.

caste [kast] -n- refers to the Hindu system of dividing society into classes; any social class.

casuistry/casuistic [cause-zhis-tree] -n/a- today, often means specious excessively subtle reason *ing intended to rationalize or mislead*; **originally**, the determination of right or wrong via principles of ethics (rather than via faith); see sophistry.

cataclysm [cat-ah-clisum] -n- *flood*//inundation; deluge; *upheaval*; *disaster*; cp conflagration (fire); holocaust (massacre); apocalypse

---

(event of far reaching proportions/day of reckoning); maelstrom (wide-reaching turmoil).

catacombs -n- *underground chamber or tunnel* with recesses for graves; cp. crypt (underground vault); honeycombs; outside Rome, early Christians celebrated Mass there to avoid detection / prosecution by the Romans.

catalepsy/tic -n/a- a *seizure*; cp. apoplexy (sudden loss of *muscular* control or *consciousness*; comatose (unconscious); sans/non compos mentis (w/o or not + control of mind).

catatonic -a- affected by schizophrenia, ***mutism***, negativity, or ***lack of movement or expression.***

catharsis [cah-<u>thar</u>-sis] -n- purging of undesirable emotions by means of art as in drama; cp. therapeutic (healing).

<u>c</u>atholic -n- of broad or general scope; *universal*; Lat./Gr. = in general; syn. ecumenical; ant. secular.

<u>C</u>atholic -n- a member of the Roman Catholic Church.

caustic -a- ***scathingly*** sarcastic; sardonic; able to corrode by chemical action; acidic / acrid / acerbic / choreric / vitriolic.

cavalcade -n- a formal procession on horseback; It. cavalcare: to ride.

caveat [<u>cah</u>-vee-aht] -n- a *warning*; a *qualification* or explanation; *advice to beware*, as of a person or thing; _____ emptor (L. beware + buyer, hence, "buyer beware").

cavil -v/n- to raise *trivial objections*; to be captious, to carp or niggle; a peccadillo (small fault); a pettifogger.

cede -v- to yield or give up; near syns. accede (grant a request) / concede (admit); cp. precede (go before).

celerity -n- swift; from Lat. celer.

celestial -a- related to the sky or heavens; L./Fr. sky.

Celsius -a- the thermometric method of measuring temperatures used in most of the word; see centigrade. Named after Andrew Celsius (c. 1850); same as centigrade, *except* divisor used is 99.99; see centigrade; in both Celsius and Centigrade, the point at which water freezes is 0 degrees (not 32) and the point at which it boils is 100.

censorious -a- tending to or expressing censure; Lat.

centigrade -n- the thermometric points at which water freezes and boils, divided by 100 degrees; approximate **syn. Celsius.**

centrifuge/al [**cent**-tri-fuge] -n/a- an apparatus consisting of a compartment spun about a central *axis to separate materials* of different densities or to stimulate gravity with _____ force.

cept -root- From Lat. v. "take" or "seize"; Exs. intercept (seize before arrival).

cerebellum -n- a part of the brain about the assize of a peach, located toward the back of the brain, but contains about 80% of the brain's neurons. Lat. little brain.

chandler -n- a dealer in supplies for boats; also a candle maker; Fr. candle.

chanticleer [**shan**-ti-clear] -n- Fr. rooster.

chapbook -n- a *small* book or *pamphlet* (containing poems, ballads, or stories); chapters book.

charade [sha-**raid**] -n- a pretense that is readily perceived; a game to guess the meaning of a gestures, akin to pantomime.

charisma [cah-ris-ma] -n- a rare power over others; *pers'l magnetism*; cp. karma (persona); cachet (distinctive style).

charismatic -a- Theol.- an alleged, *divine power to inspire others*; cp. élan [ee-**lan**] (*style; flair*; enthusiastic vigor/liveliness); cachet (individualistic characteristics); ethos (distinguishing aspect of a person, culture or thing), karma (essence/total effect); panache (flamboyance).

charivari [shar-ee-var-ee] -n- a cacophonous, mock serenade; also, as series of discordant noises; see cacophony.

chasm [<u>kas</u>-um] -n- deep opening in earth's surface; an abyss or gorge.

chaste -n- disciplined, esp. abstaining from sexual activity.

chasten [**chase**-en] -v- *reprove* or *punish* by beating (physical or verbal); *severe criticism.*

chastise [**chas**-tize] -v- generally, means criticize; near syn. diatribe / excoriation / fulmination / vilification (extreme criticism).

chauvinism/istic -n/a- *prejudiced belief in the superiority of one's group*; *fanatical* patriotism; or male bravado; e.g., He is a male _____.

cheeky -a- slang for *impertinent*, also for insolently audacious//bold// brazen//cocky.

chenille [shah-neel] -n- a *tufted chord or yarn* used to trim furniture; fabric made from same; Fr. hairy caterpillar.

chiasmus [kee-az-muss] -n- a statement that reverses the order of words: "Never let a *fool* kiss you -- or a *kiss* to fool you." Lat. crosswise; cp. anonym (a name written backwards); see acronym.

chicanery [shi-**can**-ery] -n- *trickery*; cp. legerdemain/prestidigitation (hand/card tricks).

---

clamant [klah-**mahnt**] -a- urgent; *compelling*; *loud*; e.g. the _____ traffic; Lat. to cry out.

clarion -n/a- a kind of trumpet with loud, clear notes; any sound loud and clear.

cleft -v/a/n- **verb**: past tense of cleave; *deeply divided*; **n/a**: split, crease; a _____ palate (split lip).

cliché [klee-shay] -n- a stale, overused, worn-out, hence *trite*, expression; syn. hackneyed/trope (a figure of speech often overused); see adage.

cloister -n/v- Lat. for "*closed place*"; esp. devoted to *religious seclusion*, a monastery/convent/to seclude; cp. sanctuary (sacred place free from intrusion).

cloy/ing -v/a- to injure or *maim*; to be *disgustingly sentimental*; cp. near syns. bathetic (overly sentimental); maudlin (tearfully sentimental).

coagulate -v- *to cause to thicken, viscous; conjoined*; Fr.; see congeal (liquid to solid).

coalesce/coalition -v/n- to come together; those joined together; Lat. cum = with + grow.

cockle -n- a mollusk (a shellfish) with a *heart-shaped shell* with radiating ribs.

codi/code -root- Lat. refers to writing documents; e.g. codicils (amendment to a Will); encode (to put in code); decode (to break a code).

coda -n- a concluding passage, often in music; Lat. tail.

codify -v- to put together as a code or system, as in legislation; e.g. laws; Lat. wood tablets.

cogent -a- makes a *compelling* appeal to the intellect; a _____ argument.

cogitate/tion -v/n- *to think carefully*; contemplate, meditate, muse, reflect, ruminate (think at length); Lat. intensive thought; co + agitare/agitate; cp. opine (give opinion).

cognate -n- words with a common etymological origin; Lat. co = with + natus = to be born; in law: a blood relative.

cognition/cognitive/cogitate -n/a- thinking; understanding; learning; remembering; Lat. to learn; meditate//muse//ruminate.

cognitive dissonance -term- *where beliefs conflict with actions*; e.g. opposing killing animals but eating meat.

cognoscente/i [kon-no-**shen**-tay] -n- *person(s) of superior knowledge or taste*; erudite (learned); savant(to know without being taught); polymath (*extremely* learned) pundit (teacher).

cohere/nt -v/n- to *stick together* in a mass; unite; also to be logical; Lat. together; coalesce/conjoin (bring together); cp. congeal (change fluid to solid); coagulate (thicken).

cohort -n- one who is part of your group or some identified group; Lat.

coital/coition -a/n- sexual intercourse; cp. conjugal/connubial (having to do with marriage).

Cold War -n- the 40-year, non-shooting war between the U.S. and Russian, began in the post-WWII era, around **1946** and accelerated from 1970's, until the Berlin Wall came down in 1**989**.

colloquy/quist -n- a *formal* conversation or written descant/discourse//disquisition; one who does; cp. natter//palaver//prattle (silly, meaningless chatter); banter (witty discourse); persiflage (flippant colloquy); dialectics (reasoning); polemics (debate); rigmarole (confused chatter).

colonic -n- that which cleanses the colon; ex. high ___; cp. emetic (causes vomiting); purgative (purging//cleansing); dyspeptic (indigestion or irritability).

colloquial -a- informal, esp. conversation; oddly, colloquy relates to formal conversation; no root other than "loquator" or speaker; cp. ant. colloquy.

comatose -a- in a *coma; unconscious*; cp. moribund (dying); non compos mentis (L. not control mind); cp. stolid (emotionless); torpid (numb); catatonic (no movement or expression); apoplectic (no muscle control).

comely -a- beautiful; O.E.

comestibles -n- things to eat; Fr. with + eat; victuals [vit-tals].

comet -n- small, gaseous elongated body whose tails can be stretched for millions of miles as they approach the sun and which can be seen only when they pass close to the sun. Cp. *asteroid* (rocks 1-300 mi. wide); cp. meteor; see Haley's Comet & solar system.

comity [kom-ih-tee] -n- an atmosphere of *social harmony*, esp. *courteous recognition* of others, *esp. among nations* and courts; cp.hedgemony (common interests among nations); cp. privity (a legal connection).

commiserate/tion -n- pity; sympathize with; give condolences; Lat. with + misery; cp. empathize.

commodious -a- spacious; capacious; Fr. "commode" = a chest that adds space.

Communion -n- syn. Eucharist (Lat. gratitude); wafer + wine = JC's flesh + blood.

compass -n- a *magnet* detector which, if no electrical current is flowing thru its wire, it will line up with the earth's magnetic field and, thus, point toward the North Pole. Invented by Chinese c.1000AD, altho' primitive versions existed pre-Christ. Most *modern compasses* use a Magnetized Needle (MN) or dial inside a capsule filled with a liquid (usually lamp oil or alcohol); the needle is Magnetized by rubbing it on a lodestone (a magnetite stone that possesses polarity or other magnet aligning it with the earth's magnetic field; when the MN floats in the liquid, the MN then points north.

complacent [com-**play**-cent] -a- *self-satisfied; **content; not trying;*** Lat. with + place; cp. enervated (exhausted); indolent (won't work); lethargic/phlegmatic (sluggish/indifferent).

complaisant/ance [com-**plays**-sant] -a/n- willingness to please; ***obliging;*** Lat. with + pleasure; see obeisant (bowing); cp. toady / sycophant (slavishly attentive and flattering).

complement -n- to go well with something else; cp. compliment (to applaud).

complicity/ous -n- *aiding or abetting*/being an accomplice; cp. culpable (deserving blame).

---

comport -v- how one behaves or acts. Ex. He comported himself admirably; second meaning: to be in agreement with someone or thing. Ex. His words comported with the audience's beliefs.

compos mentis -term- Lat. control + mind; ant.. comatose (unconscious) ; deranged; ant. non comos mentis.

compunction -n- sense of *guilt*; Lat. with + puncture; ant. impunity(w/o fear of punishment).

conciliate/ation/atory -v/n- to *overcome distrust* or animosity; CP. near syns.: allay; alleviate; appease; assuage; pacify; palliate; propitiate (reduce tension/make peace); reconcile; CP. ameliorate (to make better); rectify (make right).

concoct/tion -v/n- create, esp. a recipe.

concomitant -a- *to go together; parallel;* con = with / together + comitant = accompany; eg _____ interests; syn. symbiotic / mutually beneficial.

concord/ance/ant -n/a- accord; agreement; treaty; text of same; Lat. With + agreement.

concourse -n- act of *merging*; convergent; *where roads meet*; airport runways/concourse; conjoin (unite).

con-cu-pis-cent/ce [con-que-pea-cent] -n- lustful//lascivious//lecherous//libidinous; Lat. cupere=desire; see lascivious for similar words; cp. contumacious (obstinate).

confab/ulation -n- *talking*; in psychiatry: the fabrication of imaginary experiences to *make up for loss of memory*.

conflagration -n- large, destructive *fire*; root Fr. flag+to burn; see cataclysm (flood/upheaval); cp. apocalypse (an event of great importance; day of reckoning); Holocaust (massacre); maelstrom (wide reaching turmoil); pandemonium (extensive chaos).

conflate -v- combine two variant texts into one whole; cp. conjoin (connect together).

confluence/ent -n- *a flowing together* of two or more streams (of anything); with+fluid.

congeal -v- *to change from a fluid to a solid*; hence, make more substantive; cp. **coagulate** (thicken).

congenial -a- agreeable//affable//amiable; Lat. with + friendly.

congenital -a- *from birth*; innate//native//indigenous//; with genesis; cp. incipient (beginning); inchoate (not a yoke); inveterate (deeply rooted); latent (dormant).

congregation -n- a magic incantation or spell; Lat.

congeries -n- a disorderly collection, a jumble, a heap. Lat. "heap up"; cp. congress.

congress -n- an assembly of people; the act of meeting; syns: congregation;//convocation; cp. invoke (call higher power).

congruent/congruous -a- corresponding, *matching exactly;* cp. adjacent//paradigm/parallel; (contiguous); coterminous (having a common boundary); ant. incongruous.

conjoin -v- to join together; *unite*; with + join; near syn: confluent; cp. conflate (combine texts).

conjugal -a- of or relating to the married state; Fr.; syn. connubial; cp. coital.

cranium/cranial -n/a- *skull* of a vertebrate, esp. enclosing the brain; cp. cerebral (of the brain, intellect).

crapper -n- slang for toilet; origin: Thos. Crapper (c. 1900) a British plumber who popularized the use of toilets.

crass -a- beneath normal dignity; <u>*crude*</u>; cp. curt (a rude shortness of words).

craven -a- afraid; *cowardly*; pusillanimous; cp. trepid (fearful); n. poltroon (coward); ant. dauntless/undaunted/ /intrepid (fearless).

cred -root- Lat. from verb "to believe"; e.g. credible (believable); credulity (appearance of truth); creed or credo (a statement of basic beliefs); Exs. It is a credible story. He lacks credulity. That is the credo of their religion.

Crimea -n- a large peninsula on the northern border of the Black Sea; it includes So. Ukraine.

crypt -root- Gk. for hidden; e.g. decrypt (decode); encrypt (encode); cryptic (unclear); cryptography (writing messages in code).

croak -n- a deep, hoarse, guttural sound; esp. by a frog; slang for "to die".

crocodile -n- a large, ferocious, predatory reptile, similar to an alligator, but with a more narrow and longer snout. Crocodiles have salt glands in their tongues and, therefore, adapt easily to salt water.

crucible -n- a *pot for melting steel;* a *severe test*, as of patience or belief; a trial.

crucifix/tion/fy -n/v- *cross*; nailing on cross; Lat. cruciare=to torture.

cruciform -a- arranged in the form of a cross; cross+form.

crux gemmata -n- cross with 13 gems (symbolic for Christ & the 12 apostles); cp. amulet/talisman.

crypt/cryptic -n/a- an *underground vault*; something having a *hidden meaning*; cp. catacombs (chamber below ground with recesses for graves); sarcophagus (stone tomb); sepulchral (burial vault for relics).

cuckold [cuck-cold] -n/v- a man whose wife is adulterous; to make one so.

cudgel -n/v- short club; cp. truncheon (short club esp. used by cops); verb-to beat.

culpable -a- deserving blame or censure; cp. complicitous (being an accomplice); conspirator.

cupola [koo-pol-la] -n- a small dome or a dome on a dome; also a gun turret; It. cask.

curate [cure-rate] -n- a clergyman who is in charge of a parish (an area served by a Christian church); rector/vicar (Episcopal); prelate (high ranking clergyman).

curator -n- one in charge of something, esp. a museum.

curriculum vitae/CV -term- Latin for brief biography or resumé [rez-u-may].

cursory/sorily -a- *hasty*, without attention to detail; cp. capricious (impetuous, whimsical).

cybernate/netics -v/n- to *control* by machines (computers); a *system* for doing so.

cyborg -n- an abbreviation for "cybernetic organism", *a theoretical or fictional being with both organic and bio mechatronic parts*, a term coined by nerds in the 1960's; see Halacy's "Cyborg Evolution of the Superhuman".

cynosure [sigh-no-shure] -n- a person or thing that is *the center of attention or admiration*; cp. sinecure (a job with no duties, esp. in a church or government).

"D"

dactyl [dack-till] -n- Gr. *finger, toe, digit*; a *metrical foot* consisting *one long and two short syllables* (tenderly).

daunt/dauntless -v- intimidate; cp. dauntless (w/o fear).

dandle -v- to bounce anything (esp a baby) up and down.

Dark Ages -n- roughly the first half of the Middle Ages (c. 500 AD-1000 AD), limited trade and travel; art/literature waned; barter replaced coins as money; trade limited.; the law of Rome replaced by anarchy; trial by ordeal was common; see Feudal Era. D.A. followed Roman Empire (c. 200BC 300AD), which followed Greek Epoch (500-200BC).

daub -v- spread or smear a surface with a thick substance (e.g., the face with cream, a wall with graffiti.

davit -n- a small crane usually used to load and unload ship. Origin: a carpenter's tool.

d/Dean -name- describes the *head of faculty, college or church*; root is Gaelic meaning "from the valley".

debase -v- to lower in *character, quality or value;* cp. abase (lower in esteem).

debauchery/ous -n/a- *excessive **indulgence*** of sensual appetites; *see **lascivious*** for similar words. Note: In the area of sex, dictionaries give widely varied, overlapping and confusing definitions due in part to massive misuse of words.

debunk -v- to disparage or expose as a sham; no root; cp. denude; defrock.

dictionary -n- a book defining words; an Englishman, John of Garland, did the first one in 1210 but his was "a book about diction".

dictum -n- Law: the court's ruling or theory of a case; an authoritative order; cp. axiom.

didactic -n- excessively instructive; preachy; cp. pedantic (ostentatiously knowledgeable).

diffident -a- extremely shy / demure / timid; cp. taciturn (silent).

diffuse -v- to pour out or *spread* freely; cp. defuse (disarm); suffuse (*overlay* with light, color, water).

dilate -v- to expand or enlarge, esp. the pupils of the eye.

dilettante -n- one with an *amateurish or superficial interest* in the *arts*; syn. Tartuffe (Imposter, as in Moliere's play).

diluvian/diluvial -n/a- from or produced by a *flood*; Lat. to dilute; syn. alluvial; cp. cataclysm (deluge, disaster, flood); conflagration (fire).

dionysian -a- delirious; frenzied.

din -n- a mixture of *loud and discordant noises*; ex. the __ of the crowd; near syn. cacophony (discordant / dissonant sounds).

dint -n- by means of force, impact or effort; M.E.; ex. Succeed by _____ of hard work.

dipsomania/ical/iac -n/a/n- an *insatiable craving* for *alcoholic* beverages; Gr. thirst + mania

dire -a- *warning* of dreadful events; Lat. ill-omened; a ___ sound; cp. ominous / portentous (threatening).

dirge -n- a slow, *mournful music* or lament, esp. at a funeral.

disambiguation/ate/ous -n/v/a- the process of *resolving conflicts among words* and their definitions; doing same; words that are same; not + ambiguous; ant. ambiguous (multiple meanings).

disavow -v- to deny something you earlier affirmed or represented; syns. foreswear//gainsay//recant//renounce//repudiate; cp. abjure (renounce under oath).

discant -n/v- *tedious & protracted talk;* Lat. dis-not + cant-sing; cp. disquisition (a *formal* discourse, often written / colloquy / dissertation); dialectics (reasoning); banter / badinage / doggerel (comic talk); natter / chatter / palaver / prattle (idle or silly talk); persiflage (flippant conversation); polemics (debate). Descant has two meanings: one is a synonym for discant; the other is: a counterpoint or highest part sung above the melody.

disciple -n- a follower and proselytizer of another's views; see apostle.

Disciples -n- the 12 Disciples of Christ; see list at "Apostles", Matt. 10:2-4.

discombobulate -v- to throw into a state of utter *confusion*; syn. discomfit.

discomfit -v- make uneasy or embarrassed.

discommode -v- to trouble or inconvenience someone; Lat. deprive of protection.

discourse -n- *verbal* exchange of ideas//discant; cp. colloquy// disquisition (formal discourse). banter (witty); dialectics (reasoning); persiflage (flippant discourse); polemics (debate); chatter / natter / prattle (silly verbiage); rigmarole (confused or lengthy communication); to palter (v-equivocate (to be ambiguous to the point of lying).

discursive -a- fluent & expansive; covering a wide range of subjects; also, *reaching a conclusion by reason/dialectics*, not intuition; root: not + hand-writing; cp. cursive (hand writing).

dishabille -n- a state of being scantily clothed; Fr. undressed.

disingenuous -a- not straightforward; ***crafty; devious***; what a knave is; cp. ingenuous (naive, guileless).

disintermediation -n- the removal of intermediaries/middlemen; e.g. buying online has done this; blockchain seems likely to expand it exponentially; Lat. "come".

dismay -n/v- frustration; puzzled distress; consternation (anxious dismay).

disparage -v- asperse//calumniate//decry/defame//debase//denigrate//deride//derogate//malign, cp traduce (malign falsely); cp. debunk (disprove); excoriate (censure scathingly).

dispensation -n- the act of dispensing, distributing, usually things of value.

disparate [dis-par-it] -a- *dissimilar;* unequal.

disquisition -n- a *formal* discourse, often written / colloquy; Lat. investigation; cp. dialectics (reasoning); descant (tedious discussion); banter/badinage/doggerel (comic); natter//chatter//palaver//prattle (idle chatter); persiflage (flippant conversation); polemics (debate); *dissertation.*

disseminate -v- to distribute.

dissipate/tion -v/n- to exhaust; state of being spent; enervate (weaken); debilitate (render immobile)

dissolute -a- immoral//base//licentious//wanton; a libertine/reprobate; see lascivious for similar.

diurnal -a- that which occurs *daily* / quotidian.

divisive [dih-<u>VIH</u>-sive. **Not** dih-VEYE-sive] -a- dividing; fractious; cp. discordant; creating discord/dissention; do **NOT** pronounce as "dih-VIE-sive" as is the common mispronunciation.

doc/doct-root- Lat. for "teach"; e.g., document; doctrine; indoctrinate.

docent [doe-sent] -n- a person who acts as a guide, esp. in a museum, art gallery or zoo; a teacher; cp. Pundit; Ger. teach.

doggerel -a- words *loosely* styled; *irregular*; esp. for **comic** effect; also, inferior.

dogma -n- a principle/statement claimed to be the *absolute truth*; generally refers to religious doctrines; Lat. opinion; **see** "Fundamentalists Christians" (their "5 dogmas").

doleful -a- filled with grief; despondent/dolorous; lugubrious; morose; soulful.

dollop -n- a large quantity of something, esp. liquid that falls from a cloud as if a plug was pulled.

<u>do</u>lorous -a- showing sorrow or pain; cp. doleful//lugubrious/soulful (in mourning), morose (brooding).

dolt -n- a blockhead//dullard//dunce//ignoramus; cp. lout (clumsy, stupid, boring person).

---

dom -root- Lat. for "house" or "master"; e.g., domicile; dominant; dominion; Dom Perignon.

dopamine -n- a brain-secretion that gives a sense of pleasure and energy. Exercise does this: the runner's "high".

dour -a- relentlessly severe, stern, gloomy; M.E.

dowager -n- a widow with a *title* or with considerable *wealth*; cp. endow (give/bequeath wealth) **doxology** -n- a hymn of praise; Lat. glory + logia/saying; cp. dirge (song/hymn of grief).

DNS -term- domain name server; while there are hundreds of servers worldwide, in **2016**, there were 13 "authoritative domain servers" (DNS') in world (10 in U.S., 1-Sweden, 1-Holland. *Tim Berners-Lee, a physicist, in **1989**, created the first large node* (a central, originating point that interconnected URL's) *at CERN in Switzerland; see WWW.*

don -v- to put on (clothes); a contraction of "do on".

Don/don -n- a title affixed to a surname denoting an important person. Span., It.

dote -v- to be exceptionally fond of someone; to care for them.

Draconian -a- Draco was an *Athenian leader* known for *extreme punishments*. Count Dracula, a mythical character, who became a vampire, in an 1897 novel by Brian Stoker. Cp. Vlad the Impaler, aka Vlad Dracula (1400's), a Hungarian nobleman known for his cruelty, such as impaling victims.

dregs -n- the remnants of a liquid. Orig. Scandnavian.

droll -a- dry, curious, unusual, esp. relating to humor.

drone -v/n- **VERB:** make a continuous *low humming sound or buzz*; **NOUN:** a *male bee* which does not work but fertilizes queen bee; today: *a remote, pilotless aircraft*; O.E. to resound.

druid/Druid -n- an order of *Gaelic priests-prophets/sorcerers*; Irish legend.

"DT's" -term- "delirium tremens", the shakes caused by alcoholism.

dulcet -a- especially sweet and soothing, esp. a sound; Ex. the dulcet tones of band.

dusk -n- the darkest stage of twilight just before night. O.E.

Dutch -n- a mispronunciation of "Deutsch"[Doitch]/German; refers to citizens of Holland (aka Netherlands).

dyspepsia/dyspeptic -n/a- disturbed digestion' cp. emetic (causing nausea and vomiting).

dysphonia/dysphonic -n/a- difficulty in *speaking*; often related to hoarseness; cp. dipsomania (alcoholism).

dystopia/n/ic -n/a- a place or condition of total misery; ant. utopia (ideal place).

"E"

Ebonics -n- English as misspoken by uneducated blacks; from "ebony" (a blackish wood).

Ebonite -n- *a Jew who followed Jesus (but not St. Paul)*; they were the first Christians; cp. *Messianic Jews* (modern-day Jews who have converted to Christianity, i.e., followers of the Messiah).

ebonite -n- a hard, inelastic rubber, used in weights and bowling balls.

ebullient/ce -a- *enthusiastic*; bubbly; lively; engaging / effervescent / vivacious; Fr. boil, bubble.

ecclesiastical -a- of or pertaining to a church; Gr. an ***assembly*** of people or thoughts.

eclectic -a- something that *combines elements/things from a variety of sources*.

eclipse -n/v- *to surpass, block or cast a shadow*; partial or complete *block of one celestial body by another*; e.g. **solar eclipse** (moon passes between sun and earth, which lasts only a few minutes, usually in July) and **lunar** (moon goes behind earth and earth prevents sun's rays from reaching moon, which lasts several hours and usually occurs in December). See Easter and solstice.

eclogue -n- a poem in the form of a pastoral dialogue; prefixes for log/ue: ana (analogous); epi (after); pro (before); mono (solo) ____.

ecosystem -n- a biological community of interacting organisms & their environment; ex. the ocean and sea life; the desert and desert life.

ecstasy -a- intense joy; euphoria; bliss; felicity; jubilance/jocosity; cp. Elysian; blithe.

ecumenical -a- *worldwide//universal//catholic*; esp. re a Christian church; Gr. cp. *secular* (not belonging to a religious order, hence putatively not spiritual); cp. ecclesiastical (church-related group); evangelical (relating to the Gospels).

eddy -n- a current of *water running contrary to the main current*, esp. in a counterclockwise circle.

edict -n- a proclamation by an authority; cp. interdict (*prohibitory* decree); injunction (prohibitory *or* mandatory order).

efface -v- <u>erase</u>; expunge//eradicate//obliterate; cp. expurgate (erase obscene matter); purge; cp. deface (mar / disfigure).

effete [ee-feet] -a- *no longer productive, infertile*; weak; worn out//enervate; dissipated; cp. decadent (decaying); atrophied (withering); Lat. effetus-worn out by child bearing; ant. fecund; cp. impotent; fecund (fertile).

effervescent -a- bubbly; engaging; enthusiastic; syn. ebullient / vivacious; Fr. to bubble or boil; cp. effulgent (shining).

efficacy/cious -n/a- effect; ability to produce desired effects; used as "the _____ of something.

effigy -n- a painted or *sculpted likenesses*, usually of a person.

effrontery -n- *brazen & insulting boldness//temerity*; near syns: audacity//bodacious (fearless).

effluence/effluent -n- *outflow*; issue; effusion; emanation; e.g. grass fm. seed; cp. profusion (abundant outpouring).

---

effluvia/ium -n- outflow, waste, sometimes invisible, esp. related to mining and minerals.

effulgent/ce -a/n- radiant; shining; Fr. to shine; cp. ebullient/effervescent (bubbly).

effusion/effusive -n/a- out-pouring; unrestrained utterance; effluence; ex. he is ___.

egalitarian -a- believer in the social and political equality of men; Lat. Equal.

egregious -a- *flagrant;* outrageously bad.

egoism -n- *selfish;* cp. solipsistic (self, the only reality); narcissism (erotic self-love).

egotism/tistical -n/a- *conceited;* cp. egoism (selfish).

eidetic -a- denoting mental images, having unusually vivid detail; ex. an eidetic memory (a photographic memory on steroids).

ejaculate -v- to eject semen at sexual climax; also, to say something suddenly, an exclamation.

El -n- abbreviation for "**Elohim**", the 2nd most common word for God in Torah (Gen., Ex, Lev, Nms, Deut); **Adonia** is 1st; Torah also uses **YHVH** ("Yaweh") as Hebrew had no vowels (or punctuation), which some Non-Jews pronounce "**Jehovah**".

élan [ee-**lan**] -n- *style;* flair; enthusiastic vigor/liveliness; cp. cachet (individualistic characteristics); ethos (*distinguishing* aspect of a person/culture//thing); karma (essence/spirit); panache (flamboyance); charisma (rare power).

electron -n- *one of three* sub-atomic particles of an atom (protons and neutrons); a *negative* charge; cp. atom, molecule, particle, quantum, Uncertainty Principle; see elements and atom.

elegy/iac [el-eh-gee] -n/a- a *melancholy poem*; esp. memoriam; cp. eulogy (tribute to the deceased).

Eliot -n- name meaning "from God"; "iot"=from; EL is short for Elohim (the second most commonly name for God in the early versions of the OT) originally meant "the mountain", as the mountain was an early "god" for some, as was the sun, etc. Common misspellings: Elliot/Elliott.

elf -n- a *supernatural creature* from folk tales, in human form, with pointed ears & magical powers; cp. lepricon and gnome (dwarf-like creature who guards treasures).

elicit [ee-**liss**-it] -v- to induce, bring forth (as via hypnotism); Fr. to allure.

elision -n- the omission of a sound or text ("I'm" or "The book … began"); Lat. crush out; near syn. ellipsis.

ellipse/ellipsoid/ial -n/a- a *plane curve*; a surface comprised of same; geometry term; cp. aquiline.

ellipsis/ic -n/a- omission of words/elision, such as the use of three dots (…) to reveal the omission of words in a quotation; also refers to assumed or obvious words: e.g., "[You] Jump." Also, refers to a leap from one topic to another (electron-like leaps); Gk. omit; cp. desultory (jumping place-to-place).

elliptical [ee-lip-tih-cal] -a- related to an ellipse.

---

elucidate [ee-**luce**-ih-date] -v- to explain clearly; to make lucid; cp. elicit (bring forth).

Elysian/ium -a- pertaining to the *Greek's heaven*; hence, blissful, heavenly; sublime; supernal (celestial); Arcadia (blissful place, Gr.); El Dorado; U/utopia (ideal place); Valhalla (Norse heaven).

emasculate -v- to deprive spirit, strength, vigor; to weaken; L. missing + male.

emblematic -a- serving as an emblem or symbol; *representative.*

embower -v- to surround or embrace; e.g. trees embower the house; bower = shelter.

embryology -n- study of **life's** origins or embryos (any vertebrate prior to birth); egg + knowledge.

emetic -n- an agent that causes vomiting; Gk. vomit; cp. colonic; dyspeptic.

empathy/ize -n/v- using your personal experience to *understand or feel* another person's problem; cp. sympathy (compassion for another's problem w/o the benefit of personal experience).

empiricism/empirical -n/a- the philosophical pursuit of *knowledge by observation*/experience/ *experiment*; Lat. experienced; ant. a priori (without precedent or prior knowledge).

empurple -v- to color or tinge with the color purple.

empyreal/empyrean [em-pie-ree-an] -a/n- *celestial*; the highest heaven in ancient cosmology; related to emperors; Elysia; sublime; an ideal condition or place; Utopia; El Dorado; Gr.

emulate/emulous [**em**-u-late] -v/a- to imitate.

emulous -a- a desire to emulate/imitate; Lat.

encipher -v- to convert a message into "cipher" (code); to encode; ant. decipher (decode).

encomium -n- a formal speech of praise; a eulogy; Gr. en-within + komos – level; a panegyric (a public speech or text in praise of someone or something).

encrimson -v- to make or dye red; to embarrass; florid (flush with red, rosy).

Encyclopedists -n- 18th century school of dialecticians (reasoners), sophists (questioners) and atheists led by French philosophers, Diderot and Voltaire.

endeavor -v/n- to strive to do; the act of doing so.

endemic -a- *native* to a particular people OR place; cp., indigenous (native to place); cp. denizen/habitué (one who frequents a place).

endogenous [en-**dodge**-eh-nus] -a- *produced from within*, as from within a cell; ant. exogenous; cp. androgynous (male and female characteristics).

energy -n- Science: *That which makes things happen* and causes changes. It has *many forms*: chemicals, electricity, heat, light, sound, water, wind. It's invisible; cannot be made or destroyed, but, rather, only converted to other forms (as is the case with atoms).

enervate -v- deprive of strength; weaken; devitalize; dissipate; exhaust; make effete/impotent; effete (worn out) Lat. enervare; causing lassitude, languor, fecklessness; cp. stolid (emotionless); torpid (numb).

enigma/tic -n/a- *puzzling*; conundrum; near sysn. indecipherable; inscrutable; esoteric; arcane; abstruse; obscure; recondite.

enmity -n- hatred; mutual antagonism; abhorrence/imprecation/odious (hateful); execrate (curse or damn); rancor (deep ill-will).

ennui [on-wee] -n- *boredom*; listlessness/dissatisfaction resulting from lack of interest.

ensconced -v- *sheltered*; concealed; *deeply planted.*

enthrall -v- to *spellbind, captivate*; cp. enslave; Lat. to put into + slave.

entomology -n- the study of *insects*; cp. etymology (study of words).

entourage -n- a group of *attendants or associates.*

entreat/ies -v/n- to make an *earnest request*; beseech; cp. importune (beg); invoke (call for help).

entropy/entropic -n/a- *disorder*; that which measures the degree of disorder of a system (e.g., the universe); *the physicists' law* that all *things unattended fall into disarray*; ant. dharma

envisage [en-vis-edge] -v- visualize; envision; to put into + eyes.

epaulettes -n- shoulder ornaments, especially with a fringed strap worn on military uniforms.

ephemera/al -n/a- that which is *short-lived*; fleeting; cp. evanescent (vanishing); transient (passing quickly).

epicurean/ism -n- Phil. *the philosophy of luxurious living*; to *accept fate and defeat and concentrate on pleasure*(hedonist/sybarite); today, generally used to refer to one devoted to gourmet food and wine; near syns: hedonism; sybarite; ant. asceticism.

epidermis -n- the outer layer of skin; cp. hypodermis (layer of skin just below epidermis).

---

epigenetic/sis -n- *genetically* influenced *motivational* factors; e.g. patriotism; racism; religion.

epigram -n- a short *poem* expressing a single thought; also means a concise witty and often **paradoxical truth**. Ex. "Too soon old, too late smart"; cp, adage; elegy; epilogue; oxymoron.

epigraph -n- an <u>inscription</u>, esp. on a tomb, statue or building; cp. epitaph.

epilogue -n- epi = on/upon/after + log; *a short speech/writing* at the *conclusion* of a work; a post script; ant: prologue (text preceding a work); cp. analogue (an analogy to something else).

epiphany -n- a *revelation* of a *divine* being; an incarnation; <u>E</u>piphany- relig. holiday before Lent; cp. avatar (divine incarnation, but, today, any likeness of a person); apparition (ghost).

epistle/Epistles -n- a *formal* letter; e.g., books James-Jude in N.T.; cp. missive (writing from a *higher* authority).

epistemology/temic -n/a- *study of origin, nature and validity of knowledge*; the theory/science.

epitaph -n- a brief <u>written</u> <u>tribute</u> *to a deceased person* (e.g. on a tombstone); cp. eulogy(same at funeral); elegy (poetic eulogy).

epithet -n- descriptive word or phrase; Lat. epi = upon + to place.

epitome -a- an ideal of something; a brief summary; Gr. to cut short. cp. archetype//exemplar (best of type); prototype (model); see apex.

epoch/epochal -n- a particular *period of history*, especially one considered remarkable or noteworthy.

---

eponym/eponymous -n/a- a *name* of a person that relates to a *place* (Romulus//"Tex"); e.g., an eponymous restaurant; cp. acronym (WAC, WOP), anagram (God/dog, pea/ape), anonym (a name written backwards: eel ttevol); acrostic(word made from the first letters of every line of a poem) homonym (but/butt/butt).

epoxy -v/n- glue, fill or coat as with an epoxy resin.

equanimity -n/a- evenness of mind; *balanced disposition//equable*; *unflappable*; homeostatic (balanced mind and body).

equator -n- the *great circle dividing the earth's* Northern & Southern hemispheres; the *circumference* of the earth at the equator *is 25K* miles; earth's *diameter is 8K* miles.

equatorial -a- at, near, or related to, the equator.

equinox -n- either of 2 times a year *when the sun crosses the celestial equator, when day/night equal*; the "vernal equinox" is 22 Mar.; "autumnal equinox" is 22 Sept.; root: equator/equi; cp. summer and winter solstices (when the sun is at its highest or most distant point from the earth creating the longest and shortest days): 21 June/Dec.=longest/shortest days.

eradicate -v- destroy completely/decimate/obliterate; Lat. torn out by roots; cp. efface / expunge (erase).

ergo -a- therefore (in Latin).

eros/Eros -a/n- sexual love; Gr. God of love/sexuality, son of Aphrodite; cp. erotic.

erotic -a- abnormally sensitive to sexual stimulation; Eros (Gr. god of sexuality).

err -root- Lat. to make a mistake; e.g., error; aberrant (deviating from norm).

err [errr] -v- to make a mistake.

errant [air-ahnt] -a- roving in search of adventure; knight ___ (e.g. Don Quixote); (Lat. to err); cp. arrant (completely such, e.g., an arrant fool).

ersatz -a- *artificial*; Gr. *substitute*.

erstwhile -a/n- <u>former</u>; erst=first + while.

erudite -a- knowledgeable; learned; cognoscente; cp. maven (expert); pedant (ostentatiously learned); pedagogue (teacher who is ostentatiously learned); pundit (teacher/critique), sagacious (wise), savant (knows w/o being taught; polymath (super-learned at genius level).

eschatology [ess-ka-tology] -n- a *branch of theology* concerned with the last things, e.g., death, Gr. last/ology; cp. moribund (dying); necrophilia (fascination, even sex, with dead); necromancy (communication with the dead); see Rapture; cp. scatology (study of excrement).

eschew -v- shun; avoid; escape; evade.

esoteric -a- understood by the specially trained; cp.arcane (by a few); abstruse / obscure / recondite (difficult to fathom); inscrutable (not understandable); ineffable (indescribable).

esplanade -n- a level, open stretch of paved or grassy ground, esp. for walking; M.F; cp. heath.

esprit de corps [ss-**pree**-du-core] phrase Fr. spirit of the corps; team spirit.

espy [ess-spy] -v- to catch site of; *glimpse*; cp. descry (discern something difficult); cp. decry (disparage).

essay [ESS-ay] -n- short literary piece; often philosophical.

essay [ess-SAY] -v- test the quality of; to try; to ___ the gold content.

Estates:

The Three Estates -term- In the Middle Ages, the social order was sometimes referred as "the Three Estates", which referred to the Church, the nobility, and the masses; the word "estate" may refer to a prescribed area and/or other assets under common ownership.

Fourth & Fifth Estates -term- Over the last Century, *the press* has been added as the Fourth Estate, and very recently, the Fifth Estate has been added: the *non*-mainstream media, e.g. independent news organs, bloggers or any group beyond the other estates, e.g. online sources.

esthete/tic -n/a- one with *artistic* skills or appreciative of same.

estimable -a- anything worthy of respect; esteemed; Lat. to estimate; "an ___ man"; cp. revered / venerated (worshipped).

estuary -n- an *arm of a sea* that extends inland to meet the mouth of a river.

ether -n- the upper regions of space/Heavens; also the light that permeates all space/airwaves; also a light, flammable, volatile liquid C4H10O; also, loosely "the air".

ethereal -a- unusually *delicate or refined*; ether-like; syn. gossamer (gauzy, shear); cp. diaphanous (transparent); translucent/pellucid (transmitting light); ephemeral (fleeting).

ethnic/ology -n- of or pertaining to a *race, religion, cultural or national group*; Lat. national.

ethnocentric -a- placing ethnicity at the center; making it important.

ethos -n- the *distinguishing character or values* peculiar to a *person, people, culture.* or movement; cachet (individuality); cp. aura/ ambiance (distinctive atmosphere of place or person); élan (flair, style); karma (spirit/essence); panache (flamboyance in style).

etude [a-tude] -n- a piece of music played to practice technique or for its artistic valued.

etymology -n- *study* of history of linguistic forms, languages, ***mainly word***s; cp. semantics (study of definitions); lexicography (dictionary); linguistics(language); orthography (study of the way letters blend to form sounds); philology (love of learning); syntax (grammar); entomology (insect-study).

Eucharist -n- a religious ceremony commemorating the Last Supper; aka Communion; R.C. sacrament/sacred rites: bread/wafer & wine (flesh & blood of Jesus); Lat. *gratitude ;* One of the three RC sacraments (baptism, marriage, communion) which RC's say salvation requires.

euchre [u-ker] -n/v- a card game; *tricking*/cheating someone else; cp. legerdemain// prestidigitation.

eugenics -n- the science of developing the best offspring; Gr. good + genes.

eulogy [u-lo-gee] -n- a laudatory speech or written tribute, esp. at a funeral; cp. elegy (poetic tribute); syn. encomium; a panegyric (a public *speech or text in praise* of some*one* or something); epitaph (written or verbal praise of deceased); epigraph (written praise, esp. on a tombstone).

eunuch [u-nuck] -n- a *castrated* man or whose testes did not develop.

eupeptic -a- healthy digestion or good spirits; eu = well; pepten = digestion; cp. winsome (winning, *a youthful, innocent charm*); blithe (carefree joy); ant. dispetic.

euphemism -n- substitution of a *mild* term *for* a *blunt* one; understatement; cp. euph<u>u</u>ism (affected writing).

euphony/euphonic -n/a- *pleasing* to the ear; see aural (heard via ear).

euphoria/ic -n/a- extreme sense of well being; *bliss; ecstasy; exultant; felicity;* jubilant/jocose.

euphuism/tic -n- *affected* manner of writing/speaking; flowery// grandiloquent; rhetoric; orotund (pompous, pretentious writing/ speaking); cp. pedantic (ostentatious display of knowledge); bombast (overdone/empty); hyperbole (exaggerations).

Eurasia -n- countries in Asia, Eastern and Western Europe, UK, Russia & in Med; cp. Occident (Eur+Americas).

evanescent -a- *vanishing* (missing+vanished); cp. ephemeral (short lived); transient (passing quickly).

evangelical/ist -a- relating to the Christian gospel, esp. the four gospels of the NT; a member of a group *believing that salvation comes from faith* rather than from good deeds; see Calvin & Augustine, cp. Acquinas (reconciled faith & reason); proselytizing (converting)[4] ; root: from + angelos / messanger.

---

4 See "Christianity" for brief history.

evangelism -n- the *zealous preaching* of the gospel; militant zeal for a cause; CP. **gospel** (Fr. god/*good+spell tale*, generally relates to The Gospels (NT:Matt-John), loosely defined as truth or fact, although *the root Fr. word suggests a "tale" or fiction; false.*

evasion -n- *escaping* some consequence *by deceit*; cp. avoidance (doing same w/o deceit).

evince -v- display clearly; reveal; show; evidence; cp. presage (foreshadow).

eviscerate -v- to disembowel/remove a vital part/destroy; cp. flay (skin); vivisect (dissection of animals).

exacerbate [ex-ass-er-bait] -v- aggravate; make more intense; *compound.*

exaltation -n- feeling of bliss; also being elevated to a high place.

Excalibur -n- the legendary *sword* magician-Merlin gave King Arthur making him invincible.

excise -v/a- to remove by cutting/tax; cp. eradicate; expunge/efface (erase); expurgate (remove obscene lang).

excogitate -v- to think out, plan, *mentally strain*; Root: out + think; cp. muse/reflect (think) / opine (give opinion) / extrapolate (reach a conclusion by calculating data).

excommunicate -n/v- expelled from a church by *ecclesiastical* decree; cp. exile (governmental expulsion).

excoriate -v- *to censure scathingly*//fulminate//revile//vilify//vituperate; cp. asperse. calumniate; debase//decry//defame//denigrate// derogate//malign//inveigh.

---

excrement -n- *waste* discharged thru the anus/the effluent of defecation; syn. feces; cp. secretion//scat (animal excrement).

exculpate -v- to free from blame or guilt; absolve; *exonerate; vindicate.*

excursion -n- a short journey; cp. escapade (adventure).

execrable/ation -a/n- deserving hatred//abominable/enmity; extremely bad/inferior; near syn. odious (causing hatred); cp. invidious (causing jealousy).

execrate -v- to *curse / damn / hate*; cp. abhor/ abominate / imprecate (hate); ex = away; sacrare = sacrament; malediction(a curse).

excrete/tion/ment -v/n- to discharge/defecate harmful waste; the waste; cp. secretion/scat (discharge of animals).

exegesis [X-eh-gegh-sis] -n- *analysis; interpretation; critique,* esp. of a text or scripture; GK.

exeget [X-eh-jet] -n/v- an interpreter of text, esp. religious; to interpret or expound on text; Gk.

exemplar/y -n- *an ideal that serves as a pattern*; one that is worthy of imitation; a model; cp. archetype//prototype (an original model); lodestar (guiding star); paradigm (a parallel).

exhort -v- *to incite by words*/foment; advise correctly; cp. admonish (advise or reprove kindly); beseech/entreat (urge); importune (beg).

exhume -v- disinter; bring back from the grave; L. out + earth.

exiguous [ex-idge-u-us] -a- scanty/de minimis/modicum/ /paucity; ex. his exiguous assets; Lat.weigh.

exile -v- to expel from one's country; cp. extrude (force out); exorcise (cast out demons).

existential/ism/ist -a/n- a philosophy that (1) **regards human existence as inexplicable** and (2) accepts the *uniqueness and isolation* of the individual experience; (3) views the universe as *hostile or indifferent*; and (4) stresses *freedom of choice* and *responsibility for the consequences of one's acts*; the writers, Dostoyevsky and Sartre, were prominent proponents; most pantheists, humanists, agnostics atheists and even some deists classify themselves as existentialists; cp. **nihilism** (all values are baseless; nothing is knowable) see "deism" for related "ism's".

exogenous -a- *external* to the system; exo (outside) + genis (gene); ant. endogenous (within system).

exorcise -v- to cast out, as demons; cp. excise (to cut as taxes).

exotic -a- *from a distant culture*; usually refers to a beautiful woman.

expatiate -v- to speak or write at length; explicate/exposit ; perorate (summarize grandiloquently).

expedient -a- *promoting one's interests* at another's expense; Lat.; cp. ad hominine; hegemony.

expedite/tious -v/a- *act with speed*; Ex. He expedited his knee recovery by adhering to the Doctor's suggestions. Avoid confusing with expedient (promoting one's interests w/o regard to others).

expiate/tion -v/n- to make atonement //penitence//reparation// retribution (give recompense for an injury); cp. contrition (expressing sorrow for error); repentant (sorrow; change ways, make amends); conciliation / placate / propitiate / mediate (settle disputes).

explicate -v- to explain, make clear//explain//exposit; cp. expiate.

---

export -v/n- to send to another country; root: from+port; see import; cp. exile (to permanently expel a person from a country).

exposit/tion -n/v- to explain meaning or intent; explain / explicate; cp. posit (state as fact).

expositor/expostulation -n- one who *explains or exposes* the meaning.

expostulate -v- to express strong disapproval; Lat. demand; cp. postulate (assume, stipulate); posit (state as fact); propound (suggest); explicate (explain).

expunge -v- to *remove entirely*; efface//erase / eradicate; cp. annihilate / obliterate. excise(cut); expurgate (remove offensive material, e.g., porn).

expurgate -v- to remove *obscene* or objectionable material; cp. expunge (erase); excise (cut as taxes).

exquisite -a- elegant; rare; special.

extant -a- still existing.

extirpate -v- to pull up by the roots, cp. exterminate (eliminate).

extract -v- to remove, take out.

extricate -v- to *rescue* from difficulty.

extrovert -n- one who is outgoing; interested; ant. introvert.

extrude -v- to force or *push out*; expel; Fr. to thrust; cp. exile (from country); exorcise (cast out demons).

exult/ant -v/a- rejoice; blissful; felicitous; cp. ecstatic; euphoric; jubilant; jocular; jocose.

"F"

facet -n- an aspect of something; a component, a part; a _____ of a diamond.

facile/facilitate -a/v- mild mannered; compliant; *making something seem easy.*

fagot/faggot -n- a bundle of sticks bound together; slang meaning a male homosexual.

Fahrenheit -n- a thermometric method of measuring temperature created by physicist Fahrenheit c. 1725; *used only in U.S. and a few other countries.* To convert Fahrenheit to centigrade/Celsius, subtract 30 and divide by two; e.g. 90 degrees F = 30 centigrade/Celsius (90-30=60/2=30); see centigrade. In reverse, to convert C to F: 10C=10x2+30=50F.

fain -a- happily; preferably; willingly; wont; Gr. happy; ex. He is fain/wont to do; cp. feign (pretend); deign (condescend); vouchsafe (grant privilege).

faith/Faith -n/name- *belief in something that cannot be proved,* "Faith is the *substance* of things *hoped* for and the *evidence* of things *not seen.*" Hebrews 11:1. "And now abideth faith, hope and charity... the greatest of these is charity." I Corinthians 13:14. Some enjoy Twain's priceless comment on point, "Faith is what you believe that you know ain't so."

fathom -n/v- *a unit of length equal to 6 feet* in the measurement of *marine* depth; also, to determine the depth of; to sound, hence, to understand; cp. league (3 statute miles/4.3 km) or a group of states/competitors; twain (a set of two, esp. 2 fathoms or 12 feet); furlong (220 yds); meter (3.3 feet).

fatuous -a- foolish//insensate; cp. inane (empty).

faux pas -idiom- Fr. a social blunder.

fealty -n- loyalty//fidelity//troth.

febrile [feh-breel] -a- feverish; Lat. fever.

fecal/feces -a/n- waste discharged thru the anus; see excrement; cp. secretion//scat(animal excrement).

feckless -a- *lacking purpose* or vitality; *careless*; effect-less; cp. insipid/flat/dull/vapid; hapless(hopeless).

fecund [fee-**kund**] -a- fertile; fruitful; productive; ant. effete (worn out/infertile).

feign [fain] -v- to *pretend* or fabricate; cp. fain (happily); deign (condescend); vouchsafe (grant privilege).

felicity/felicitous -n/a- bliss; happiness; agreeable; blissful; cp. euphoria; ecstasy; exultant; jubilant; fain (happily); genial (cheerful); congenial (agreeable).

fellah -n- a *peasant laborer* in Arabic countries; Anglicized to "fellow"; cp. churl (peasant); serf (worker bound to the land/an indentured servant, under a feudal lord); proletariat (laboring class).

feral -a- existing in the *wild; untamed;* e.g., a ___ cat.

ferret -n/v- a prairie-dog/hound dog like animal that constantly searches; to search.

festination -n- a series of accelerated small steps or other movements common to PD patients, as well depicted by Tim Conway on the Carol Burnet TV Show.

festoon -n/v- *things hung in a string; garland* (same but only of flowers).

fete [fet] -n/v- a celebration or festival; to entertain or honor lavishly; Fr. feast.

fetid -a- having an offensive smell; *malodorous;* fusty (stale, decaying); miasma (unhealthy); putrid (decaying smell); mephitic (rotten odors from the earth); ant. aroma (pleasant scent); cp. olfactory (sense of smell).

fetish -n- obsession; an object of worship.

fetter -n/v- a chain/shackle; restraint; encumber; impediment; obstruction; to do aforesaid.

fettle -n/v- a condition of health, fitness, wholeness; to set in order/get ready; Fr./Old Eng.

fez -n- man's felt cap in shape of a flat-topped cone with a tassel; Shriners; Middle Eastern; a town in Morocco.

fiacre [fee-ach-rah] -n- small, *four*-wheeled carriage for *hire*; named after Fr. hotel where first rented; cp. surrey (same but *not* for hire); hackney (4-wheeled carriage for *hire* but drawn by 2 horses; today often refers to a taxi or taxi driver as "hack").

fiasco -n- an event that is a miserable, ridiculous *failure.*

fiat -n- an *arbitrary* order or decree; Lat. let it be done (regardless of harm).

fickle -a- *erratic*, especially with attachments to people; cp. capricious (whimsical).

---

fid -root- Lat. for faith or trust; e.g. affidavit (sworn written statement); perfidy (disloyalty).

fidelity -n- *loyalty//fealty//troth*; fealty; *exactness*, as in a copy; clarity of *sound*/image.

filch -v- to appropriate furtively; to *steal*/pinch//purloin; ME.

filial [fill-ee-al] -a- relating to a <u>child</u>; cp. familial.

filament [fill-ah-ment] -n- a slender, *threadlike object or fiber*; a variant of filigree.

fillip -n- something that *stimulates or boosts an activity*. Reading is a fillip to knowledge.

fission [fish-shun] -n- the process of dividing or splitting apart.; cp. fusion (joining things).

fissure [fish-shure] -n- a long, narrow opening, or crack or cleft; aperture (gap, opening)/orifice (vent, hole or mouth); interstice (space between things); lesion (skin-wound); orifice (hole, outh, vent); rictus (hole or bird's beak).

flaccid -a- *lacking firmness* or resilience; e.g. _____ cheeks or muscles.

flagellation/ate/ant -n/v- *whipping*; punishing; one who is whips or is whipped//flogged; cp. flail.

flagrant [flay-grant] -a- extremely offensive or wrong; Fr. to burn; cp. conflagration(destroy by fire).

flail -n/v- a stick with a chain on the end, used to whip wheat (or people).

flamboyant/ce -a/n- elaborate or *colorful* display or conduct; Fr. to flame; panache. (flamboyant style); cp. cachet (distinctive characteristics); élan (style); ethos//karma(essence/spirit).

flatter -v- insincerely compliment; cp. compliment (sincere praise); blandish/inveigle/wheedle (to coax by flattery).

flax/en -n/a- a widely cultivated plant with blue flowers, the seeds of which are used to make textiles (linen) and oil; *ground flax seeds are blond in color*, and may refer to "flaxen hair"; wheat and other light-colored hair are similarly blond.

flay -v- to *strip off the skin or money or criticize* severely; cp. fillet (cut into narrow strips); depredate (plunder, loosely rape); rapine (rape).

fledgling -n- a young bird; an immature person; M.E. to fly; neophyte; novice; recruit; rookie; squire; tyro.

fleet -a/n- fast, nimble in movement; ex. _____ of foot. NOUN: ships under control of one Cmdr.

florid -a- flushed with *rosy* color; *ruddy*; cp. redolent (aromatic).

flotsam -n- floating debris; Fr. to float.

flout -v- to openly disregard a rule, law or convention; scoff; Dutch.

foil -v/n- to *trick, to prevent* from being successful; a *fencing sword*, a thin sheet of metal; *one by whose strong contrast underscores the distinctive characteristics of another*; the straight man in a comedy team.

foist -v- to impose something, esp. surreptitiously; ex. Obama foisted the Muslims on America.

folderol/falderal -n- *foolishness; nonsense;* trivial or nonsensical language, behavior or ideas; rubbish.

folly -a- foolishness; Fr. madness; cp. fatuous/insensate (foolish).

fop -n- a man concerned with his clothes; one affects feminism; a dandy, esp. a gay.

foray -n- *a sudden raid* or military advance; syn. incursion; Scan.; cp. fray/scuffle/brawl; melee (hand-to-hand combat); imbroglio (argument); sortie (armed attack going from defense to offense).

force majeure -Legal term- An event beyond human control; an act of God; a major force.

forensic -a- evidence/data employed in arguments or legal proceedings; Lat. forum.

forsake -v- to abandon; cp. forlorn (sad/lonely/doleful/morose/soulful).

forswear/foreswear -v- to *disavow//renounce//*relinquish//reject// forgo//disavow even under oath; aka abjure//recant; gainsay (deny or contradict); repudiate (to challenge or deny something).

forte [for-tay] -n- some endeavor in which one exceeds; one's strongsuit. Ex. Chess is his forte.

fortitude -a- strength of mind; ability to withstand pain.

fortnight -n- two weeks; "fourteen nights"; cp. one score (20).

four score -n- four times a score (20) or 80; see Lincoln's *Gettysburg Address*.

fractious -a- creating fractures, anything divisive; *irritated;* ill-tempered; cp. choleric (easily angered; ill-tempered / bilious / irascible); volatile (changeable).

fratricide/al -n- killing one's brother; cp. matricide, patricide; genocide (group); homicide.

fray -n/v- scuffle or brawl; a dispute; to wear away as the edges of fabric; cp. foray, melee, sortie.

frankincense -n- an oil or aromatic gum from trees that is burned as incense; syn. myrrh.

frenetic -a- frantic; frenzied; Gr. brain disease; syn. madding.

fug -root- from Lat. to flee/escape; e.g., refugee; fugitive.

fulcrum -n- Mech. the support around which a lever turns; also, the *cause of the action*; the stem-winder; near syns: cog (a tooth on gear); catalyst (something that causes change); pinion (bird's wing).

fulgent -a- dizzyingly bright; Lat; syn. refulgent; cp. coruscating (flashing/sparkling).

fulminate -n- to make a *thunderous verbal attack*; excoriate; revile; vilify, vituperate etc.; cp. calumniate (slander).

Furher -n- Ger. "leader"; Hitler's name for himself; Gr.; syn. "Il Duce" [Doo-chay], Mussolini.

furlong -n- 220 yards/201 meters; see league (3 statute miles), fathom (6 ft); see meter (3.3 ft.).

furrow -n- a long, narrow *trench* made in the ground by a plow; a crease, wrinkle; see fissure.

furtive -a- clandestine, *covert*; *surreptitious*; done secretly, stealthily; cp. cowled (hooded).

fusion -n- the process of *joining* two or more atomic nuclei to form a single heavier nucleus, thus releasing large quantities of energy; fusion is the process that powers the stars, hydrogen bombs and some experimental devices for electrical generation. *Nuclear fission* refers to the *splitting* of the atoms to create energy; cp. fissure (crack/cleft). Fission (the process of dividing something).

fustian -a- pompous or pretentious speech or prose/**orotund**; Lat. pillow-padding; cp. bombast (empty speech); euphuistic (affected speech/prose).

fusty -a- smelling *stale*, damp, decaying/putrid; also old fashioned in attitude, style, speech.

gabble/gab -v- to talk rapidly and unintelligibly; cp. banter (speak in *humorous* way; chatter//natter// palaver//prattle (to *talk idly*); colloquy (formal convsation); persiflage (flippant colloquy); prate (talk foolishly or tediously); rigmarole (confused talk); cp malaprop/ism (comically misused words).

gaffe -n/v- a long stick with a sharp hook on one end, to grab fish from the water; Fr.; to stick, cheat; cp. flail (stick with a chain on end; also meaning to strike the wheat).

Gaelic -a- from Scotland, Ireland or surrounding islands; orig. Celtic fm Ireland & Scottish Highlands.

gaggle -n- a flock of *geese*; a cluster or group.

gainsay -v- to declare false; deny//disavow//foreswear//recant; O.E.; abjure (deny under oath); recant; renounce; repudiate (deny); cp. rescind (reverse decision); vouchsafe (to grant a privilege; remise (release a claim).

galaxy -n- a cluster of stars; see Milky Way, Aquarius & universe.

gall -n/v- a chronic skin sore; today, *impudent behavior*; also the contents of the gallbladder / bile (known for excessive bitterness and stench); to fret or *wear down or make sore by friction*; M.E., O.E.

gallinipper -n- a large mosquito inflicting a painful bite; humorous Civil War term for mosquitoes so large that they could "nip" a "gallon" of blood in one bite.

gambit -n- a chess move to sacrifice a minor piece for a major one; *a winning strategy*; Lat. leg, to trip.

gambol -v- to run or jump playfully; frolic; Lat. leg; cp. gamble (bet).

galvanize -v- to *stimulate* or shock with an *electric* current; to *move to action*.

garland -n- string of *flowers*, festoon (anything hung in a string).

garrulous -n- *tiresomely* talkative; cp. loquacious (talkative); prolix/verbose (wordy); cp. voluble (easy flow of speech); ant. laconic//pithy//sententious//succinct/terse (concise and brief with words).

gauche [go-shsh] -a- Fr. lacking social graces//crude//*tactless*; Fr. root: left.

gaucherie [go-sharee] -n- awkward, embarrassing, unsophisticated ways.

geld -v- castrate, neuter, desex; deprive of vitality; M.E.

genial -a- friendly, cheerful; syn. congenial//cordial; of similar genes; cp. felicitous (happy).

genesis -n- the coming into being of anything.

genital/ilia -n- male / female *sexual organs*.

gentile -n- a non-Jew; a goyim (Heb. For gentile).

genocide -n- the *assassination of a group* (racial, political or cultural); syn. holocaust.

genome -n- an organism's *complete set of genetic code*; the human genetic code consists of *3 billion base pairs organized into 50-80K genes*.

genuflect -v- bend the knee/kneel; esp. in worship,

georgic -n- a poem or book dealing with rural life or agriculture; Virgil's epic poem, "Georgics", likely origin of the name "George".

gerontology/phobia -n- the *study of aging* (physiological and pathological); fear of same; geriatric (old, outmoded).

gerontocracy -n- rule by elders; cp. autocracy, democracy, plutocracy.

gerund -n- v*erb* form with "*ing*" ending, used as a *NOUN*; e.g., flying is fun; cp. participle (adj. form, flying fish).

gesticulate -v- make gestures with your hands; cp. legerdemain/ prestidigitation (slight of hand, crafty).

ghoul [gool] -n- an evil spirit or phantom; or one who robs graves and eats dead bodies.

gist [jihst] -n- the *central idea*; Law: basis of the case; Lat.; cp. jest (joke).

glib -a- taking for granted//*presume*; cavalier//flippant(casual, dismissive); cp. assume (believe/accept); insouciant//nonchalant.

gloaming -n- twilight/after sunset before dark; Ger. to glow.

glut -n- syns. plethora; superfluity/surfeit (*excess*); **cp**. plentitude/ profusion (*abundance*); spate (overflow).

gluten -n- an elastic substance from wheat that gives cohesiveness, e.g., in dough.

gluteus maximum -n- the outermost muscle of the buttocks.

glyph -n- an ornamental, verticle groove, esp. in a Doric frieze (an artifact imbedded in an edifice); also, a symbolic figure or character used in ancient systems of writing; cp. hieroglyphics (a system of writing in pictoral characters; Gk. pictures = carvings).

gni/gno -root- Gk. "to know"; e.g., recognize; cognitive (related to mind); agnostic; incognito (not known/disguised); prognosis (before knowledge, a prediction).

gnome/ic [nome] -n/a- *fabled* race of *dwarflike* creatures who lived underground guarding treasures; a/k/a Swiss bankers; also means a pithy saying/aphorism etc.

goad -n/v- a spiked stick/prod for driving cattle; to prod or stimulate movement.

goblin -n- an ugly, mischievous, dwarflike creature from English folk lore; cp. gnome.

google/googol -n- 1 followed by 100 zeros; math: 1 to the 1000th power; 10 to the 100th power;

gorge -n/v- a ravine or large open space; -v- to eat excessively or voraciously.

Gospel(s) -n- *teachings of Jesus/hisApostles*; the first four books of N.T.; Fr./O.E. godspell / god / good + spell a tale; currently used to mean a teaching accepted as true; cp. evangel (Gr. good news); evangelism.

gossamer -n- a soft *sheer, gauzy, delicate* (*fabric* or thing) / ethereal/ refined/delicate / diaphanous (transparent); cp. translucent// pellucid (transmitting light).

goyim [**goy**-yim] -n- Heb. for gentile.

gourmand -n- a gourmet to the excess.

gourmet [gour-may] -n- a *connoisseur* of fine food and drink; epicure.

grandiloquent -a- extravagant, pompous; overdone speech; fustian/orotund; cp. bombast (empty); euphuistic (affected writing); hyperbole (exaggerated wording).

graph -n/v- Gk. "to write"; e.g., calligraphy (beautiful writing); choreography (designing dance); lithography (writing on stone, early printing).

grant a privilege -v- vouchsafe; cp. remise (release a claim); deign (condescend); fain (happily).

gravitas -n- gravity; *tendency to be grave*/serious; ex. the ___ of a politician.

gregarious -a- belonging to, attracted to, or moving in a group/flock/herd; Lat. flock; cp. gaggle

grouse -v- complain; grumble; syn. querulous.

grovel -v- to lie or move abjectly on the ground with face downward; *to obtain forgiveness or favor*; cp. fawning/genuflecting/obsequious/servile.

gurney -n- a horse-drawn cab with a rear entrance (named after its inventor); also, a stretcher on wheels.

guerrilla -n- a member of an irregular military force, operating in a *small group*; Sp. guerra-*war*.

guile [gile] -a- cunning; *skillful deceit;* cp. covert//furtive//surreptitious (stealthy).

gulag [goo-lag] -n- Russian acronym for "slave camp", popularized in *Gulag Archipelago,* Alexander Solzhenitsyn's book about the string of slave camps across Russia during Joseph Stalin's bloody reign

(1929-53), during which an estimated 20 million Russians were liquidated largely as enemies of the State.

gullible -a- easily deceived; cp. naïve (innocent).

gumption -n- shrewed or spirited *initiative/resourcefulness*. Scottish.

gustatory [**Gus**-tah-tory] -a- relating to the sense of *taste*; Lat. taste.

gusto [guss-toe] -a- vigorous *enjoyment*; *pleasure*; Lat. taste.

gynecologist -n- doctor for women; Gr. "gyne"=female reproductive organ.

H2O -n- 2 atoms of hydrogen + 1 atom of oxygen combine to create water.

hackney -n- a *horse* with a bent-leg gate; a *carriage* for hire, drawn by two horses; cp. fiacre(small, 4-wheeled carriage for hire) ; surrey(4-wheeled carriage not for hire).

halcyon [hal-see-on] -n/a- *tranquil; a fabled bird* with power to calm the wind/waves; a *kingfisher;* the ___days; today, *anything that is* **calm and exceptionally pleasant**.

hale -a/v- healthy; firm; Old English; verb: to compel to go (German); ___ a taxi; cp. hail (ice-rain).

Hanukkah -n- Jewish celebration of the return of the light of God to the temple; it occurs in December; cp. <u>Yom Kipper</u> (Day of Atonement in Sept.); <u>Passover</u> (anniversary of Moses' emancipation in April).

hapless -a- very *unfortunate;* root unknown but "happy-less"; cp. feckless (lacking purpose).

harlequin/ade -n/a- a clown; buffoon; being such.

harangue [hah-rang] -n- a lengthy, aggressive lecture or speech; cp. diatribe (bitter invective).

harem -n- the women's quarters in an Arabian palace; syn. seraglio (a Muslim harem); Lat.

harridan -n- a strict, bossy old woman; belligerent. Fr. "old horse".

harrow/ing -v/a/n- to cultivate with a hoe; to *torment / hassle / harass / vex*; that which is vexing; a large blade with teeth used to rake over soil to break up clods; cp. furrow (a long narrow trench made for planting; to make one).

hassock [has-sock] -n- a thick, firmly padded *cushion*, esp. for kneeling in church; also a footstool; O.E.

hauteur -n- *haughtiness* in attitude; *arrogance*; cp. haut couture (high fashion); cp. hubris.

havoc -n- wide general *destruction*; M.E.; maelstrom (wide-reaching turmoil); cp. cataclysm (flood); conflagration (fire); holocaust (massacre); apocalypse (event of far reaching proportions/day of reckoning).

hebdomadal -n- weekly; Gr. hepta=seven; cp. diurnal / quotidian (daily).

heath -n- an area of open uncultivated land, wasteland, esp. for drainage; cp. lea (open, grassy land).

Hebrides [heb-brih-dees] -n- a group of 500 or so islands NW of Scotland.

hectare [heck-tar] -n- a metric unit equal to **2.5** acres.

hector -n/v- a bully/to bully (Greek mythology).

hedonic/s [hee-don-ick] -a/n- that which *deals with pleasant/ unpleasant sensations*; the study of same; "_____ adjustments" in the CPI; cp. hedonism.

hedonism [hee-don-ism] -n/a- the doctrine that all behavior is motivated by the pursuit of pleasure; Gr. pleasure; syn. epicure or **sybarite**; cp. solipsistic (self as only reality); ant. asceticism (self-denial); cp. stoicism (indifference to pain or pleasure); Epicureus: "Eat, drink and be merry…"

hegemony -n- the predominant *influence* of one State over another; cp expedient (promote one's interests).

heinous [hay-nuss] -a- grossly *wicked*; Old French: to hate; ex. a _____ crime.

hieroglyphics -n- a system of writing in pictorial characters; Gk. pictures=carvings); esp. refers to BCE writings in Egyptian pyramids.

helter-skelter -a- disorderly/*chaotic*/confused/hectic; M.E. to hasten; also refers to the insane murderer, Charles Manson, who, c. 1970, directed his Helter Skelter Cult to murder the stunningly beautiful actress, Sharon Tate and others in brutal, torturous ways.

hemisphere -n- half + (celestial) sphere, divided by the equator/the celestial equator; hence, usually refers to north and south of the equator OR east and west of a meridian; Gr. half + sphere.

hemophilia [hee-mo-feel-ya] -n- a *disease* evidenced by *excessive*, spontaneous **bleeding**; Lat. hemo – blood; cp. phlebotomy (draw blood); lobotomy (now discredited surgical removal of part of brain to combat mental illness).

henotheism -n- a tribal (Jewish) monotheism that recognized lesser gods (e.g. those permitted by King Solomon to placate his many thousand wives some of whom weren't Jews).

heresy/etic/etical -n/a- at variance with established beliefs, esp. religious; controversial views; heterodoxy; cp. atheist.

hermaphrodite -n- one having *male and female sex organs*; see androgynous (m/f characteristics).

hermetic/hermit -a- living in solitude; sealed from escape or entry; Lat. solitary.

heterodox/y -n/a- contrary to some established standard like the Bible, a creed; *hereticalheter / hetero = different*; ant. orthodox.

heterogeneous -a- *diverse* character or content; motley; different + genes; ant. homogenous.

heteronomy/ous -n- being subject to *a law or standard external to oneself*; Kant expanded it to mean *acting in accordance with one's own wishes rather than by reason or morality*. Root: **hetero** = different or other; **onomy or nomy** = rules or laws; cp. hubris (excessive *pride*; *arrogance*//hauteur); egotistic (conceited); supercilious (haughty *disdain*); solipsistic (self the only reality) [also cp. anonymous (w/o name)].

hew/ler -v/n- to cut with heavy blows, as with an axe; M.E.; sometimes "to conform"; one doing so.

hexameter -n- poetry with "*six* feet" per line; each "foot" being 2 long or one short + two long syllables per line; common to classic (Greek and Roman poetry); iambic pentameter uses "*five* feet per line", with each iamb (one short syllable followed by one long) and is the cadence used by English-speaking poets, e.g. Shakespeare, the Romantic poets, etc.

Hezbollah -n- "Party of Allah"; Muslim terrorist group in M.E.; see ISIS.

hieroglyhphics -a- Egyptian. A system of writing using symbols to represent words and sounds; cp. Aramaic and Ancient Hebrew (neither had vowels or punctuation); Sanscrit (ancient language of the Hindu scriptures, akin to today's Hindi).

hippocampus -n- an area of the brain believed to be *the situs of emotion*; Gk. hippo/sea monster.

hoary/hoar -a/n- gray or white as with age; ancient; aka cobwebs; cp. whore.

hoarfrost -n- greyish white crystalline frozen water on vegetation, fences, etc.

hobo -n- bum, itinerant unemployed; thought to come from "Ho, boy", a call to bums riding the rails.

Hobson's Choice -term- a free choice in which only one option is offered, hence a "*Take it or leave it" offe*r. Thomas *Hobson (C.1600) operated a large livery stable* but he only allowed customers to take the horse in the closest stall or none at all, which practice became dubbed "Hobson's Choice".

hocus/hocus-pocus -n- trick; Lat. for slight-of-hand; syns. legerdemain / prestidigitation.

hoi polloi [hoy-pahloy] -n- Gr. the many; the *common* people, *masses*; throng (large group), to which Dickens pricelessly referred as "the great unwashed".

hokum -n- a *hoax*; something that *seems impressive but is untrue* or insincere;specious*;* cp humbug (nonsense).

hol/holo -root- Gk. "whole"; holistic (a complete system); holocaust (massacre of all).

holocaust -n- *a massive slaughter*; cp. cataclysm (flood/disaster); conflagration (fire).

Holocaust -n- Hitler's genocide of 6M Jews in WWII; cp. Stalin's murder of 8M kulaks; some maintain that Stalin's rule led to the liquidation of as many as 20M Russians.

homo -n- any of the genus homo, hominid that includes modern man and various extinct species; slang for "gay" or homosexual.

homeopathy/ic -n- a system of medicine that treats diseases by *administering small doses of the disease;* also refers to treatment of disease using home remedies.

homeostatic/sis -a/n- a state of physiological (like+unwavering) equilibrium (emotional or intellectual balance); equanimity; equable (balanced mind); Obama projects it.

homily/istic -n- a *tedious, moralizing lecture*/sermon; Gr. discourse to a crowd; cp. litany (prayer with responses from crowd); simile; metaphor.

homogeneous -a- man and genes of the *same* kind; *consisting of similar parts*; ant. heterogeneous.

homonym -n- one of two words with the *same sound or spelling but with different meanings* (there/their, sun/son, great/grate, do/due/ dew, baud/bawd; but/butt/butt, complacent/complaisant, feign/ fain, nave/knave; cp. *acronym* (WAC/WOP); *anagram* (pea/ ape;God/dog); *acrostic* (first letter of each word in a verse forms a word); **anonym** (name written backwards); *eponym* (Romulus/ Tex); pseudonym (nom de plume).

homo sapiens -n- modern man; Lat. homo-man + *sapere-to know*; see evolution; see hominids. See hominid. The alleged dates for Adam, Eve et al are given in many older Bibles, e.g. The Lovett Family Bible (1886), which the author still has. See evolution.

homosexual -n- one who prefers sex with one's own sex, most commonly a male.

horizontal -a- parallel to, or in the plane of, the horizon; e. to w.; ant. vertical.

hospice -n- a *shelter for travelers*, providing for *physical and emotional* needs; Fr. host; today, where those with a few weeks to live go to die; cp. triage (a place for the injured or disadvantaged).

hostel -n- inexpensive lodging; cp. **hostelier** (innkeeper); hostile (relating to an enemy); ostler (one takes care of the horses at an inn).

hot tempered -term- bilious/choleric/irascible/volatile; cp. scabrous (difficult).

hubris/tic [hoo-briss] -n/a- excessive *pride*; *arrogance*//hauteur; cp. egotistic (conceited); effrontery (insolence) supercilious (haughty *disdain*); heteronymous (sacrificing reason and morality to personal wishes); solipsistic (self the only reality).

Humanism -n- a cousin of pantheism; a philosophy asserting that Nature is our source, our; and this earth and this life are enough." Epictetus, Lucretius, Socrates, Seneca, Voltaire, Hume, Kant, Hegal, Thoreau, Freud et al concurred.

humbug/gery -a/n- *nonsense*; rubbish; English slang; popularized by Scrooge in Dickens' *Christmas Carol;* cp. hoax//hokum//specious (seeming truth but false); spurious (false).

humiliate -v- abash; *embarrass*, disconcert; to + bash; to be so; cp. denigrate.

Hun -n- (1) a member of the warring Asiatic nomads who ravaged Europe in the 4th-5th centuries, Attila the Hun being their most infamous leader; (2) a derogatory nickname given to all Germans in WWI.

husbandry/husband -n/v- the raising of livestock; *careful management*; man in wedlock.

hydrogen -n- colorless, highly flammable gaseous element; the simplest atomic element No. 1 (one proton, one electron); most of the universe is a vacuum; atmosphere/air exists around planets; hydrogen comprises 92% of air in *universe's planet's* atmosphere; cp. nitrogen (78% of air of *earth*, oxygen 21%) See H20 (2 atoms of hydrogen + one atom oxygen=water). The oxygen we breathe comes from plants; without them, we don't breathe. **If you scream in space, can you be heard?** No. Sound cannot be heard in a vacuum.

hyperbole/ic -a/n- *exaggerations*; hyper=above/beyond; ballein=throw; cp. bombast (overdone / empty words).

hyperdermis/ic -n/a- the highest layer of cells beneath the epidermis (the outer layer of skin).

hypergamy/ous -n/a- marriage into a higher social class or caste; Lat. above + marriage.

hypochondriac -n- one who complains about imaginary ills; hypo = under/down + cartlidge.

hypothalamus -n- *the part of the brain **below** the thalamus, which regulates cell* processes *and sends messages* (hormones) through the blood stream.

hypothecate -v- pledge; beneath + place. Ex. Pledge collateral for a loan.

hypothesis -n- the *rationale* for a set of facts; ***below*** + thesis; posit (state as fact); see postulate (assume/accept as true); presume (take for granted); propound (suggest); hypothetical (assumed for sake of discussion).

"I"

iamb/ic -n- iamb = *metric foot*, consisting of a short syllable followed by a long one; ex. tra-**peze.**

iambic pentameter -term- a line of verse including *pentameter = five* metric feet (syllables); IP consists of five sets of unstressed syllables followed by five of stressed syllables: "But soft, what light through yonder window breaks" (R&J); "Now is the winter of our discontent." (Richard III).

iconoclast -n- a breaker of icons/images; one who attacks cherished beliefs.

iconograph/y -n- *pictorial illustration* of a given subject; Gr. likeness/images + description.

id -Lat. word- *repressed, antisocial*, aggressive ***desires***; Freudian term; Lat.-it; cp. libido (sexual desire).

idiopathic -a- a condition for which the cause is unknown. Gk. peculiar + path.

idiom/atic -n/a- word/expression peculiar to *a region or group*; similar to dialect / slang / vernacular (characteristic of speech of a *region*); cp. parlance (peculiar to an *activity*, eg legal); shibboleth (language peculiar to a *group*); jargon (incoherent or *hybrid*).

idiosyncratic/cy -a/n- behavior *peculiar to one individual;* idio (personal) + sync (harmony).

idyll/idyllic -n/a- a short *poem* describing a *peaceful, happy, picturesque,* usually *rustic, pastoral, country scene*; a scene that is so; cp. quixotic (idealistic).

ignoble -a- dishonorable//disgraceful//opprobrious; prefix is "I", short for in/not + ignoblis (Gk. for noble).

ignominy/ious -n/a- *disgrace*, dishonor; opprobrium.

imbibe/ ation -v/n- to drink; cp. libation (liquid poured, esp. alcohol).

imbroglio [im-**brogue**-lee-o] -n- a difficult situation, heated *quarrel*; cp. fray (scuffle); foray/incursion (sudden attack); melee (hand-to-hand fighting); sortie (armed attack); Ger.

imbue -v- to permeate or influence deeply; cp. infuse (to inject or permeate for the better).

immemorial -a- extending beyond the reach of memory or record.

immolate/tion -v/n- *kill; destroy*; offer in sacrifice; cp. execrate/ imprecate (hate).

immoral -a- not + moral; a person who has morals but chooses to violate them ; base; dissolute, licentious, a libertine, wanton; cp. amoral (without + morals); amoral generally refers to one who has no morals, hence lacks a conscience or any remorse (e.g., a serial killer).

immure -v- to confine, especially walls; Lat. walled; cp. inure (to benefit).

immutable -a- not changeable; without + mutation (change); cp. implacable / inexorable (unmovable); intransigent / intractable (inflexible).

impair -v- weaken; damage; not + a pair; cp. impede (to obstruct/ hinder); Lat.

impale/ment -v/n- to pierce with a sharp stick; to torture or kill thus.

impalpable -n- not perceptible to the touch; not easily grasped; ant. palpable, tactile.

impecunious -a- *penniless*; Lat. without + pecunia = wealth; cp. destiture / privation (want of necessities).

impel -v- to *set or keep in motion; to stir* to action; *incite*; cp. compel(force); propel (drive forward).

imperious -a- *domineering*; dictatorial; Lat. without+peers; cp. supercilious (disdainful arrogance).

impertinent -a- *ill-mannered*; cp. impudent (disrespectful/rude), insolent (insulting); cp. effrontery (bold).

impetuous -a- capricious/impulsive/precipitous/whimsical and unpredictable.

impinge -v- *encroach*; infringe; trespass.

implacable [imPLAKable] -a- *unmovable*; w/o being able to placate; syn. inexorable; cp. ineluctable/indomitable (not to be overthrown); immutable (unchangeable); resolute (determined).

implore -v- to call upon earnestly to do something//beseech//entreat; cp. admonish//exhort (urge strongly); entice; genuflect (ask on bended knee); importune (beg); supplicate (plea slavishly).

import -v/a- to bring in; Fr. in+carry; as an adj.= significance; ant. export (send out).

importune/ate/ing -v/a- *beg*; *too persistent* in request; beseech/entreat/ implore; cp. supplicate (pray, entreat); a mendicant (beggar); blandish/inveigle/wheedle (induce by flattery).

impost -n- tax or other compulsory payment; the weight carried by a horse as a handicap.

impotent -a- lacking strength; enervated; esp. incapable of sexual intercourse; cp. effete (infertile); incontinent (can't control bodily excretions).

imprecate/tion -v/n- to *abhor/hate*; execrate (curse/damn); cp. malediction (curse); cp. deprecate (disapprove); immolate (kill).

imprimatur [impriMAHTture] -n- "stamp of approval"; sanction; license; Lat. let it be printed.

impudence/t -n/a- *disrespectful;* rude; cp. impertinent (ill-mannered); insolent (insulting).

impugn [im-**pune**] -v- to challenge as false; ex. they ____ his integrity.

impunity -a- Lat. *w/o penalty* or fear of penalty; ex. he did it with ____.

inane [in-**nain**] -a- *empty*; lacking sense or substance; cp. fatuous// insensate (foolish); innocuous (harmless/benign).

inanition -n- lack of spiritual vigor or enthusiasm; apathy; cp. inanimate.

inanimate -a- lifeless; Lat. not + alive; cp. inert (sluggish/lethargic/ phlegmatic).

inapposite -a- inappropriate, *not pertinent*; cp. specious (seeming truth); spurious (false).

incandescent -a- *emitting visible **light by being heated***; not + candle; e.g. *all light bulbs*; cp. opalescent (multi colored); pellucid/ translucent(transmitting light); fluorescent light//neon light (gas in a glass tube).

incantation -n- ritualistic *recitation of spells* to produce a *magical* effect; not + sing.

incarnate -a/v- a *deity appearing in the flesh; anything in an extreme form*; Lat. not + flesh; e.g. capitalism incarnate.

incarnation/ate -n/a- a bodily manifestation of a supernatural being; one who personifies a given abstract quality or idea; cp. apparition (ghostly figure); epiphany (a revelation/sighting of a divine being); ex. He is the _____ of Christ; cp. epiphany.

inchoate [in-ko-at] -a- in *early stage; incipient;* near syns. embryonic/ nascent (being born/undeveloped); Lat. not +a yoke; congenital (from birth).

incipient [in-**sip**-ee-ent] -a- undeveloped; beginning; not + begin; inchoate; nascent.

incisive [in-**sigh**-sive] -a- *sharp mental perception;* that which cuts (root is misleading).

incite -v- to *provoke to action*; Lat. go forward; foment.

incontinent -a- *unable to restrain bodily functions* (esp. excretions) or appetites; cp. impotent.

incorrigible -a- incapable of being reformed; Lat. in = not + corrigere = to correct; cp.recalcitrant.

incubus -n- a male demon believed to have sexual intercourse with sleeping women; also, a cause of distress or angst; Lat. nightmare; ex. Debt is an incubus, cp. necrophiliac (sex with dead).

incumbent -n/a- *an elected official; also, any requirement/obligation,* e.g., "It is ___ upon you to study."

incursion -n- a sudden *invasion* of another's territory; syn. foray; cp. fray/scuffle/brawl; imbroglio (argument); mêlée (hand combat); sortie (armed attack).

---

indenture -v/n- *to bind* one person *to work* for another; bondage; a document that defines the terms of control.

indigenous -a- *native* to an *area*; cp. *endemic* (native to a people OR place); denizen / habitué (a frequenter of a place); coterminous (having the same boundaries).

indolent -n- *habitually lazy*; cp. malingerer (feins illness to avoid work); languor // lethargic // phlegmatic (sluggish, indifferent); torpor (inactive); torpid (numbing) ; inert (slow to move); enervated (weakened).

indomitable -a- unconquerable; irrepressible; ineluctable/insuperable; Lat. *not* + *to dominate;* cp. implacable/inexorable (can't move or placate).

Indonesia -n- all of the *islands* in *the Indian Ocean*, s. of China; colonized by the Dutch; population of 235M; ethnically Oriental; religion, almost all Muslim.

induce -v- to move by *persuasion*; to effect; Fr; cp. deduce (to conclude by reason).

ineffable -a- *indescribable*; cp. arcane (known to a few); inscrutable (not to be understood); see abstruse/recondite (difficult to grasp// fathom); esoteric (understood by the trained).

ineluctable -a- *not to be overcome*; syn. indomitable/insuperable; cp. inexorable/implacable (unmovable).

inert -a- slow to move; sluggish; lethargic//phlegmatic; cp. languid/ torpor (inactive); torpid (numb).

inexorable -a- *unmovable//implacable*; unbending; cp. immutable; intractable/intransigent; indomitable//ineluctable/insuperable (unconquerable); obdurate (stubborn); recalcitrant(disobedient).

inextricable/y -a- not able to extricate (free or remove).

infernal -a- of or relating to Hell; Fr. Hell; cp. abominable (detestable); devilish; fiendish.

infidel -n- disloyal (esp in marriage or religion); one who has no religious beliefs; cp. apostate (abandoned his religion); cp. agnostic/atheist.

infidelity -n- breach of trust; syns. adultery//perfidy//perfidious// unfaithful.

inflection -n- an alteration in pitch or tone; *a change of direction*; ex. an ___ point.

ingenuous/ingénue -a/n- *naive; innocent; guileless*; actress being same; cp. disingenuous (devious).

ingest -v- to take in for digesting.

inhibit/ed/tion/or -v/a/n- to make fearful; the state of being fearful; a fear; one who imposes fear.

inimical [in-<u>nim</u>-ih-cal] -a- adverse to; hostile to; unfavorable to; Lat. enemy; cp. antipathetical (aversion to).

inimitable [ih-nim-it-tahble] -a- defying imitation; matchless; peerless/imperious; Lat. not + imitate.

iniquity/ous -n/a- *wicked; sinful*; Fr. not + even; ignominious (disgraceful).

injunction -n- a directive; a *prohibitory* OR *mandatory* decree; syn. sanction; cp. interdict (prohibitory).

inamorata/o [in-am-or-ahtah/ahto] -n- a female or male lover; Italian.

innocuous -a- harmless; benign; cp. inane (empty); fatuous//insensate (foolish); banal (commonplace).

inundate -v- flood; overwhelm; bury; Fr. in + wave; cp. cataclysm (disaster esp. flood).

inquire/quisition/or -v/n- Lat. to ask questions; the act of doing so; one who does so.

insatiable -a- one who can't be satisfied; Lat. not + satiety/fullness.

insensate -a- foolish//fatuous; Lat. without + sense; cp. inane (empty); ludicrous (ridiculous); inane (empty).

insidious -a- spreading in a *subtle but harmful* way; more dangerous than it seems; Lat. to sit.

insignia -n- a badge, distinguishing mark; the "in" prefix is deceiving; cp. imprimatur (stamp of approval).

insipid -a- tasteless; spiritless; dull; flat; vapid/wan; without + spirit.

inscrutable -a- not understandable/incomporehensiable //obscure// Delphic; recondite; cp. arcane (known only to a few); esoteric (known only to the specially trained; ineffable (indescribable).

insolent -a- *insulting*; cp. impertinent (ill mannered); cp. impudent (disrespectful/rude).

insomnia -n- chronic sleeplessness; L. not + somnolent/sleepy.

insouciant [in-**sue**-sant] -a- blithely *unconcerned*; **nonchalant**; flippant; in-not + soucier-to trouble; near syns. apathy (indifferent); complacent (satisfied); blithe (carefree).

insular/ity -a- *isolated*; detached; narrow.

insuperable -a- impossible to overcome/ indomitable/ineluctable; invincible; not + super.

insurgent -a/n- one who revolts against civil authority or a government; *rebellious*.

insurrection -n- an act of *open revolt* against civil authority; ant. moderate.

intangible -a- without/not tangible/touchable or perceptible to the senses; impalpable.

integral/er -a/n- Lat. entire, *an essential part;* whole numbers.

intelligentsia -n- the educated/smart classes.

intemperate -a- not temperate; excessive; immoderate; cp. asceticism; ant. abstemious.

inter [in-ture] -v- to place in the ground, as a corpse.

inter alia -Lat. phrase- among other things.

intercede -v- *to come between*; cp. inject; interject; cp. interpolate/ interpose.

interdict/ion -n- a *prohibitory* decree; cp. injunction (prohibitory or obligatory decree); sanction (license).

interjection -n- the act of putting in between; also, an exclamation ("Heavens!", "Dear me!", "Wow!")

interlocutor -n- one who takes part in a conversation; a *moderator* Lat. between + speak.

intermittent -a- sporadic; off and on; starting and stopping.

internecine -a- *mutually destructive*, as in warfare; fatal to both; cp. Pyrrhic Victory.

Internet -aka World Wide Web- see details at WWW.

interpolate -v- ***insert** a point between*; between + poles; cp. intercede/ interpose/interject; **intersection**/intersect -n/v- where lines/ courses/roads etc. cross; to cross or divide.

interstice(s)/tial -n- a small or narrow *space* between things; see aperture (gap); fissure (crack); orifice (vent/mouth); lesion (skin-tear); rictus (bird's beak, gaping hole).

intervene -v- come between for the purpose of disrupting; cp. intercede.

intone/ate/ation -v/a/n- to utter long tones, esp. musical; to be in tune; cp. monotone (one tone).

intractable/intransigent -a- *inflexible*; *obdurate/stubborn*, uncompromising; / refractory / restive; (resists control); cp. contumacious// recalcitrant (disobedient); cp. unswerving (committed).

intrepid -a- courageous; fearless; undaunted; not + fearful; ant. trepid/ timorous; craven/daunted/pusillanimous (cowardly).

introvert -n- one who is self-conscious or shy; not + to find; diffident (shy); taciturn (silent).

inure -v- *reflect upon*; to benefit; syn. redound; cp. immure (to confine, especially in walls).

140   LEE G. LOVETT I AND III

invaluable -a- *beyond* value; priceless; inestimable value.

invective -n- a denunciatory or *abusive commentary*; chastise / chasten/ diatribe / excoriation / vilification / vituperation.

inveigh [in-vay] -v- to *protest* vehemently; Lat. attack; ex. Don't _____ against your gov't.

inveigle -v- to win over by flattery; syns. blandish/wheedle (OFr. To blind); see toady/sychophant.

inverse -n- the *opposite* / antipodal position; cp. obverse (*the more obvious* of two points; facing the observer; the "heads" of a coin); reverse (turn back); root: vertere – Fr. to turn.

inveterate -a- firmly established; deep-rooted.

invictus -a- unconquerable/indomitable/ineluctable/insuperable; Lat.; see the revered poem of that name by Wm. Ernest Henley.

invidious -a- tending to arouse **resentment** or envy/jeolousy; cp. animosity; jaundice (envy/hostility) odious / execrable (causing hatred).

inviolate/able -a/adv- not to be profaned or violated; sacred; sacrosanct; not to violate for religious reasons.

invocation -n- grace; calling for help from *a higher power*; cp. convocation (convene assembly).

invoke -v- to *call for help*; cp. convoke/cation (cause to assemble); cp. evoke (cause).

involute/tion -a- curled spirally or inward; *complex*; cp. convolute (fold together, *confuse*).

ion/ization [eye-on] -n- an *atom, group of atoms* (or molecule) that has acquired *a net electric charge* by the addition or removal of electrons; the formation of ions; see atom.

iot -suffix- meaning *of or from* a place; e.g. "Eliot" = god + from; El and Elohim (OT, Hebrew name for God.

iota [eye-oh-ta] -n- least bit; a very small amount; whit; modicum; 9th letter of Gr. alphabet.

ipso facto -Lat. term- fact speaks for itself; itself + fact; hence, *self-explanatory*.

irascible -a- hot tempered; short fuse; prone to outbursts of temper / bilious / choleric / volatile; cp. scabrous (difficult).

irate -a- enraged.

ire [eye-er] -n- anger; rath; Lat.

Irene -name- Greek for "peace"; syn. serene.

irenics -n- a belief system that attempts to unify Christianity's beliefs with reason. Gk. peace; also refers to pacifists, esp. those seeking unity among Christian sects.

iridescence -a- showing *luminous colors* which *vary* as seen at different *angles*; Lat. iris (rainbow).

Iris -name- Lat. for rainbow.

irony/ic/al -n/a- an event/result (or use of words that defies logic; cp. oxymoron (a contradiction in terms e.g., the speedy turtle; paradoxical (contradictory "Zhivago" (means lively in Russian).

ISIS -terrorist group- acronym for "Islamic States Iraq and Syria"; cp. **ISIL** ("Islamic State of Iraq and the Levant" and Levant is a large area in SW Asia); **Al Qaeda** ("the base", refers to the late Osama Bin Laden's military group); **Hezbollah** (Party of Allah, a Shi Islamic terrorist group from Lebanon); **Taliban** (means student) are terrorists from Afghanistan); all are guerilla-type armies committed to converting "infidels" to Islam, killing those who will not convert or who interfere.

As the they steal everything in sight and enslave, kill or conscript the rest into their "army", this is a relatively easy way to make a living for the fighters, as those they conquer are unarmed. This robbing and bullying process is typical of of many of history's "great conquerers", e.g. Ghengis Khan, Attila the Hun, Mohammed, Napoleon, Hitler, Stalin.

i/Iscariot -n- as in Judas ___, Heb. For *traitor or assassin*; not actually Judas' name.

Ishtar -n- ancient Babylonian *goddess of love, fertility*; see Aphrodite.

Islam -n- an Arabic word meaning "submission (to Allah)", the faith founded by Mohammad c. 610AD; Arabic verb "**aslama**" = I surrender. *Koran/Quran* means "recitation"; the words "Moslem" and "**Muslim**" mean followers of Islam; see Mohammed. In practice, Muslims, from Mohammed forward, have expanded their base by force: Convert or die; this makes it less a religion and more a method of seizing the assets of others and enslaving them. **Name the *three, principal Muslim sects: Shiites, Sufis and Sunnis*. SHIITES** believe that all caliphs (successors to Muhammed) should be his *direct descendants* and, hence, divinely inspired like the Pope. Disagreements over descendants have led to more splinter groups. One descendent, known as "the Divorcer" had 90 wives 'n 100 concubines. M. allowed himself eleven wives, altho' M's *Koran limits men to four each*. Each major country has a "caliph"; **SUNNIS** chooses the most learned to lead them. **SUFIS** are less literal interpreters of the Koran) and are viewed as pagans. Sufis also have the Order of Whirling Dirvishes, who perform a well known dance emulating the planet's movements towards heaven.

isthmus [iss-mus] -n- a narrow strip of land connecting two larger bodies of land: Panama, connecting No. and So. America is the largest example; Gk.

ism -**suffix**- *a distinctive doctrine or theory*; often a discriminatory belief systems, deism v. theism, monism, humanism, Buddhism; Catholicism; Confucianism, Taoism, Judaism.

isotope -n- an atom with an abnormal number of neutrons (In 1953, geologist Clair Paterson was the first to accurately date the earth (at 4.55B yrs) by counting the isotopes in igneous rocks. Same year as Watson and Crick discovered DNA).

ISP -n- acronym for Internet Service Provider.

itinerary/ant -a/n- *a schedule* of one's travels from place to place; *one* who travels; cp. peregrinate / tion (to travel, travels); peripatetic (walking about).

"J"

jane/Jane -n- a woman; "plain Jane" (an unattractive woman); Jane Doe (an anonymous woman, esp. in a lawsuit); Jane Eyre, a "plain Jane" heroin of Charlotte Bronte's outstanding classic novel.

Janis/Janice -name- Heb. gift from God.

janissary -n- a member of a group of loyal troops or supporters. Turkish.

jaundice/d -n/v- a *disease* causing *yellow skin*; an attitude of *envy or hostility*; cp. invidious (causing envy); odious/execrable (causing hatred).

jeer -v- to speak or shout derisively; mock; ridicule.

"jen" -n- *humanness*; association with and *loving* others (Confucius).

Jew -n- a person whose traditional religion is Judaism and who traces their origins to the people of Israel to Abraham. Origin: via Aramaic from Judah.

jingo/istic -n- belligerent/militant nationalism/war monger (sold to the masses by the U.S. government leaders as "patriotism" or "defense of freedom" and pushed by the enormous military-industrial complex for purely economic reasons).

jocose/sity/ **jocular/jocund** -n/a- *being merry*; jubilant; cp. ecstatic// euphoric (extreme joy) cp. blithe (carefree).

Jove -n- Gr. God of Gods, aka Jupiter; used to *express surprise or excitement*, ex. "by __"

jubilee/ant -n/a- a *special anniversary,"* esp. the 50ᵗʰ; a joyous celebration.

J/juggernaut -n- the title of the Hindu deity Krishna; generally refers to an *overwhelming or irresistible force or movement*; anything that elicits blind devotion.

Judeo-Christian -n- any Jew who has converted to Christianity; cp. *Ebonite*, the first Jews who followed Jesus (but not St. Paul). Also see "*Messianic Jews*" (a post-Jesus Jew who converts to Christianity).

Judas -n- the disciple who allegedly betrayed Jesus; Iscariot means traitor.

jur -root- Lat. to swear or take an oath; adjure; abjure; jurisprudence (philosophy of law).

juxtapose -v- place side-by-side or near; Lat.; "juxta" = near.

kakistocracy -n- *government by the worst* of men; Gr; ochlocracy (mob rule).

karma -n- the *total effect* of a person / *aura* / ethos / feeling; atmosphere (Buddhism/Hinduism); the Hindus have 4 Yogas: karma-yoga (based on one's *actions* and thoughts).; see yoga; cp. cachet (distinctive characteristics); élan (style); mantra (magical power); panache (flamboyance); zeitgeist (the culture or spirit of an society or era).

keen -a- eager; enthusiastic.

k/Ken -n/v- perception, ***understanding***; v: to recognize, know (O.E.); family name.

ketosis/ic -n/a- where the body is burning/expelling fetid carbohydrates (often via mouth); a phenomenon of the Atkins diet; ex. He has ___ breath.

kinetic [kin-et-ick]/kinesis [kin-ee-sis] -a/n- relating to motion; psychokinesis (mind moving objects); Gr. movement.

kleptomania/iac -n- an irresistible urge to steal; one who does so.

knell [nell] -n/v- a *mournful bell's* sound, as for a funeral; to *make mournful.*

knave -n- an unprincipled, crafty person; the Jack in card games; crafty, disingenuous; devious.

Krishna -n- a Hindu word for God in human form, but Hindu words often have many confusing meanings; Krishna also refers to "black"; The Dark One or he who draws us to Himself; *the inner*

Lord who personifies spiritual love and lives in the hearts of all beings; *an incarnation of Vishnu*; "Hari" is another word for it. See Bhagavad-Gita.

"L"

labyrinth -n- a complicated, irregular network of passages; a maze.

lachrymose [la-kree-mous] -a- tearful; Lat. lacrima-tears; ex. her _____ expression; disconsolate (dejected); petulant (pouting); cp. repining/rueful/lamentable/lugubrious / soulful.

laconic -a- brief; concise; pithy; succinct; terse; cp. truncate/ apostrophize (shorten).

laity -n- laymen collectively, parishioners, as distinguished from the clergy.

languor/id/ish -n/a- *lacking energy*; exhauste / lassitude(exhausted)// listless; cp. effete; enervated (weakened); cp. lethargic / phlegmatic (sluggish); quiescent / torpor (inactive); torpid (numb); indolent (lazy).

lapidary -n- one who *cuts* and/or engraves precious *gems*; gemologist (specialist in gems/fine stones).

lapis -n- *semi-precious stone* rich azure *blue* in color, often with spangles; e.g. obsidian lapis eyes.

lascivious -a- *lustful* / concupiscent / lecherous / libidinous; *cp. related words:* **excessive indulgence** in sexual activity: debauchery *immoral:* base, depraved; dissolute, licentious, a libertine / reprobate / turpitude; wanton **sexually stimulating** sexual desire: erotic/lubricious/prurient/salacious (e.g. pornography) **vulgar, crude** conduct/speech: lewd; ribald, cp. scurrilous (insulting to one's reputation)

Note re sex: dictionaries give *widely varied and overlapping definitions*. The above compromise among several.

laser -acronym- for Light Amplification by Stimulated Emission Radiation A laser emits light via optical amplification on the stimulated emission of electronic radiation. Cp. **LED** (light emitting diode) and **LCD** (liquid crystal display), all use light. Lasers, in myriad forms, are now being used experimentally to cure many organic problems; cp. diode (a semi-conductor with 2 terminals).

lassitude -n- *exhaustion*/languid/languor/listless; effete (infertile); enervated (weakened); stolid (emotionless); quiescent/torpor (inactive); torpid (numbed); lethargic/phlegmatic(sluggish).

lateral -n/v- a sideways pass/toss; that which is on the side; to put something to the side.

latitude -n- one's freedom from normal restraints; **cartographically**: the parallel lines running *east_and west*, parallel to the Equator; cp. longitude / meridian (great circle N-S) ; Lat. wide. Latitude & longitude tell us the precise location of anything by measuring their distance, respectively, east and west (latitude) and north and south (longitude) of the equator.

LCD -acronym- "liquid crystal display"; an LCD contains a liquid crystal (transparent glass) that becomes opaque (cloudy); electrical current is applied; colors and shapes can be created by controlling the electrical current.

lea -n- an open area of *grassy* land; cp. heath (uncultivated land, drainage area); cp. lee (an area sheltered by wind).

league -n- a group of similar things; also, **three** statute miles; cp. fathom (6 ft.); furlong (220*yds*); score (20); see Jules Verne's *20,000 Leagues under the Sea*; the *deepest part of the ocean* is in the Marianas Islands (So. of Japan in Pacific Ocean), almost 36K feet (about *6.8 miles*); so, Verne was dreaming; cp. meter (3.3 feet); foot (0.3 meters); yard (3 feet); twain (two); fathom (6 feet).

lecherous -a- lustful/lascivious/libidinous/concupiscent;/preoccupied with sex; see lascivious.

Lee/lee -name- Historically, from "lea"; Old English, meaning dwelling near the woods; "**lee**", not as a name, means "sheltered from the wind"; e.g. a boat in the lee; originally, *the name seems to have implied "one who shelters or protects".*

legerdemain -n- artful *deception/artifice* or trick; *slight-of-hand*; Lat. read + hand; syn. hocus-pocus; prestidigitation.

lepricon -n- a mischievious, bearded, tiny man in green; Irish folklore; cp. elf; gnome.

lesion -n- a *wound* or tear; change in skin tissue; aperture (gap); cp. fissure; orifice; rictus (hole or bird's beak.

lethal -a- *deadly*; pernicious/truculent; cp. venonmous/virulent (poisonous); cp. bane (great distress).

lethargic/y -a/n- *sluggish, apathetic*/indifferent; syn. phlegmatic, cp. indolent (won't work); inert (can't move); see lassitude (exhaustion); stolid (emotionless); torpid (numb); quiescent / torpor (inactive).

leviathan -n- a sea monster; Heb. aka something huge or formidable; elephantine, gargantuan; gothic; titanic.

Leviticus -n- Gr. for "about the Levites"; 3rd book of Torah/OT; a manual for ethical life and *personal hygiene and rules about food.*

lewd -a- vulgar/ribald; cp./scurrilous (damaging to reputation); see lascivious for similar words.

lexicography -n- the process of compiling a dictionary; a lexicon (list of words) cp. philology (love of knowledge); linguistics (relating to language); etymology/semantics (study of words, language forms and their histories, also grammar); syntax (grammar).

lexicon -n- a dictionary; the vocabulary of a person or group; Lat. words; cp. parlance (wds of a trade).

"li" [lie] -n- Chin. word for the *attitude* with which things are done (Confucius).

libation -n- an *alcoholic* drink (originally poured in honor of a god); Liber-Roman god of wine; potation (a synonym that also may refer to a bout of drinking).

liberal/ism -n- *those favoring change*; a belief in change; ant. conservative.

libertine -n- one who is immoral; a reprobate; base/depraved// dissolute/licentious/wanton (w/o morals); cp. lascivious.

libidinous -a- lustful/ concupiscent/ lascivious/lecherous; see lascivious for closely-related words.

libido -n- sexual desire; springs from Freud's term "id" (repressed, antisocial desires).

licentiate -n- one holding a license to do something.

licentious -a- *sexually immoral*; base / dissolute / wanton / a libertine/ reprobate; see lascivious for relative terms.

ligature [lig-gah-chur] -n- something that binds, esp. a thread in surgery Lat. to bind.

light (speed) -n- travels at *186K miles/second*; a "light year" equals roughly six trillion miles; light takes 1.3 seconds to reach the moon (225K miles), 8 minutes to reach the sun (90M+ miles), and 100,000 calendar years to escape the most distant part of the Milky Way Galaxy, in which our solar system is located; see Einstein.

limerick -n- short poem.

limpid -a- completely clear; unclouded; e.g. eyes; lucid also means clear but is not used to refer to physical things; cp. opaque(cloudy); obsidian (dark, clear glass).

lintel -n- a threshold; the supporting structure over a doorway that holds the door together; hence, something that provides structural support.

litany/tanical -n- *prayer with responses* from the congregation; cp. homily (tedious moralizing lecture / sermon); liturgy (religious service).

litmus -n- *a failsafe test; a test for acids*; a test certain to determine the truth; Scandinavian: Dying.

liturgy/ical -n- the prescribed ***form*** for a religious service; the Eucharist/Communion; to show gratitude; cp homily.

lodestar -n- a *star by which one charts his course*; a *model*/exemplar/ inspiration; O.E.; cp. archtype/exemplar/protype (models).

lodestone -n- something that strongly *attracts; the stone-magnetite which possesses polarity*, used to rub the needle for a compass to

---

enable it point in the direction of the earth's magnetic field/north; see compass.

log -root- Gk. for "word"; e.g, dialogue; epilogue; monologue; cp. blog (web log).

longitude -n- refers to the *great circles or meridians* which run to the No./So. Poles; Prime Meridian chosen at Greenwich, England in 1888 (Paris had been it before); John Harrison in 1750 created the first timepiece that would work at sea, enabling sailors to mark longitude and, therefore, to accurately navigate at sea other than by the stars; see book ("Longitude") by Dava Sobel.

Lord's Prayer -n- Mathew 6:8-15; part of Jesus' *Sermon on the [unnamed] Mount* (Matt 5-7).

loquacious -a- *talkative*; Lat. to speak; cp. garrulous (***too*** talkative); prolix/verbose (too wordy); cp. voluble (fluent/flowing speach); ant. laconic/sententious.

lout/ish -n/a- one who is clumsy, *stupid, boring*; cp. dolt (dunce, blockhead/ignoramus).

lubricious -a- intended to arouse sexual desire; syn. erotic/salacious/ prurient.

lucre [loo-ker] -n- monetary gain; profit; OE reward; cp. eucre (a card game or trick).

lucubration [luke-oo-bray-tion] -n- study or work *at night;* akin to Lat. light+work.

Luddites -n- British workmen in **1811-16** who destroyed machinery to try to save their jobs; Ned Ludd led them.

ludicrous -a- ridiculous; cp. fatuous/insensate(foolish); idiosyncratic; bizarre.

lugubrious -a- *mournful*; *doleful*; dolorous; grief stricken; bereaved; soulful; woeful; cp.disconsolate; morose (melancholy).

lum -root- Lat. from noun meaning "light"; luminary, luminescent, illuminate.

Luke/Lucas -name- Fm. Gr. "light' or "giving light"; St. Lukc; Lucas derived from Luke; also meaning "a man from Lucania (a region of Italy).

lupine -a- *wolf like*; ravenous; Lat. wolf; cp. lupus (an enigmatic disease); cp. vulpine (fox-like).

lurid -a- causing shock, horror or revulsion; *stressing violence or sensationalism*; see lascivious.

lust/ful -n/a- sexual desire; near syns: concupiscent, lascivious, lecherous, libidinous.

"M"

macabre -a- *suggesting* the *horror* of *death and decay; gruesome;* cp. morbid, moribund, eschatology.

mach speed [mahk] -math term- roughly means the *speed of sound* or 761 mph; Mach=v/a or velocity/sound; named after Austrian physicist, Ernst Mach. Most commonly used in reference to aircraft speeds.

machinate/tion -v/n- to ***plot***; plotting; cabal (to plot, a group in one).

madding -a- *frantic//frenetic//frenzied;* cp. maddening (irritating); *Far From The Madding Crowd"* was the name of Thos. Hardy's famous novel; the title was based on a poem that contrasted rural life which was "far from the madding crowd" in urban areas.

maelstrom -n- *turmoil* of wide-reaching effect; syn. havoc; pandemonium (extensive chaos); cp. cataclysm (flood/upheaval); conflagration (fire); cp. fray (brawl); melee (hand-to-hand combat); cp. holocaust (slaughter); apocalypse (violent event, revelation).

magistrate -n- *a civil officer* with the power to enforce law. Lat. master; cp. ombudsman (official who investigates).

magma -n- the *molten matter* under the earth's crust from which igneous rock is formed by cooling; solids with enough liquid to form a pasty mass; *residue of fruits* after squeezing juice; Lat. knead; cp. pith/y.

magna -root- meaning great, e.g., Magna Carta, magnanimous (giving), magnificent/wonderful; magnate (a person of great influence); magnanimous (giving); magnum (large bottle); magnum opus (great work).

Magna Carta -document- Lat. Great Charter; was the first document setting rules for man's basic rights on a King of England by his feudal lords to protect themselves from the King's tyranny; signed in **1215** by King John.

magpie -n- one of many of various birds in the "jay" family, who chatter noisily; hence, *any noisy talker.*

malaprops/ism -n- from Fr. mal a propos (inappropriate); an *intentional & humorous misuse of a word or phrase*; "Texas has lots of electrical votes" (rather than electoral), as Yogi Berra (the famous NY Yankee catcher put it); based on a character, Mrs. Malaprop, in Sheridan's 1775 play, *The Rivals*; Yogi Berra (the famous NY Yankee catcher) was known as "Mr. Malaprop"; Fr. mal a propos. Malapropism is also called *Dogberryism* (from Officer Dogberry, a character in Shakespeare's *Much Ado About Nothing*, who made similar verbal boo-boos. George Bush's: "Weapons of mass production" (when he meant "destruction") and Bush's" It takes time to restore law and chaos" (order).

malediction -n- a *curse*; bad+edict; cp. imprecation//execration (hatred).

malevolent -a- *evil*; bad+evolve; heinous (grossly wicked) cp. baleful (deadly / lethal / pernicious / truculent). **malicide** -n- killing the bad; usually refers to killing of "infidels" by a religious group.

malinger/er [mah-LING-er] -v/n- *feigning illness or other excuses to avoid work*; one who does so; bad + lingerer; cp hypochondriac; indolent (won't work).

malign -v- speak evil against; asperse // defame // denigrate // deprecate // derogate // disparage // slander; traduce; cp. excoriate; revile; vilify; vituperate (scathing rebuke).

malignant -a- having a tendency to *cause great harm*; bad + causing.

malleable -a- susceptible to being molded; tractable/transigent; ants. intractable/intransigent.

malodorous -a- bad smell; syn. fetid; miasma (unhealthy smell); mephitic (same from the earth); putrid (decaying smell).

mammal -n- not reptiles or birds or most fish, but, rather, usually *warm blooded animals, born alive* who gives milk to its young and has hair at some point, e.g., humans, chimps, dogs, cats, bats, rats, even whales, porpoises, seals; Lat. mamma=teat, pap; cp. vertebrate (a creature with *a spine*; Lat. jointed; includes mammals, amphibians, birds, fish and reptiles).

mammon -n- riches, avarice, *worldly gain*, any *false god*, evil influence (from the NT and Milton).

man -n- humorously defined as "protoplasmal (living jellylike matter) primordial [1st in time] atomic globules" (by Gilbert Sullivan (1880's) in *Mikado*) TO what I define as : upright, sentient (feeling), polymathic (extraordinarily learned), polemic (debater) homo sapiens; Lat. proto=first; see "evolution" for chronology of mankind.

mania -n- an *insanely intense desire for or against something*.

maniac/al -n/a- one who is affected by *mania*; mad; insane.

manic depressive -term- one whose moods leap between extreme joy and depression/bi-polar.

---

manifest -n/v/a- to show or *make plain*; document that does so; self-evident/apparent/beyond doubt/apodictic/obverse.

manifesto -n- *a public declaration* of principles or intentions.

mansard -n- a roof with four sloping sides, two nearly vertical; Fr. after F. Mansart. Fr. designed to lower realty taxes, as space was measured to the cornice(any horizontal decorative molding on a building, door or window).

mantle -n- *that which covers*; the layer of earth *between the crust and the core;* see earth.

mantra [mahn-trah] -n- a *statement, sound, slogan,* chant or sacred formula (or anything) *with magical power;* origin: Hindu religion; today, also words/slogans repeated to change conduct; cp. aura; karma.

manumit -v- set free (as slaves); manus-hand + mittere-send; Ex. Lincoln wanted to manumit the slaves without moving them from their States.

marginalia [margin-**ail**-ee-yah] -n- notes written in the margins.

marmoreal -a- *like marble*, as smooth, white, hard; Lat. marble.

marsupial -n- *mammals with long tails and pouches* to carry their young while they complete development outside the womb, including kangaroos, possums, etc.

martinet -n- *a rigid, military **disciplinarian***; named after a Fr. military officer, Jean __ (c. 1650); *punctilious* (acts in exact accord with prescribed conventions, mores, rules); punctual (on time).

masochism -n- sexual perversion, *hurting self* (fm. Ger. Novelist Sacher-Masoch); cp. sadism-hurting others sexually (Count Sade the Impaler –basis of Dracula legend, 1890).

masticate -v- to chew, crush; Gr. to grind the teeth.

matriarch -n- a woman ruler of a family, group or state; mother+rule; cp. patriarch.

matriculate -v- *to be admitted* to a group, e.g. a college.

matrix -n- a ***situation*** or surrounding ***substance*** within which something else *germinates//is contained*; cp. metrics (*statistics and math-analysis*).

matter -n- Science: any and all physical substances; there are *4 states* of matter: solid, liquid, gas and plasma (atoms without electrons); compare to 5 Elements (Taoist): wood, fire, soil, metal and water; see atom, molecule, elements, plasma.

matzot (balls) -n- *unleavened bread*; Jewish custom caused by lack of time to bake as they fled Egypt (c. 1140BC); bagel (extremely dense, heavy, sweetened, high calorie bread).

maudlin -a- *tearfully* sentimental; cp. bathotic (overly sentimental); cloying (disgustingly sentimental).

maunder/er -v/n- *move slowly*; *speak* indistinctly; mutter or mumble.

mausoleum -n- large, stately *tomb* or *building* housing same; cp. sarcophagus, catacombs.

maven -n- one with special knowledge, an *expert* (Yiddish); cp. pundit (teacher/critic); pedant (ostentatiously learned); savant (knows w/o being taught); polymath (extraordinary brilliance in many areas).

maw -n- the mouth or throat of a voracious animal; O.E. stomach.

Maya [My-yah] -n- the **Gr.** goddess of *illusion*; hence, illusion, appearance rather than reality; also the *creative power of god*. *Hindu*: the origin / mother of the world; **Lat**: *goddess*.

meager -a- *deficient* in quality or fullness; scant; paltry; cp.modicum (small portion).

Mecca -n- *where Muhammad was born*, the site of Muslim's annual pilgrimage; *any goal*; cp. Nirvana.

mega -a- Gr. vast; of the highest level; important.

megalomania/iac -n- obsession to be the best; *one who believes that he/she is the best*; cp. egomania (a maniacal level of egocentricity/ self-centeredness); solipsistic (self is only reality).

melancholia/y/ic -n- one in extreme *depression*; Gr., black/dark+bile.

mélange -n- Fr. mixture; a blend.

melee [may-lay] -n- confused *hand-to-hand fighting*; a *tumultuous mingling* in a crowd; cp. foray (sudden attack); fray (scuffle); sortie (armed attack) ; maelstrom (wide-reaching turmoil).

mellifluous -a- flowing with honey/sweetness; sweet + flowing; as "_____ sound".

meme [maim] -n- an element or system of *behavior* that can be *passed by imitation*; also a *humorous image*, video, text that is copied rapidly and spread by Internet users; Gk.

menagerie -n- *a collection of wild animals* kept in captivity for exhibition.

mendacious/acity -a/n- untruthful (prevarication, prevaricator); cp. perfidious (unfaithful).

mendicant -a/n- depending on alms for a living; a beggar / panderer; Fr. to beg; cp. solicitor.

mensa -n- *Astronomy*: A faint, southern constellation containing part of the Large Magellanic Cloud. The Large and Small Magellanic Clouds are irregular, dwarf galaxies visible from the southern hemisphere, which may be orbiting our Milky Way Galaxy. *Group: A person belonging to an international society of those with IQ scores in the 99 percentile.*

mephitis/ic -n/a- a foul smell, esp. a pestilential one coming from the earth; syns.. fetid; / malodorous; cp. miasma (unhealthy smell); putrid/putrescent (decaying).

Messiah -n- Fm. Heb "Mashiach" is Christos in Gr. And "unctus" in Lat, and means *"anointed"* as in anointed with **oil**; to be the *anticipated deliver/liberator* of the Jews; Christ to Christians; cp."mess", slang.

Messianic Jew -term- Jews who considered themselves ethnically Jewish but who have converted to Christianity; most mainstream Jewish converts today are called simply "Christian Jews"; cp. Ebonite's (the first Jews who adopted Jesus' teachings, i.e., in Jesus' lifetime, but rejected those of St. Paul, the putative author of 13 books of the New Testament).

metamorphosis/ose -n/v- a *transformation* in character or composition, often as if by magic/sorcery; Lat. above + change.

metaphor -n- *figure of speech transferring meaning by analogy*; "winter of discontent", evening of life; celestial thoughts; cp. **simile**=a figure of speech *comparing two unlike things*, often using "as" or "like" e.g. he is strong as a bull; limpid grace; singing syllables; mankind's mirror.

metaphysics/al -n/a- meta = above or denoting + physics=external nature; near syn. Preternatural (before nature); supernatural (above nature); numinous (things that surpass nature); cp. ontology (deals with the essence of being).

mete [meet] -v- to measure, dispense, allocate, esp. in measured proportions.

meteor -n- *a luminous trail or streak* that is caused by a meteoroid; seems like a syn. for comet; KT Meteor / meteriord (c. 65MYA) is believed to have extinguished the dinosaurs.

meteoroid -n- an object (from a spec of dust to a large asteroid) that causes the luminous tale; meteor + likeness.

meter -n- Gk. for "measure"; a measure of distance that equals 1.09 yards or 3.28 feet; 1KM = 1,000 meters = 3,280 feet = .62 miles; 10K = 6.2 miles.

metrics -n- *a method of measuring things by statistics or math*; cp. matrix.

miasma [my-asma] -n- an *unhealthy* smell or stench; cp. fetid / malodorous (a vile smell); putrid / putrescent/ce (decaying); mephistic (pestilential smell from the earth).

microbe -n- things that can be seen only with microscopes and which account for 20 of the 23 divisions (and 80%) of all of living forms; see life forms and atom.

mien [mean] -n- a person's look or mannerisms or conduct//demeanor; cp. karma etc.

milieu [mill-you] -n- French word for *environment*; setting; cp. ambiance (atmosphere/mood).

minion [min-yun] -n- a servile dependent or *underling*; cp. servitor; varlet; acolyte.

minutiae [min-ue-shay] -n- a *small or trivial* detail; cp. iota / modicum (small amount); whit (the least bit); a miniscule amount.

minx -n- a pert (attractive, lively, cheeky, *flirtatious* young girl), sometimes cunning or impudent (rude); cp. soubrette (coquettish maid).

misanthrope [MIS-an-thrope] -n- Lat. hate + mankind.

miscreant [miss-cree-ant] -n- one who imposes hatred; commonly, an *evildoer*; a villain; bad + doer.

misogamy -n- hatred + marriage.

misogyny/ist -n- hatred + women; one who does so; cp. gynecologist (women's doctor).

missive -n- a *written* communication, esp. from a *superior* authority; OE letter; cp. epistle (formal letter).

mnemonics/ist [nee-monics] -n- a system used to enhance the *memory*.

modicum -n- a small portion; cp. iota//minuscule (infinitesimally small); cp. minutia; molecule, nano (one billionth); whit (the least bit); moitt (one-half).

modus operendi/vivendi -Lat. phrase- method of operating/// method of living.

moiety [moy-eh-tee] -n- one half or a lesser portion; cp. modicum, minutia, iota, whit.

Moira -name- Gr. for fate/destiny; a girl's name, usually Gaelic, esp. Irish.

molecule -n- a *stable* configuration of *groups of atoms* bound together by electromagnetic forces; hence, a small particle, bit (Lat. moles); *man-made molecules* include plastic, synthetic fibers. In the air, *in every cubic inch*, there are 45 billion-billion molecules. See atom.

monarch/y -n- government by a *sole, absolute* ruler; root: man + ruler; syn. autocrat/cy; near syns: potentate (ne with absolut power); tyrant (a cruel, absolute ruler) / despot.

monastery/monastic -n/a- where monks live in seclusion under religious vows; doing same.

money/currencies -n- the coin of the realm; the medium of exchange in commercial transactions; slang words: boodle, bucks, clams, greenbacks, moolah; cp. loot / lucre (ill-gotten money); pap (a payment made as a bribe).

moniker/monicker -n- a *personal* name or nickname; cp. appellation (title); rubric (chap. heading); sobriquet (humorous or affectionate nickname for a person or a thing).

monism -n- a metaphysical belief system in which things are viewed in a unified whole; a form of humanism; root: man + belief; Lat to warn; cp. agnosticism, atheism, deism, theism.

moola/moolah -n- slang for money; see money.

mordant/cy -a/n- bitingly sarcastic/sardonic or painful; n. a *corrosive* substance; also a dye to set colors in fabric; from Lat. to bite.

morgue -n- *where the dead are kept until buried*; syn. mortuary; **cp.** catacombs (underground burial site); crypt (recessed areas for bodies); mausoleum (a building full of tombs), sarcophagus (stone tomb).

moribund -a- about to die; dying; Lat. to die; cp. eschatology (study of dead); macabre (suggesting death).

morose -a- extreme *melancholy* by disposition; cp.bereaved//doleful// lugubrious//mournful// soulful//woeful (grief stricken).

morph -root/v- Gk. for "shape"; e.g., amorphous (no shape); to change; cp. metamorphosis (change/evolve).

mortuary -n- where bodies are kept *prior* to burial or cremation; syn. morgue; Lat. dead.

mosaic -n- of or pertaining to Moses, his laws; *something of many colors* (like Moses' temperament).

Moslem / Muslim -n- Names for followers of Islam; see Islam.

motif -n- decorative design on anything; a distinctive feature or dominant idea in an artistic or literary composition.

motley -a- having *diverse and varied components*; heterogeneous; multifaceted; ex. a ____ crew.

mottle/mottled -v- to *mark with colored spots* or varied blotches; often used in past tense.

moulder -v- to decay or disintegrate from neglect; cp. mold (to shape); *mould (a fungus)*.

mull -v- to *consider/cogitate/contemplate/meditate/muse/ponder/reflect/ ruminate;* cp. opine give opinion); mull also means to grind or mix; *also* to heat, sweeten and flavor, as with spices; cp. masticate (chew).

multifarious -a- having great diversity; many parts; motley// multifaceted//heterogeneous; cp. nefarious (wicked).

mummery -n- excessive ceremony; esp. religious; O.E. mummer (actor, mimist).

mundane -a- typical; *ordinary; commonplace;* sy. banal/plebian/ prosaic.

munificent -a- exceedingly generous; Lat. make+gift; beneficent, benevolent.

muse -v/n- to contemplate, ponder/mull; **-n-** any of nine Gr. gods of the arts; M.E.

Muslim/Moslem -n- *a believer in Islam;* the faith founded by Mohammed c. 610AD;. see Koran (recitation); primary sects: Shiite, Sufi, Sunni.

muster -v- *summon, assemble* (as in troops); convene/convoke/marshal.

mutable/ation -a- liable to change; *protean//* vicissitudinous; cp. volatile; tractable.

myrmidon [mar-mih-don] -n- Gk. one who executes orders without question; a hired ruffian/body guard or unscrupulous subordinate; Gr. a member of a warlike Thessalonian people led by Achilles at the siege of Troy; see Thessalonians in New Testament.

myrrh -n- *an aromatic gum* from trees/shrubs from which *perfume* is made; Heb. *frankincense* is the same but from different trees; Fr. franc = superior + incense.

mystic -n- one who reaches beyond human understanding to the supernatural; being superstitious.

mysticism -n- *vague or ill-defined beliefs*; myth/mysticism/mystery all come from a Gr. verb meaning to close the eyes or mouth. **Myth** has come to mean a *story, fable, fantasy or lie*; cp. **superstition** (*a belief held in spite of contrary evidence*). Examples of some stunning long-accepted superstitions or myths include: The earth is the center of the Solar System; the *earth is flat*; the *universe is static* (doesn't change or expand); the *earth is a few thousand years old*, then a few million vs. 4.6 billion today; there *is only one galaxy* (the Milky Way) vs. 140 billion or so; Adam & Eve were the *first humans and were created in 4009BC and Noah 2948 BC*, as repeatedly dated in many Christian Bibles until 1950 or so, when the errors became noticeable to most, as paleontologists can date monkeys at 8M and human-like beings 4M or so years ago (so far) and homo erectus 150KYA, and homo sapiens 50-100KYA; and fossil and now DNA discoveries keep pushing the dates farther into the past.

"N"

nadir -n- Hindu term for opposite the highest point, hence *the lowest point*; plinth; ME opposite; <u>ant</u>. acme//apex//pinnacle//zenith/ Horeb height; cp. apogee (most distant point in orbit); solstice.

nano -n- one **b**illionth; extremely small; a ____second; Lat. dwarf; minute/miniscule/minutae.

nanotechnology -n- the branch of physics that is expected to revolutionize medicine, science, computers, etc. in the 21st Century; cp. nanocar (a nanoparticle that can be remotely controlled like a drone and used inside the body with nanorobots to destroy cancel cell).

nape -n- the back of the neck; M.E.; syn. scruff.

narcolepsy -n- an extreme tendency to go to sleep, even during conversations; Gk. numbness; cp. epilepsy (sporadic loss of consciousness).

nascent -a- coming into existence, emerging; embryonic (being born); Lat. to be born; sim. inchoate / incipient (beginning); embryonic; congenital (from birth); neophyte / novice / novitiate / rookie / plebe (beginner) / tyro (inexperienced person); cp. metamorphose/ is (change in composition or character).

natal -a- relating to the time or place of one's birth; cp. nascent (from birth); congenital (from genes) inchoate (from egg); incipient (beginning).

natter -v- to *talk idly*; chatter; palaver; prattle; rigmarole (confused or meaningless chatter); cp. maunder (mutter, speak indistinctly); persiflage (flippant banter).

nave -n- *the central part* of a church; the hub of a wheel; cp. navel/belly button; knave (crafty, dishonest person).

nebbish -n- a pitifully ineffectual/feckless/timid/timorous or submissive person; Yiddish.

Nebuchadnezzar -n- a large *wine bottle*, equivalent to 20; also, *King of Babylon* c. 600BC, who built a huge walled city, conquered Jerusalem and enslaved many.

nebula/lous -n/a- a *cloud, mist, fog*; hence *vague*.

necro -root- Gr. meaning "dead body".

necrology -n- a *list* of recent deaths; syn. obituary; Lat. corpse + knowledge.

necromancy -n- *communicating with the dead* to predict the future; black magic; sorcery; Lat. corpse + divination; cp. occult (secret, hidden, especially re the dead).

necrophilia -n- an *obsessive **fascination with death*** and corpses; ***sex** with corpses*; see incubus (a demon who has sex with sleeping women); cp. eschatology (study of dead things).

nefarious -a- *extremely wicked* or infamous [Lat. crime]; cp. multifarious (many facets).

neophyte -n- a beginner or novice; Gr. new + plant; syn. novitiate; cp. apprentice, plebe, tyro.

neologism/y -n- a newly coined word, phrase or expression; *a meaningless expression of a psychotic.*

nemesis -n- Gk. an **unbeatable** rival; Gr. mythology; cp. Achilles heel.

neon light -term- for a type of light: a light switch sends electricity through a tube of gas, exciting the atoms, which then decay back to their original state, releasing light in the process.

neural -a- nerves situated on the same side of the body as the brain.

neuro -root- Gr. *nerve*; nervous system.

neuron -n- a cell transmitting *nerve* impulses; a nerve cell; Gk. tendon, sinew.

neurogenic -a- having to do with *nervous disorders*.

neuroplasticity -a- the brain's plasticity (or ability to change itself and be re-mapped).

neurosurgeon -n- brain surgeon.

neurosis/neurotic -n/a- any of a number of *mental or emotional disorders* of the mind.

nemen -n- the spirit or divine power presiding over a thing or place.

nexus -n- a link or connection.

nib -n- the point of a pen or anything; Norse (Norweigan).

his/her Nibs -n- a facetious reference to a person in authority, esp. a demanding person; Norse.

niche [nee-shh] -n- a shallow recess, esp. to dispay a statue or ornament; a small area; often *mispronounced as 'nitch" which is not a word*; ex. He found his niche in life; Lat. nest.

nicker -n/v- a horse's whinny; M.E.; hence a plaintiff sigh.

---

niggard/ly -n/a- stingy/parsimonious; Scandinavian word that has nothing to do with negroes or the slang word "nigger"; cp. frugal (slow to spend); cp. nigger (black person, variation for negro/oid and a reference to Nigeria, from *whence the earliest slaves emanated*, being sold by their tribes for trinkets to traders).

niggle/ing -v/a- to make *trifling/petty* points; syns. carp; pettifogger / captious (trivial objections).

nihil -root- Lat. means "nothing"; Ital. nullo/niente.

nihilism -n- doctrine that *all values are baseless* and *nothing is knowable*; nihil = nothing; cp. existentialism.

Nirvana -n- a **Buddhist** religious tenet; *the goal of life*; *extinction of the human spirit* (or quest for human pleasures) and absorption into supreme spirit; ascetism; fm: Sanskrit: the extinguishing of a fire when the fuel is gone; i.e., *when human cravings go and bliss arrives*; hence, *the ultimate blissful state*; ant. cp. hedonist / sybarite/ Epicurean (devoted to pleasure above all else).

nitrogen -n- Symbol "N", atomic element 7, comprises 78% of the **earth's** *air*, oxygen 21%; cp. elements; (**hydrogen**, which is the most prevalent element (93%) of the air in the *universe'* atmosphere).

nomenclature -n- a system of names for *logging scientific data*; Lat. name + assign.

non compos mentis -Lat. phrase- not + control + mind; cp. comatose (unconscious); deranged.

nonpareil -a- having *no equal*; *peerless*; a *paragon*; e.g. _____ beauty/ excellence.

non sequitur -n- a conclusion that does not follow from the premises or evidence; Lat. not + follow.

nostalgia/ic -n/a- longing for the past; Gr. return home + akin to.

nostrum [no-strum] -n- a *quack* medicine; a popular but untested remedy for problems; nostra = quack; the term is an adaptation of Nostradamus' name.

notional -a- existing only in theory or as a suggestion, idea or notion; syn. hypothetical.

nouveau riche -Fr. term- those who have gained wealth quickly and lack culture/refinement; near syn. parvenue (one who become wealthy or famous quickly).

novice [nah-viss] -n- *beginner*/freshman/plebe//rookie/squire; cp. acolyte; apprentice /neophyte/ novitiate//tyro.

novitiate -n- a *novice*; OR the *place* where one lives as a novice; a priest in training; syn. neophyte.

nubile [new-beel] -a- marriageable; attractive; *sexually appealing*; her ___breasts/face, etc.

nugatory -n/a- *unimportant*; without force; *invalid*; nullity; nugget: a lump of unshaped rock.

Numbers -n- Gr. for "in the wilderness"; 4th book of OT; repetitively chronicles Moses' 40 years there.

numerology -n- the study of the significance of numbers, mainly for occult purposes.

numen -n- the spirit or divine power presiding over a thing or place; Lat. divinity.

---

numin/numinous -n/a- of or pertaining to *religion / supernatural /* metaphysical (above nature) / mysterious / preternatural; Lat.; cp. superstition/ious (beliefs in things for which there is no proof, often due to a fear of the unknown).

numismatist -n- coin collector; cp. philatelist (stamp collector).

nylon -n- a tough, lightweight, elastic, synthetic (man-made) polymer (a chain of many molecules) with a protein-like chemical structure.

nymph -n- a ghostlike image of a woman, a phantom, especially one inhabiting rivers or woods. O.E.

nymphomania/c -n- uncontrollable sexual desires; a woman with same; Lat. inner lips of vulvae + mania.

"O"

obdurate -a- contumacious / *obstinate* / *stubborn* / pertinacious; hardhearted; unyielding; intractable / intransigent (inflexible); refractory/restive (resists control); cp. immutable / implacable (unchangeable); recalcitrant (disobedient).

obeisance/obeisant -n/a- a bow; *homage*; genuflection; act of deference; one who is; obsequious (fawning); Fr. to obey; cp. sycophant // toady (flatter); complaisant (obliging/to please).

obelisk -n- a tall, four-sided *shaft of stone*, tapering at top; the sign of a dagger.

oblation -n- an offering mainly to God; cp. ablution (washing one's body).

obloquy [**ob**-blow-kwee] -n- abusively *detractive* / *derisive* language; pejoration; vilification.

obscure/ity -a- *unclear* / abstruse / vague; opaque (deficient in light/dark); oblique (slanted, hence hard to see or grasp); *indistinct*; cp. arcane (understood by a few); esoteric (understood by those trained); ant. lucid/transparent/translucent/diaphanous.

obsidian [ob-sid-ee-an] -a- a dark, clear natural glass from cooling of molten lava; Gr. stone; his ___ eye obsidian lapis eyes (a term for a empty, cold blue eyes; lapis = azure/sky blue.

obstetrics/ian -n- dealing with childbirth; a doctor who does; Fr. midwife.

obsequious -a- fawning; cringing; too polite; servile/subservient; obeisant/genuflecting (bowing, scraping); unctuous (oily); cp. sycophant/toady (flatterer).

obstreperous -n- unruly; noisy; boisterous // disorderly // rambunctious // rumbustious.

obtuse -a- not acute; imperceptive; mentally slow; a dolt.

obtrude/obtrusive -v/A- become noticeable in an unwelcome or intrusive way; Lat. to push. Syn. intrude.

obverse -a/n- *the more **obvious** of two points*; facing the observer; the "head" of a coin; cp. patent [pay-tent] / manifest (self-evident); cp. apodictic (irrefutable); inverse (opposite or contrary position); the counterpart of a fact or truth.

obvious -a- easy to see/grasp; cp. apodictic/irrefutable/indisputable/ patent (beyond dispute).

Occident/al -n/a- countries of *Europe & Western Hemisphere (Americas_*; cp. Eurasia (Eur.+Asia). **occlude/occlusion** -v/n- to block/obstruct; something that does; Lat. to close. **occult** -a- secret; hidden; mysterious; inscrutable; usually dealing with afterlife / séances cp. necromancy (communicating with the dead).

ochlocracy [**ah**-klo-cracee] -n- mob rule; cp. anarchy (w/o govt.) anomie (collapse of social structure); kakistocracy (rule by the worst).

ocular/ist -a/n- relating to or for the eyes; one who deals with *diseases* of the eye.

odious/odium -a/n- inciting ***hatred*** or repugnance//abominable// execrable; the state of hating; Lat. hate; syn. enmity; cp. abhor;

---

imprecate/execrate (curse/hate); invidious (inspiring resentment/ jealousy).

o/Odyssey -n- Homer's epic poem (c. 800BC); a long wandering, Achilles' return home; cp. Illiad (Homer's epic poem about the Trojan war).

oedipal [eed-dih-pal] -a- relating to an intense relationship with (or sexual attraction to) one's mother; cp. electoral (same with father); both terms originated in Gk. mythology.

Oedipus complex [eed-dih-pus] -n- son loves mother; Gr., popularized in Sophocles' play, *Oedipus Rex:* the son, *abandoned* at birth, unwittingly killed his *father* and fell in love with and *married* his mothe; cp. **Electra complex** (attachment to father), a term coined by Freud and Jung, based Gk mythology.

offal -n- *waste parts*, esp. of animals; *rubbish*; source of "awful"; scat (animal feces).

oid -suffix- Gr. similar to but the same as; a likeness; ex. humanoid, meteoroid, steroid.

olfactory -a- relating to the sense of *smell*; Lat. to smell+to do; fetid/malodorous (bad smell); miasma (unhealthy smell); putrid (decaying smell); cp. mephitic (rotten odors from the earth); ant. aroma (pleasant scent); redolent (fragrant).

oligarchy -n- *rule* by a few; L. few+ruler; cp. autocracy/monarchy; despotism / tyranny (a single, cruel ruler); ochlocracy (mob rule); kakistocracy (rule by worst); anomie (collapse of social structure).

oligopoly -n- a market with so few sellers that the actions of any move it; L. few + market.

ology -suffix- study or knowledge of; e.g. astrology, biology, philology, theology.

ombudsman -n- a *govt. official,* esp. one who investigates complaints; cp. magistrate.

ominous -a- *threatening;* dire; foreboding; portentous.

omni -root- *all;* e.g., omnipotent (all powerful); omniscient (all knowing); omnipresent, etc.

omnibus -n- an anthology (collection) of all the works of *one* author (usually on related subjects); an __ law; cp. analects (collection of works).

omnivore/ous -n/a- an animal whose diet includes plants and animals; cp. fruitarian; vegan / vegetarian / herbivore.

ontogeny -n- the *history* of development of an *individual organism;* see gene.

ontology -n- study of the branch of ***philosophy* that deals with *the essence of being;*** Gr. to be; cp. *metaphysics.*

onus -n- *burden;* something burdensome; the ____ is on you; Lat. blame.

opalescent -a- reflecting an incandescent light; opal-like; cp. pellucid/ translucent (transmitting light); diaphanous (transparent); opaque.

opaque/opacity -a/n- *cloudy/foggy; not reflecting light; unintelligible;* cp. obscure (vague); oblique (at an angle, hence unclear).

ophidiophobia/ic [oh-fid-eo-phobia] -n/a- fear of snakes.

ophis/dian/diophobia -n- Gr., relating to *snakes;* fear of same (snakes + phobia).

---

opine -v- *express an opinion*; cp. cogitate/contemplate/meditate/mull/ muse/ ponder/reflect/ruminate (think).

opium/opiate -n- A highly addictive drug obtained from the poppy plant; other drugs (such as morphine) are derived from it; an opiate is taken from or resembles opium; cp. opiod (any drug derived from or similar to opium).

opprobrium/ious -n/a- disgrace; shame; ignominy; infamy.

optician -n- one who *makes lenses* for glasses; cp. oculist (detects eye-diseases).

optometrist -n- a doctor who *measures vision and prescribes* lenses or treatments; cp. ophthalmologist (doctor specializing in diseases of the eyes); oculist is an almost arhaic term that refers to both optometrists AND/OR opthalmologists, which are defined specialities of oculist.

opt/ion -v/n- to make a choice; I ____ to read; to have a choice.

opulent -a- possessing or exhibiting great wealth; affluent; cp. decadent (decay caused by wealth).

opus -n- a *creative work*, esp. a *musical* composition numbered to designate the order of the composer's works; e.g. magnum ____ (best work); cp. symphony/sonata.

Opus Dei [day] -n- Latin for "work of God"; wealthy cult of Catholics who still put women down for "original sin"; some refer to as the "Catholic Mafia".

oracle/oracular -n/a- a person who *transmits prophesies from a deity*, often from a shrine Buffet is the ____ of Omaha; he makes _____ statements.

oral -n- related to mouth/speech; cp. aural (re ear/hearing); cp. verbal (related to speaking).

orb/icular -n/a- *sphere*, esp. a celestial sphere; something round; an area/circle of endeavor.

orgiastic -a- to celebrate orgasms; Gr. orgasms.

orifice -n- a hole, mouth or vent; *opening/aperture*; Lat. mouth+make; cp. fissure (crack or cleft); lesion (tear in skin).

Orion -n- one of 88 constellations; Gr. Myth. A giant *hunter*, pursuer of Pleiades (the 7 daughters of Atlas who metamorphosed into stars); killed by Artemis; (aka one of Dumas' 3 Musketeers); see Zodiak.

ornithology -n- study of birds; Gr. bird + knowledge of.

orthodontist -n- teeth doctor; root is too varied to be helpful; cp. endodontist (rootcanals).

orthodox/y -a/n- *adhering to accepted traditions* or faiths, esp. religious; "true meaning"; Gr. customary + opinion.

orthography -n- a language or system of *spelling;* Lat. ortho = correct + graphia = writing.

orotund -a- writing or speaking in a pompous, pretentious manner/**fustian**; Lat. a rounded mouth; cp. euphuistic (affected writing), bombast(empty), hyperbole(exaggerated), pedantic (ostentatious about knowledge); Pooh Bah (pompous official, fm Gilbert&Sullivan's *Mikado).*

oscillate -v- to move back and forth at regular intervals, like a pendulum of fan.

---

ossify -v- to change into bone; make boney; Lat. bone + make; cp. atrophy (deteriorate); petrify (turn to stone).

ostensible -a- represented as such; *seeming to be*; alleged/professed/purports/averred to be; putative.

ostentatious/tion -a/n- showy; pretentious; cp. pompous (self-important).

ostler -n- one who takes care of horses; origin: hostelier/hotelier.

ostracize -v- to exclude or ban from a group; cp. exile (from country); excommunicate (from church).

otolaryngology [oto-lair-in-ology] -n- the medical study/knowledge of ear (oto), throat (larynx).

overt -a- not concealed; intentionally revealed.

oxymoron -n- an expression with *incongruous or contradictory* words; R. oxy=sharp + moros=fool; ex. a deafening silence/speedy turtle; cp. epigram (short, witty, often *paradoxical* truth; e.g. "Too soon old, Too late smart"; *paradox* (contradictory but true, e.g. "Be tough to be kind," "a wise fool").

pacific -a- calm, peaceful, tranquil.

pacify -v- ameliorate//appease//assuage//calm//conciliate//palliate// placate//propitiate; cp. mitigate (lessen).

paladin -n- a *knight* revered for *bravery*; a *hero*; fm Charlamagne's Court (c. 768-814 AD), King of Francs (parts of Germany and France) and Emperor of Rome.

palaver -v/n- to *talk idly*; chatter; natter//prattle; cp. rigmarole (confused or meaningless chatter); cp. banter/badinage/repartee (humorous talk); maunder (mutter, speak indistinctly); persiflage (flippant); prate (speak foolishly or tediously); cp. malapropism (misuse of words).

paleontology/ist -n- the study of fossils; those who do, called "librarians" by some; have enabled us to *track the evolution of human-like creatures now as far back as 2M years*; cp. cladistics (classifying organisms); taxonomy (classifying species); taxidermy (preparing & mounting animal skins).

pall -v/n- to become *insipid*, boring; n. a *cover* for a coffin; also a cloud or smoke; see pallid/pale.

palliate/tive -v/n- *to make less severe* (as a crime); cp. ameliorate/ pacify; placate/propitiate (appease).

pallid -a- having an *abnormally pale* or wan complexion; insipid(spiritless); cp. pall.

palpable -a- capable of being _**felt**_, *touched*; *tangible*; *tactile*.

palpitate/tion -v- throb; flutter; rapid beating; pulsate.

palter -v- *equivocate or prevaricate*/lie, esp. in speech.

pan -n/v- many meanings as a noun; Gr. for God, hence pantheism (seeing Nature as God); criticize; filter (gold); scan (horizon); panoply (a complete collection of things).

panacea -n- a universal cure for a disease or problem; Gr. all + remedy.

panache -a- dash, *flamboyance* in *style* or action; orig. ornament in headdress; cachet (mark of distinction); élan (style); ethos (distinguishing feature of a person); karma (essence).

pandemic/emonium -n- widespread, general; Gr. of all (pan) the people (demos).; disorder/uproar.

pander/er -v/n- **beg**/importune; beseech; entreat; cp. mendicant (a beggar); genuflect (beg on knees).

pangaea [pan-gee-ah] -n- a single land mass that is believed to have included all the earth's continents (in the Paleozoic era 500-250MYA, long before dinosaurs); all + earth.

panoply -n- that which *protects* completely; a soldier's armor; a ___ of love; all+cover; cp. aegis (shield); chrysalis (covering, esp. of a butterfly).

panoptic -a- including everything in one view; Gr. all-seeing; all + view; ant. myopic.

pantheism -n- the doctrine that universe is god; or that there is no supernatural being that created the universe, save the combined forces of nature; all + theism; cp. theism, deism, agnosticism, atheism, humanism, monotheism.

Pantheon -n- Gr. a temple for all the gods; all + gods.

---

pap -n- teat, nipple or something resembling one; baby food; something lacking substance; slang-money, bribes.

papist [pay-pist] -n- a derogatory term for a Roman Catholic, suggesting *extreme adherence.*

papyrus -n- *paper made from stems of a water plant* by Egyptians (began c. 400BC); cp. parchment (writing material made from dried animal skins, began c. 1BC; sturdier, lasted longer).

parable -n- a simple story illustrating a *moral;* Lat. beside + ballein / to throw; cp. proverb / axiom / epigram (short statement of a general truth).

paradigm -n- an *example, pattern, model*; para=alongside, digm=to show; cp prototype; archetype; also, a fundamental change in approach in underlying assumptions.

paradox/ical -n/a- Gr. a *seemingly contradictory statement that is true*; e.g., "Too soon old…"; an epigram is a rhymed co; cp. oxymoron (contradictory words whether true or false).

paragon -n- *a peerless example of perfection*; nonpareil; a __ of virtue; Gr. along + the point.

paranoia -n- irrational *persecution complex*; Fr. beside+mind; cp. psychosis (mental disorder).

parapet -n- a low protective wall, along the edge of a roof, balcony, etc.; Lat. shield/chest.

parchment -n- stiff material *made from animal skins*, once used for writing; see papyrus.

pariah -n- a social outcast; outcast; Indian: lowest class.

parlance -n- speech peculiar to an *activity*, eg law, medicine; shibboleth (language peculiar to a *group*); jargon (incoherent or *hybrid* term); dialect/vernacular (characteristic speech of a region); palaver (idle chatter).

parley -n/v- a *conference* to resolve a dispute; e.g., for a treaty or armistice; Lat. parlare / to speak.

parlous/ly -a- perilous; M.E. alteration of perilous; cp. precipitous (dangerously high or steep).

parody -n- *an artistic work* that *mimics and ridicules* another author's work; a *performance* so bad as to be *intentional mockery;* "The trial was a ___ of justice."

paroxysm -n- a *sudden outburst of emotion* or action, a sudden attack; a ___ of tears/laughter.

parricide -n- one who murders his parent; cp. patricide (father), matricide (mother); fratricide (brother); genocide (group); homicide (human); suicide.

parse -v- to break a sentence into its component parts and explain the relationship of the words; e.g. diagram sentences; Lat. part of speech.

parsimony/ious -n/a- excessive frugality//niggardly//stingy; Lat. to spare.

participle -n- a *verb* with an "*ing*" ending that is used as an *adjective*; e.g. flying fish. cp. gerund: a verb ending in "ing" used as a noun: Flying is fun.

particles -n- small parts of things; Physics: *things that make up atoms.* See quarks. Tiny, swift, evanescent (vanishing) elements that pass thru everything (including us) in fractions of a second. As Carl Sagan speculated in *Cosmos*, if you could travel down or up inside an electron, you might find universes w/ universes, endlessly; cp. **quark** (particles that make up particles).

parvenue -n- one who gained wealth or celebrity; Lat. to come/reach; cp. nouveau riche.

passel -n- a large group of people or things; a derivation of parcel.

pastiche [pah-steech] -n- Fr. a musical, literary or other *artistic work that imitates* a prior work; cp. vignette *(a short literary work or scene).*

pastille [pass-steel] -a- a small pellet of aromatic paste burned as perfume or deodorizer.

pathology -n/a- the *study* of the nature or path of *disease*; Lat. path+knowledge; eschatology (study of death).

pathological -a- *disordered behavior*; the anatomical manifestation of disease; a ____ liar; path + outside logic.

patina -a- a grey or brown film, *a gloss or sheen*, due to age or oxidation.

patrician/Pat -n- a *member of the noble families* of ancient Rome; cp. patriarch (male leader); patron (supporter).

patronize -v- to provide support ; generally used to mean to be *condescending.*

paucity -n- fewness; *dearth*; insufficiency; iota; modicum/whit; **ant.** profusion, plethora; plentitude.

peal -n- a loud ringing of bell(s); *any loud noise*; esp. of laughter; M.E. from "appeal".

---

peccadillo -n- a small *sin or fault*; cp. v-cavil; captious (pointing out same); pettifogger/niggler (one who does).

ped -root- Gk. for "child"; also for "foot"; e.g. biped; pedestrian.

pedagogue -n- one who *teaches* in a pedantic way; Gr. pais = boy + agogus = leader [of]; cp. pedant (ostentatiously learned); pundit (teacher, critic); demagogue (leads by appealing to mass emotions).

pedant/antic -n/a- one who makes an ostentatious *display* of learning; cp. erudite/polymath/ic (very learned); cp. savant (knows w/o study); pedagogue (pedantic teacher).

pedestrian -n- one who walks; one of *lower, humble*, plebian means. tastes or knowledge.

pejoration/ative [pah-**jor**-ah-tive] -n/a- a *worsening*; disparaging// derisive remark; cp. obloquy (abusive language); e.g.., a pejorative comment; or to engage in pejoration.

pel -root- Lat. to move; e.g., compel/constrain (force), impel (to inspire movement), repel (block).

pelisse [peh-leese] -n- a woman's cloak with arm holes.

pellucid/ity -a/n- *emitting light* / translucent; Lat. to shine; _____ eyes; cp. opalescent (transmitting an *incandescent* light); diaphanous (transparent); evanescent (vanishing).

pen/s -root- to hang or weigh.

penal/ize -a/v- related to punishment; to punish.

pend -root- Lat. to weigh; e.g. pending.

Penelope -name- from Homer's Odyssey, *a faithful wife*.

penetralium -n- the inner most parts of a building or a secret place; Lat. interior.

penicillin -n- a series of antibiotics based on fungus; the first effective antibiotic; formally discovered in 1928 by Alexander Fleming, Nobel Laureat for same.

penitent/iary -a/n- feeling remorse; one who does; where one does it; contrite; cp.expiate (atone) / give retribution/recompense (pay back); repentant.

pent -root- Gk. "five"; pentagon; pentacle.

pentagon -n- a polygon (closed plane) having five sides; one exists inside a pentacle.

Pentateuch -n- "five scrolls"; another name for Genesis-Exodus-Leviticus-Numbers-Deuteronomy, aka the Torah (law or guidance); cp. Tanuch (OT); Talmud (OT +25 other Rabbinical writings).

Pentecost/al -n- *a religious ceremony* at the end of Lent, falling 10 days after JC's putative "Ascension" (making it on the 7th Sunday after Easter/Christ's resurrection, first full moon after 3/21), *celebrating the descent of the Holy Ghost upon the 11 disciples* (Judas had hanged himself); a congregation seeking same; Gr. for fiftieth day (7x7+1) after The Resurrection; some RCC's claim this as "the birthday" of the RCC.

penetralium -n- the innermost parts of a building; a secret or hidden place cp. lair; this word is not in some dictionaries.

penultimate -a- next to last (Lat. almost + last).

penumbra -n- L. almost + shadow; the *shaded area* around a sun spot, hence *partial illumination*; cp. umbra (dark area/shadow).

penury/ious -n/a- extreme poverty; impecunious (without + wealth); cp. privation (deprivation of necessities).

peptic -a- relating to *digestion*; cp. dyspeptic (causing indigestion); emetic (causing vomiting); colonic (purge the colon); purgative (purging//cleansing); eupeptic (healthy good spirits).

perdition -n- the *loss of soul; eternal damnation*; Hell; Lat. to lose; see Calvinism.

peregrinate/tion [pear-egg-grin-aa-tion] -v/n- to take a long journey or period of wandering; Gk. to travel abroad; near syn. travel.

peremptory -a- any act or words that are *decisive; final*; Fr. thoroughly+to take; e.g., a ___ strike or blow; e.g. "Just do it!"

perfidy/ious -n/a- deliberate *breach of trust; syns. adulterous//infidelity; treachery* cp. mendacity/prevarication (lying).

perforce -a- M.E.; by force; forced by circumstances; cp. cursorily (hastily).

perfunctory/orily -a- *done quickly* and often carelessly; root is misleading.

peripatetic -n- *walking about*, followers of Aristotle's logic; cp. itinerant; peregrinate (travel).

pernicious/ly/ness -a/n- highly *injurious* or destructive *of character*; bane//*lethal*//truculent; virulent (poisonous).

perorate/tion [pear-o-rate] -v/n- to give a *summary at the end* of a speech; to speak at length or grandiloquently; expatiate (speak or write at length); cp. bombast (empty rhetoric); hyperbole (exaggerated wording).

perpendicular -a- standing at right angles to the horizon / upright / vertical.

persiflage -n- a *flippant* mocking conversation; Fr. thoroughly + to banter; near syns. badinage (witty conversation); natter // palaver // prattle (silly chatter); prate (speak foolishly or tediously); rigmarole (confused, meaningless); cp. colloquy (formal discourse); polemics (debate); dialectics (reasoning); peroration (grandeloquent summary); prosaic/prosy (banal speech or writing); cp. malapropism (humorous misuse of words).

perspicacity/cious -n/a- acuteness of sight or discernment; cp. prescience (foresightedness); clairvoyance (magical foresightedness); intuitive; savant (know w/o learning).

pertinacious -a- holding firmly to an opinion or course of action; *contumacious* / obdurate / obstinate / *stubborn* / restive; Lat. per = from + tenacious; intractable / intransigent (inflexible).

perturbations -n- actions that cause one to be *perturbed* / disturbed.

PET -scientific acronym- Position-Emission Tomography = *scanning regional blood flow* in the brain via devices like fMRI (functional MRI's); cp. **TMS** (transcranial magnetic stimulation, using magnets to measure brain activity).

petrify -v- to make stiff/stoney (esp. make stiff *with fear*); Lat. make; cp. atrophy (withering); ossify (make boney); liquefy (make liquid); mortify (frighten to death).

pettifogger/petty -n/a- a person who quibbles over trivia; niggler; an unscrupulous lawyer; captious//cavil (v/n for same); peccadillo (small fault).

petulant -a- sulking; pouting childishly; cp. querulous/complaining; whining/grumbling/grousing.

phantasm -n- a mental image of a real object.

phantasmagoria/ic -n- a *shifting succession* of things *imagined* by fever; hallucination.

pharisaical/ic -n- *outwardly religious*; hypocritical; i.e., like the Pharohs.

phenomenal/non -a- *extraordinary*; philos: derived from the *senses not the mind*.

phenomenology -n- the study of all possible phenomena/*appearances* in human experience.

philatelist -n- stamp collector.

phile [file] -suffix- admirer &/or imitator; e.g., Anglophile; Francophile (those imitating Brits / French); pedophile.

philistine/Philistine -n- a person who is *hostile or indifferent to the arts*; the current meaning is quite a stretch from its roots: a member of a non-Semitic group from ancient, southern Palestine, who had conflicts with the Israelites in the 12th Century B.C. (e.g., David and Goliath).

philology -n- love of historical *linguistics*; love of speech/learning; (Gr. love+study); cp. epistemology (study of origin and validity of knowledge); etymology (study of words) and lexicography (graphing words/dictionaries).

philosophy -n- the ***love of wisdom***; *active* culture; Lat: philos-loving, sophia – wisdom;

philosophy includes ***five fields of study***:

esthetics -study of the ideal form of beauty.

ethics -study of ideal conduct; of good and evil.

logic -art and method of clear thinking.

metaphysics -study of the nature of matter and mind; (meta=above; physics=external nature).

politics -the study of the ideal form of government.

See **syllogism:** major premise, minor premise, & conclusion; ex. Men are foolish; I am a man; I am foolish.

philter -n- a drink supposed to excite sexual love; Gr. to love; cp. aphrodisiac.

phlebotomy/ist -n- *blood letting*; one who does so; Lat. phleps-vain + tomos - cut; cp. lobotomy.

phlegmatic -a- *sluggish; apathetic*; impassive; indifferent; syn. lethargic; cp. indolent (won't work); inert (can't move); see lassitude (exhaustion); stolid (emotionless); torpid (numb); quiescent/torpor (inactive).

phobe [foab] / phobia -suffix/n- extreme *aversion to, dislike, fear*; e.g., Anglophobe; acrophobia (fear of heights); agoraphobia (open spaces); ailurophobia (cats); apiaphobia (bees); arachnophobia (spiders); aviaphobia (birds); claustrophobia; homophobia (of men, usually of "gays"); ophidiophobia (snakes).

Phoebe [fee-bee] -n- Gr. myth, the goddess; the *moon*; hence *shinning*; also, a species of bird.

---

phon -root- Gk. sound/voice/speech; e.g. phonics (learning to read by sound), phonetics (study of speech sounds).

photons -n- *light particles*; the quantum (a quantity or unit of energy) of electromagnetic *energy having zero mass*, and has no electric charge and an indefinitely long lifetime.

phrenology -n- the study of the size and shape of the brain; Gk. mind + study.

phylogeny/ic [fill-**loge**-ihny] -n/a- *evolutionary development* of a plant, animal, tribe or race; Gr. phylo/species + gene / origins.

phylum [file-lum] -n- Biol. A taxonomic (classification) *division* of species of animal kingdom OR plant kingdom; cp. cladistics (classify organisms; taxonomy (classification, esp. of species).

physics -n- the branch of science studying the nature and properties of matter and energy.

physiognomy -n- *facial expressions or features*; the art of *judging character from same;* Lat. (physique + gnome / interpreter).

physiology -n- the biological study of life's processes, functions and organs; Lat. *nature+knowledge / study*; cp. homeostatic (physiological equilibrium).

physis -root- Gr. nature; physics=analyzing nature, the way the universe works.

piety/pious -n/a- devotion to worship of a higher being, devout; L. worship.

pilgrim/age -n- a *religious devotee* who *journeys to sacred shrine*; the journey to same.

Pilgrim -n- English who founded Plymouth Rock, N.E. (1620).

pinion -n/v- a bird's wing; a cogwheel (a wheel with cogs/teeth on the rim); to "pin"/hold someone.

pinnacle -n- highest point; acme; apex; epitome; Horeb (Sinai) height; peak; summit; vertex; *zenith*; cp. apogee (most distant point in orbit); apotheosis (highest point in orbit); solstice (sun's highest point).

pinnace [**pin'**/iss] -n- a small <u>sailing</u> boat; cp. tender (one kept on board), or punt (open, flat bottomed boat) dinghy (*any small boat*, sail, motor, or row).

piquant -a- *pleasantly* pungent (penetrating) in *taste* or odor; spicy; cp. aromatic (pleasant, distinctive); redolent (fragrant); pungent (strong taste or smell).

pit -n- a deep hole OR referring to fruit: the *hard seed* in the center of some fruits.

pith/y -n/a/v- *spongy tissue* in the center of most vascular (with vessels) plants; something soft, spongy; to kill by severing the spinal cord, esp cattle.

pith helmet -n- aka "topee"; a helmet originally made of piths, now of cork, covered in white cloth.

placate -v- to *allay anger by yielding concessions*; ameliorate; appease; assuage/conciliate/mollify/ pacify/propitiate.

placebo -n- Lat. "I shall please"; refers to sugar pills given in lieu of therapeutic drugs; cp. nocebo ("I shall harm").

placer [plah-sir] -n- a glacial or alluvial (water)/diluvial(flood) *deposit of valuable minerals*.

plagiarize [**play**-jar-ize] -v- to copy or steal.

pope/Pope -n- Lat. a child's word for father, papa; the head of the R.C.C. The elected successor to Saint Peter to whom Jesus is said to have given the keys to Heaven. The office of Pope is called the "papacy". His jurisdiction is often called the "Holy See". At times, Popes have used armies to impose their will. Pope Benedict (reigned 2005-13) was widely-known in Italy as a homosexual, explaining his effective refusal to reprimand pedophiliac priests; his secretary was said by many Italians to be his lover and to be in control of The Church. Benedict was the only Pope to resign, putatively forced to do so by his Cardinals and laity.

porcine -a- anything related to pigs. Ex. His porcine manners are disgusting.

portent/portend -n/a/v- indicative of a coming event; an omen/ominous; cp. presage (foreshadow).

portentous -a- usually an unfavorable sign; cp. ominous//dire (threatening); but also "pompous, overdone" cp. augur (foretell); auspice (favorable sign).

portmanteau -n- a large trunk/suitcase that opens into two parts; anything blending multiple parts.

posit -v- to *state* as a fact or truth; cp. postulate (assume/stipulate); propound (suggest); cp. exposit (explain).

postprandial -a- the period after dinner or lunch; Lat. prandium (a meal).

postulate/ant -v/n- to *assume / concede / stipulate* as true or evident; a proposition advanced as axiomatic; cp. posit (state as fact); propound (suggest); presume (take for granted/overconfident).

---

potation -n- a drink//libation; also *a bout of alcoholic drinking*; Lat. to drink.

potentate -n- one with the power to rule over others; potent; cp. plenipotentiary/procurator (one with full powers); monarch/autocrat; Poo Bah.

potpourri [poh-pooree] -n- a mixture of dried, naturally fragrant flowers; a diverse mixture of things.

poulstice -n- a moist mass of plant material applied to the body to reduce soreness; cp. pap (baby food or something lacking substance); cp. pith (the spongy center of vascular plants).

prate -v- talk foolishly or tediously; cp. banter (speak *humorously*); chatter // natter // palaver // prattle (to *talk idly*); colloquy (formal convsation); persiflage (flippant colloquy); rigmarole (confused talk); cp. badinage (playful repartee); malapropism (misuse of words).

pratfall -n- a fall on the buttocks; slang of unknown origin.

prattle -n- trifling, meaningless talk // chatter // natter // palaver; cp. rigmarole (confused talk); persiflage (flippant talk); doggerel (irregular, comic speech).

praxis -n- *habitual practice or custom*; M.E. action + to do.

prayer -n- a reverent request made to a deity or any higher power.

pre -root- before.

precept/tor -n- a *principle* or general rule of action; a teacher; cp. pundit (teacher or critic).

precipitous -a- *dangerously* high or steep; perilous/parlous (dangerous).

---

precocious -a- advanced beyond one's years; a *prodigy*.

precursor -n- something that precedes/precedent; cp. presage/portend (to warn/foreshadow).

predicament -n- a *difficult situation*; cp. predicate (the part of a sentence that describes the subject.

predict -v- to foretell; *before + to say*; presage (foreshadow); portend (warn).

predilection -n- reference; *predisposition*; affinity; attraction; prone; wont (custom); cp. propensity.

preen -v- to straighten and clean, as does a bird or cat; cp. groom; prune

prefixes -n- the first syllable of words; *the numerical prefixes are:* uni / mono = 1; bi = 2; tri = 3; quadra = 4; quint /penta = 5; hex / ses = 6; hept / sept = 7; octo = 8; novem = 9; deci / deka = 10; cent/ hector = 100; milli / kilo = 1,000; mega = million; giga = billion.

prelate -n- *high ranking clergyman*; curate (in charge of a parish); rector/vicor (Episcopal curate); cp. sexton.

premonition -n- feeling that something is going to happen; cp. presage.

presage -n/v- to *foreshadow;* cp. portend/warn; an omen//warning; auspice (favorable sign).

prescient/ce -a/n- *foresight;* before + knowledge; perspicacious (acuteness of sight); intuitive; cp. savant (knows w/o being taught; clairvoyant (sees the future/psychic).

presentment -n- intuitive feeling about the future/premonition; prescience; clairvoyance.

---

prestidigitation -n- *manual skill/dexterity* in the art of tricks / sleight of hand; legerdemain.

presume/umption -v- to be *overconfident, take for granted / expect*; to be glib; *cp. assume*; postulate (assume); propound (suggest).

pretentious/tion -a/n- given to outward show; syn. ostentatious; cp. pompous (self-important).

preternatural -n- before nature; *supernatural*; transcending matter; syn. metaphysics (above nature) / numinous.

primate -n- the order/phylum that includes man, monkeys and apes; the *bishop* of highest rank in the region.

primordial -n- *first* in time; existing from the beginning; see man.

pristine -a- *original, unspoiled,* primitive; e.g. It is in _____ condition.

privation -n- deprivation of *necessities*; abject poverty; cp. penury // impecunious (penniless).

privity -n- a *relationship; joint knowledge* of a matter; a shared interest; M.E. private; ____ of contact.

probity -a- adherence to the highest standards of morality; Lat. honest.

procure/r -v/n- to obtain, acquire; one who does so.

procreate/or -v/n- to create; to *beget offspring*; Lat. forward + create; cp. progenitor (originator of a lineage).

procrustean -a- Gk. mythology; ruthless disregard of individual differences.

procurator -n- an *agent* having *power of attorney*; an official with delegated authority; near syn. plenipotentiary (with full power, ambassador); cp. curator (administrator, esp. of a museum).

prodigal -n/a- *recklessly wasteful*; extravagant; profuse giver; "the ___ son"; cp profligate (dissipating).

prodigious -a- huge; vast; a _____ producer; cp. prolific (produce freely), fecund (fertile).

prodigy -n- one with extraordinary talents, esp. a child; cp. precocious (advanced for one's age).

prodrome/dronic -n/a- an early symptom of a disease; pro = before + dromos = act of running.

profane/ity -a/n- vulgar or irreverent language; syn. scurrilous/ribald (vulgar).

proffer -v- *to offer / tender* for acceptance, *as evidence in a trial.*

profligate -a- given to *dissipation*; cp. prodigal (extravagantly wasteful).

profusion -n- abundant supply; copious; plentitude; replete/tion (plentiful); cp. glut / plethora / superfluity / surfeit (excess); prodigious (huge producer).

progenitor -n- *an originator / procreator of a line* of descent; a direct forbearer; Lat. to beget; cp. atavist (ancestor).

pro hac vice [pro-hock-veechay] -Lat term- "for this event to speak", esp. the admission of a lawyer to try a case in a jurisdiction where he is not licensed.

proletariat -n- laboring class; cp. bourgeois (middle class,); kulac, capitalist); Bolshevic (Communist Party member).

prolific -a- *producing freely*; fertile/fecund; cp. prodigious (huge, vast).

prolix/ity -a/n- wordy; verbose; long-winded; cp. euphuistic (affected), loquacious (talkative), garrulous (too talkative); voluble (fluent); ant. laconic / pithy / sententious / succinct / terse.

Prometheus / promethean [pro-mee-theeus] -n/a- Gr. mythology, meaning "fore thinker"; P stole fire from the god-Zeus and gave it to man; hence, any P suggests *any heroic person or deed.*

promiscuous -a- *indiscriminate*; casual; irregular; today, sexually loose.

promontory -n- *cliff*; high point; cp. acme, apex, apogee, capstone, Horeb height pinnacle, solstice, summit/vertex.

promulgate -v- to announce, promote or make known. Ex. The agency promulgated rules. Near syns. broadcast; disseminate; propagate.

propensity -a- a natural inclination,/proclivity/predisposition/ preference to *think in a certain way*; pre − before + pensare − to think; predilection (disposition to like something).

propinquity [pro-pink-quit-tee] -n- nearness, *kinship*; Lat. near; cp. atavistic (ancestor-like); forebearer; progenitor.

propitiate/tious -v/n- ameliorate; appease-specially a gov't.; assuage; conciliate; mollify; pacify; placate; cp. palliate (make less severe.)

propound -v- to *suggest*; cp. posit (state as fact), postulate (assume/ stipulate); presume (expect).

prosaic/prosy -a- ordinary, esp. of speech or prose; having no imagination; commonplace; trite; banal /mundane / pedestrian / plebian; mundane; pedestrian; cp. quotidian (daily, commonplace).

proselytize/proselyte -v/n- *to convert* from one faith/belief system to another; one who is converted; tendentious (prejudiced, promoting a cause).

prosody -n- the study of the metrical structure of verse/poetry.

---

protagonist -n- the *leading* figure in a drama or **cause** (Gr. first + actor); cp. proponent (advocate).

protean -a- able to change frequently or easily; fickle / *mutable* / given to vicissitude; Gk. "Proteus" was the Gk. sea-god who assumed different shapes to avoid answering questions; cp. desultory; malleable. Ex. His protean disposition rendered him unreliable.

prot/proto -root- Gr. first in time; primitive; syn. primordial.

proton -n- the *positive* charge in an atom; with electrons (negative) and neutrons (no charge). comprises an atom; the dot on this "i" can hold 500T protons; see atom (500M can hide behind one hair).

protoplasm/al -n/a- a complex, *jellylike* substance constituting the *living* matter of plant or animal **cells**, performing the basic life functions (e.g., amoeba); "**man** = primordial protoplasmal atomic globules" (Gilbert and Sullivan in *Macado*) TO sentient, polemic, polymathic homo sapiens; cp. poultice & pith.

prototype -n- first of a type/architype; exemplar; *model* from which others are made; cp. paradigm (parallel).

protozoa -n- *single cell creatures* (pre-animals); now called "protests".

provenance -n- the place of origin or earliest known history of something; Lat.; cp. provident.

proverb/axiom -n- short, pithy saying expressing a well-known **_truth_** or fact; axiom; "A stitch in time saves nine." cp. adage/apothegm/aphorism, maxim (rule); tenet (rule of a group).

provident/ce -n- preparation in advance; *prudent management*; w/ capital "P" = God.

provost -n/a- the *head officer* of a college or cathedral; e.g., provost guard or marshal; cp. prelate.

prudent/tial -a/n- to *plan for the future*; one who does; origin of name Prudence; cp. wise/ judicious/sagacious (to make the right decisions).

prurient -a- *stimulating* sexual desire; lubricious / salacious (e.g., pornography)

lustful; concupiscent; lascivious; lecherous; libidinous; compare the following similar words

excessive indulgence in sexual activity: debauchery

immoral: base, dissolute, licentious, a libertine/reprobate; wanton

sensationalistic/sexually shocking: lurid; e.g., lurid newspaper articles

vulgar conduct/speech: lewd; profane; ribald, scurrilous

Note: In the area of sex, dictionaries give widely varied, overlapping definitions. The above compromise among several.

psalm -n- sacred song; hymn; gita = song in Hindi; see Bhagivad Gita (song of God).

psychedelics -n- that which causes hallucinations; *drugs*; giving psychosis (mental disorders).

psychic -a/n- relating to telepathy, clairvoyance or other inexplicable powers; a fortune teller.

psychopath/ic -n/a- one evincing *chronic abnormal* or *violent* behavior; cp. sociopath (anti-social).

psychosis/otic -n/a- severe mental disorder (neurosis) affecting intellectual and social functioning.

puckish -a- playful, esp. mischievously.

puerile/puerility -a/n- belonging to *childhood*; childish; juvenile; immature; pubescent (in puberty).

pugnacious -n- disposed to fight, belligerent, bellicose, militant; cp. jingoistic (belligerently nationalistic.

punctilious -a- *showing great attention to detail or conventions/correct behavior*; cp. martinet (rigid disciplinarian).

punctual -a- prompt; timely.

pundit -n- a learned *teacher* or *critic*; cp. maven (expert); pedant (ostentatious display of learning); pedagogue (pedantic teacher); polymath (extremely learned); preceptor (teacher); savant (learned w/o study).

pungent -a- a penetrating or biting smell; cp.aromatic/piquant (pleasantly pungent); redolent (fragrant).

purgative -n/a- a laxative; tending to cleanse or purge; med. cleanse the bowels//colonic; cp. cathartic (purge undesirable emotions thru art/drama); therapeutic (healing); emetic (causing vomiting).

Puritan -n- syn. pilgrim; English Puritan who founded Plymouth Rock in 1620.

purl -n/v- soft sound of a swirling stream; to make a sound like that; cp. purr (sound of a pleased cat).

purser -n- an officer on a ship who keeps the accounts; hence bookkeeper; also, a head steward.

pusillanimous -a- lacking courage; craven; pussill = *weak*; animus = *courage*/purpose/spirit; ant. intrepid//undaunted.

put -root- from Lat. to think or believe; e.g., compute, impute, repute.

putative [pew-ta-tive] -a- alleged / *asserted* / *averred* / *ostensible* / *purported* /*reputed.*

"Pygmalion Effect" -term- Belief: *When people believe in themselves, they perform much better.* Geo. Bernard **Shaw's play** of the same name (which was converted into the famous musical, *My Fair Lady)*; Pygmalion came from Ovid's *Metamorphes*, where Pygmalion was a sculptor who fell in love with one of his statues.

pyre [pie-er] -n- a heap of combustibles in which corpses are burned.

pyro/**technics** -n- fire or heat; art of *making or setting off fireworks.*

pyric [**peer**-ick] -a- of or relating to burning; e.g., a ___ victory; see Pyrrhic.

Pyrrhic victory -n- a victory that is rendered valueless by staggering losses; from the victory of Pyrrhus (279 B.C.), king of Epirus over the Romans at Asculum; see "zero sum game" (where no one wins).

"Q"

quad -root- four; e.g., quadrangle (4-angles); quadruped (4-feet); quadrilateral (4-sided).

quagmire -n- swamp; bog; marshy tract; cp. quay (warf); labyrinth (confused maze).

quango -n- quasi autonomous **non**-governmental org that operates arms-length fm govt.

quark -n- particles that make up particles; any of a group of hypothetical **subatomic** *particles* having the electric charge of 1/3 to 2/3 of an electron. "Three quarks for Master Mark", a line from *Finn* see particle; atom and string theory.

quarry -n/v- *a large, open pit for excavation* (of stone, ore, etc.); to dig one.

quasar -n- a quasi-stellar object (quasi + stellar (stella-Lat. star); the acronym of "quasi-steller

radio source:" also refers to massive *explosions or collisions of stars*; cp supernova.

quasi [kwa-zee] -a- resembling to some degree; e.g. a quasi artist, doctor, etc.

quay -n- a *wharf* or *place* where ships load and unload, esp, a pier of wood or rock.

querulous -a- complaining; whining grumbling; syn. to grouse; cp. petulant (pouting); Fr. to complain; remonstrate (oppose).

queue -v/n- waiting line; a line; pigtail; cp. plait.

quid pro quo -Lat. phrase- "this for that"; something given in exchange for something else.

quiescent/ce/quiet -a- inactive; *still*; dormant; syn. torpor/languor (inactive); cp. indolent (lazy) languor (slow); lethargic/phlegmatic (sluggish); torpid (numb).

quinquennial -a- recurring every *five* years; **cp.** biennial (2 yrs), tricennial (3yrs) quadrennial (4yrs), septennial (7yrs), decennial (10yrs), vicennial (20yrs), centennial (100 yrs,millennial (1000 yrs), perennial (forever).

quintessence/quintessential -n/a- the pure, highly *concentrated or distilled essence* of something

quis -root- Lat. to seek; exs. inquisition (question); acquisitive (greed); requisition (demand).

quisling -n- a traitor; named after a Norwegian officer who ruled Norway as a Hitler-puppet; cp. Judas (Escariot); heretic (renouncer of faith or group).

quixotic -a- *idealistic*; ***too** romantic*; e.g., Cervantes' Don Quixote; *cp.* idyllic (romantic, picturesque).

quo -obs- a variant of who; whether; to what place; to whom; cp. qui = who in Italian.

quo fata ferunt -Lat. phrase- Bermuda's motto; "To where or to whom do the fates take us?"

quota -n- a proportional share; a *required* amount.

quotidian -a- occurring daily/diurnal; hence, ordinary, commonplace, banal/prosiac; Fr. "as many as" + days.

quo vadis -Lat. phrase- "Where do you go?" from the 1895 novel re Nero's insane rein over Rome.

"R"

rabbi -n- ordained spiritual *leader* of a *Jewish* congregation; Gr. master; cp. curate / paster / priest / vicar / rector.

rabble -n- a disorderly mob; socially inferior or uncouth; M.E.

raconteur -n- story teller; Fr. to tell; cp. recount/repeat.

rampant -a- extending unchecked, *unrestrained;* the disease was rampant; cp. rife (plentiful).

rampart -n- an elevation, structure or *something that protects* or defends; cp. redoubt (fortress).

rancor /ous -n- bitter, *deep-seeded ill will;* deeply malevolent; cp. enmity (hatred); odious (hateful).

rank -a- an offensive smell, esp from vegetation; fetid/fusty/malodorous (bad smell); putrid (decaying); mephitic (bad smell from the earth); miasma (bad smell from disease or health).

rapacious -a- *that which takes by force;* also *plundering,* rape; greedy; depredating.

rapine -v- *violent seizure of someone's property;* syns. depredate; pillage; plunder; rapacious; cp. flay (skin); repine/ing (discontented).

rapprochement -n- Fr. to bring together; reconciliation; semi-syn. denouement (solution to a complex matter).

rapture -n- intense joy; euphoria; ecstasy.

rarified [rare-ih-fied] -a- *elevated* in style or character; lofty; rarified air.

---

rationalize -v- to *justify* (one's acts, opinions, etc.) by *plausible* reasoning, if attenuated.

rebarbative -a- unattractive; objectionable; Fr. beard to beard.

recalcitrant -a- willfully disobedient//*contumacious*//rebellious; cp. *refractory/restive (resists control);* intransigent/intractable (inflexible); obdurate (stubborn).

recant -v- Lat. to sing-back; make a formal retraction; abjure/ foreswear (do so under oath); cp. (promise not to do); gainsay (contradict or deny not under oath); repudiate (refuse to accept); rescind (cancel).

recessive -a- receding; cp. regressive/retrograde; (returning or reverting to a worse position).

recondite -a- not easily understood/inscrutable; near syn. abstruse/ obscure/Delphic; cp. arcane (known to few); esoteric (known by specially trained).

reconnoiter -v- to scout for others; to make preliminary inspection.

reconnaissance -n- a noun form of reconnoiter.

recrimination/tory -n- a retaliatory *accusation*.

rect -root- Lat. to make right/honest.

rectify -v- Fr. to make right; to correct.

rectitude -n- *moral uprightness/rightousness; honesty* of purpose; virtue.

recumbent -a- lying down, reclining, idle; syn. supine; cp. prone/ prostate (lying flat); incumbent (obligatory).

recursive/ion -a/n- running backwards (math); see algorithm (a computational procedure running backwards).

---

recuse -v- to *disqualify oneself* as a judge in a particular case.

redact/ors -v/n- to draw up; frame (in a proclamation); to alter or *materially reduce a document*.

redeemed -v- *to be forgiven for error and restored* to one's prior position.

redemption/ive -n/a- *being freed after payment of debt*; cp. expiation// pennitence//retribution (payment).

redolent -a- *fragrant*; aromatic; also strongly suggestive of something; cp. piquant (pleasant/spicey aroma/taste); pungent (penetrating, negative); cp. fetid / malodorous / rank (stinky); mephitic (foul odors from the earth; miasmic (unhealthy smell).

redound -v- to *inure*; to have an effect/consequence; *reflect upon*; Ex. deeds that *redound* to one's discredit or credit.

redoubt -n- a defensive *fortification*; rampart.

redoubtable -a- arousing *fear or awe*; *formidable*; deserving respect; Lat. doubt.

reductive/ism/ist -a/n- that which *reduces/oversimplifies* something complex; syn. minimalism; everything is matter-energy in space-time and can be reduced to the same thing; see E = MC2.

redundant/cy -n/a- repeated/ing; cp. tautology (needless repetition).

redux -a- brought back; Fr. to bring back; _____ music; resuscitated; resurrected.

refectory -n- a room where meals are served; Lat. to refresh.

reflex/reflexive -n/a- an instinctive response or reaction.

reflexive -a- pertaining to a reflex; Grammar: ____ tense -- where the subject and object of a verb are the same; e.g. "She dressed herself." "It is I." "This is he." Syn. predicate nominative (PN).

reflux -n- flowing back; Lat: back+flow; acid ____ (burping acid).

refractory/refract -a/v- resists control; contumacious / restive; in science: resistant to a process or stimulus; cp. intractable / intransigent / inflexible); obdurate (stubborn); recalcitrant (disobedient).

refugee -n- one who flees one country for refuge (protection) in another.

refulgent -a- shining brightly; fulgere (to shine); a *refulgent* smile; cp. coruscating (flashing/sparkling).

regale [re-gail] -v- to amuse; to do so lavishly; cp. regal (kingly).

regime [**ray**-geem] -n- a period of rule; a pattern of conduct or behavior.

regimen [**rej**-jih-min] -n- a systematic plan (a diet, exercise, etc.).

regress/ive -v/a- return, usually to a worse position; syn. retrograde; cp. ingress; egress; recessive (receding).

rejoinder -n- a response to a reply; Law. A *second* answer; cp. riposte (quick thrust/reply/retort).

religion/ious -n- **Western**: belief in a supernatural power as creator & governor of the universe;

Eastern: a belief in the oneness of Mother Nature, man, all creatures with little focus on creation; see

theism (belief in a Creator who rules the universe) and **deism** (a Creator who abandoned the world) and **pantheism** (belief that life evolved from natural causes, "Mother Nature"). Root: Lat. to restrain, tie back, rely.

reliquary -n- a vase/coffer that *holds ashes* from cremations (cremanes); fm Lat. sacred relics.

remediation -n- the *act of remedying* problems; Root: again = mediate / settle / resolve.

reminisce/cence -v/n- a recollection from the past; the act of doing so.

remise -v- to give, grant, *release a claim*; Fr. to put back.

remonstrance/trate -n/v- to *oppose*; something that *highlights a fault* or deficiency; captious; to niggle; pettifogger.

rend -v- to tear into pieces; to cause great pain as to a person, esp. their heart.

reparation -n- compensation//atonement (act of) // expiation // penitence // retribution; cp. redemption (an act of forgiveness or one justifying same); cp. contrition (repentant).

repayment -v- restitution//retribution; cp. reprisal (something repossessed).

repertory -a- a repertoire; a theater in which a resident company performs from its repertoire; the *repertory* players.

repetition -n- redundancy; cp. tautology (needless repetition).

repine/ing -v- discontented/*sad*/rueful/lamenting/lugubrious/soulful; Lat. again + pine; cp. rapine. (plunder/depredate); **lachrymose** [la-kree-mous] (tearful); cp. rapine.

replete/tion -a/n- abundance//plentiful//copious//myriad//plenti-tude//profusion; cp. plethora//satiety//surfeit//superfluity (excess/saturation).

repose -v- temporarily rest or sleep; supine//recline.

reprehensible -a- deserving of *censure*; M.E.

reprisal -n- an action that *takes back* // repossesses; cp. a restitution; often retaliatory; retribution (to repay).

reprise -n- a *deduction* or charge, often annually as a tax; a recurrence or renewal of something; Fr. re-again; prendre – to take.

reproach -v- to blame; Lat; cp. denigrate et al; cp. rapprochement (agreement).

reprobate -n- a morally unprincipled person; Theol. rejected by God; Lat. to reprove; base; licentious; wanton.

reprove -v- to *chide//chastise//scold//rebuke//reprimand //reproach*; Lat. *reverse* + approve.

reptile/ian -n- a snake; cp. ophidiophobia (fear of snakes).

repugnant -a- very offensive; Fr. again+fight; cp. pugnacious; anathema (hated thing/person);

requiem -n- a *musical* piece or service for the *dead*.

rescind -v- cancel formally; recant/retract/take back; cp. abjure (renounce under oath); forswear//gainsay//repudiate (deny not under oath).

residual -a- the remainder; root: to reside.

resorb/tion -v/n- to absorb again; the act of doing so; ex. a tooth absorbing its inner structure.

resuscitate -v- bring back to life; esp. mouth-to-mouth breathing / *revive / rejuvenate.*

restive -a- *resisting control* / contumacious / pertinacious / refractory; cp. obdurate (stubborn); recalcitrant (disobedient); intransigent / intractable (inflexible).

reticule -n- a woman's *draw string* purse.

retinue -n- a group of advisers or others accompanying an important person//entourage; Fr. keep back/retain.

retribution -n- to repay/restitution; Lat. again+to pay; cp. expiation (atone); contrite//penitence (feel remorse).

retrograde -a/v- moving backward/regress//retrogress; recessive (recede), inverted.

retrogress/regress/ion -v- returning to an earlier, less desirable position; retrograde.

revanche/ist/istic/ist -n/a/n- to retaliate; revenge; Fr.

revenant -n- a person who has returned, esp. from the dead; Fr.

revere -v- *worship;* to regard with **awe**, great respect or **devotion**; Lat. respect; cp. adore (love); adulate (extreme praise); redoubtable (arousing fear or awe).

reverie -n- abstracted musing; *daydreaming.*

revert -v- to return, come back, reply; Lat. nouns: response//riposte// rejoinder.

revile -v- to denounce with *abusive language*; c. excoriate//fulminate; vilify, vituperate; cp. malign (discredit).

revive -v- to bring back to life or resuscitate; rejuvenate; resurrect; Fr. again + to live.

rhetoric -n- *affected, insincere or pretentious speech*; cp. bombast (overblown, empty); hyperbole (exaggerate); dialectics (reasoning); polemics (debate); colloquy (formal discourse).

rheum -n- a watery discharge from the eyes or nose.

ribald -a- indulging in *vulgarities*; syn. lewd//scurrilous; see lascivious for similar words.

rick -n- stack of hay, corn, straw, etc. built into a shape (e.g. tied in middle).

rictus -n- a gaping *hole*, a *gaping grimace;* also, a bird's beak.

rife -a- abundant/abounding/prevalent; near syns. profuse/myriad/ plentitude/replete (abundant); cp. plethora/surfeit, superfluity (excess).

rigmarole -n- lengthy or confused talk or procedure; cp. banter (witty talk); syns: chatter; natter; palaver; prattle (all silly talk); cp. persiflage (flippant/mocking).

rigor mortis -Lat. term- the stiffening that occurs after death to corpses.

rill(e) -n- a stream, a flow of water or of something / runnel.

riposte -n- a *quick thrust* given *after parrying* an opponent's lunge; same verbally.

rive/riven [riv] -v- split or torn apart violently; cp. cleave/cloven (split apart).

---

river -n- a body of water that flows into an ocean, sea or another river; cp. brook / rivulet / stream / tributary (smaller bodies of water that flow into larger bodies (rivers or lakes).

rivulet -n- a brook or small stream; Lat.

rococo [roeko-ko] -n- excessively ornate décor, painting, & furnishings in the Baroque (17ᵗʰ Century) style.

roil -v- to make muddy/cloudy by stirring up sediment.

roister -v- to celebrate in noisy/boisterous manner / rollick.

rook/rookery -n/v- a crow; a breeding place for birds; verb-slang for to cheat; the castle in Chess.

root -n/v- As noun: the basic cause, source or origin of anything (a plant, a society, a word); as a verb: to cause anything to grow. Etymologically: the basic syllable of any word; e.g., "defatig" in indefatigable.

rosacea [rose-aa-shah] -n- a common disease of facial skin, causing redness, swelling and disfigurement.

rotatory -a- moving in a circle around an axis; the noun form of the verb rotate.

rote [wrote] -n- mechanical, unthinking, sometimes *joyless repetition* and/or one from memory.

roulade [rue-laid] -n- a musical rapid-run of *several notes to one syllable*; a ___ of her voice.

rubicon -n- an irrevocable step; the river Hitler crossed.

rubicund -a- ruddy, rosy, esp. complexion; Lat. to be red.

rubric -n- chapter-*heading*; *title*; cp. appellation (name or title); moniker (nickname).

rueful -a- *causing pity*; doleful/repining/lamenting; cp. lachrymose (tearful); woeful//lugubrious//morose (very sad).

rumbustious -a- *unruly//* boisterous / disorderly / obstreperous / *rambunctious*.

ruminate -v- L. to chew the cud;, to *cogitate / contemplate / meditate / muse/ponder, reflect upon*.

runnel -n- a narrow channel i9n the ground to transport water; also, a brook/stream; Orig. "run."

ruse -n- an action intended to deceive or trick; near syn. artifice.

russet -n- a moderate to *strong brown*.

rust -root/v- to oxidize from age and non-use.

rusticate -v- to spend time in the country; to be inactive; languish; cp. repose (rest); atrophy (wither); ossify (turn to bone); petrify (stone).

ruth -n- a feeling of pity, distress or grief; Ger. root; cp. rue (dread, regret).

Sabbath -n- the Hebrew word for religious observance and abstinence from work from Friday evening thru Saturday evening; Christians use the word to refer to Sunday.

S/sacrament -n- a *formal religious rite* (e.g., baptism, marriage, Eucharist); aka "last rites"; a key to salvation for R.C.C.'s; Lat. sacred + make; see Eucharist / Communion.

sacrilegious -a- *irreverent* or disrespectful towards something sacred.

sacristy -n- *a room in a church* housing sacred vessels, vestments; syn. vestry.

sacrosanct -a- not to be violated; inviolable; inviolate.

sadistic/ism -a/n- to gain pleasure from *inflicting pain on others*, esp. related to sexual activity; Origin: Fr. the Marquis de Sade (1888); cp. masochism (hurting self).

sadomasochism -n- sadism + masochism; *self*-inflicted suffering.

salacious -a- *arousing* sexual desire; lubricious//prurient; see lascivious for related terms; erotic.

salient -a- prominent; notably significant; noteworthy; Fr. salire (to leap).

sallow -a- grayish-greenish yellow color, murky; an unhealthy, corps-like skin color M.E. murky.

sally/Sally -n/v/name- the act of leaping or bursting forth; Fr. salire (to leap).

salmonella -a- bacteria causing food poisoning; named after a surgeon, Dr. Salmon who discovered it c. 1900; cp. botulism (food poisoning caused by bacterial growing in canned food).

salubrious -a- conducive to *health*; cp. salutary (beneficial), sanguine (positive).

salutAry [sal-**u**-tarey] -a- producing a *beneficial* effect; cp. efficacious (causing a desired effect), salubrious; sanguine.

salutatory [sah-**lute**-ta-toree] -a/n- a polite *greeting* / salutation; an opening comment.

salve errore et omission -Lat. phrase- "save/except for errors and omissions"; abbrv: "SE&O".

Samaritan -n- a native of Samaria; one who helps those in distress (Luke 10:25).

Samantha -a first name- from Biblical "Good Samaritan" and from Samaria, an area named after samarium, a rare, silvery-earth element that is now used in lasers, Atomic Elem. 62 ; Samuel.

sanction -v/n- to *allow/authorize/*permit; a *penalty* **OR** *reward* for breaking/observing the law; cp. injunction (prohibitory **OR** mandatory decree), interdict (prohibitory decree).

sanctum/sanctuary -n- a sacred place; a shrine; also, a private place.

sanguine -a- warm; confident; optimistic; *having a positive effect*; cp. efficacious, salubrious (healthy), salutAry (beneficial//efficacious); salutatOry (a greeting).

sanctimonious -a- one who *feigns piety* (religious devotion). Ex. Those who attend Church only on Christmas are sanctimonious.

sanctum & sanctuary -n- a *sacred* place that's free from intrusion; monastery; cp. cloister (closed place); cp. sacristy.

sanctorum -n- the holiest of holy sanctums; cp. sacristy/vestry.

Sanskrit/Sanskrit -n- ancient Hindu, liturgical language.

sarcastic/ism -a- *caustic (sharp) rebuke*; cutting jibe; syn. mordant; cp. sardonic (bitterly scornful).

sarcophagus -n- stone coffin; Lat. flesh + eat; cp. catacomb (underground tunnel with recesses for graves), crypt (underground vault), mausoleum (stately tombs or bldg. housing same); sepulchral (burial vault).

sardonic -a- *grimly mocking*; sneeringly disdainful; cp. mordant / sarcastic; cynical (distrustful).

Sarte, Jean Paul, who was he? A renowned French philosopher (1905-80) and *existentialist* who held that, even if God exists, it is necessary to reject him, since the idea of God negates our freedom (to reject obvious myths). **Voltaire** (like most philosophers), even though an agnostic or atheist, asserted (for physical safety), "Even if God didn't exist, we should have had to invent him...*as an absence of a belief in God would be fatal to human virtue.*" Thus, religion (except the Islamic faith) should reduce crime, and is worth supporting; this logic is dispositive and affords compelling support for religions.

sartorial -a- pertaining to a tailor or tailoring; cp. togs / vestments (clothing).

sate/satiate/satiety -v/n- to indulge until full; cp. glut/plethora/ surfeit/ superfluity (excess).

satellite -n- a small body orbiting a planet or moon; a follower; a manmade spacecraft.

saturnine -a- *melancholy* or sullen; one born under the alleged astrological influence of Saturn; Lat.

savant -n- one *who knows w/o being taught*; pundit (teacher/critic); cp. maven (expert). pedant/pedagogue; sophists (scholar, teacher, questioner, now a fallacious reasoner)' polymath (brilliantly learned).

savoir faire -French expression- to know + to do; hence, *sophisticated*, polished, worldly.

scabrous -a- *difficult;* rough to the touch; scaly; scab-like; *knotty;* indescent; off-color, i.e., *dealing with difficult themes;* e.g.,. a ___ person, attitude or situation; cp. acrimonious; ascerbic//choleric; contentious; irascible; mercurial.

scalawag -n- a rascal often in an amusing way; rogue; cp. hooligan (violent troublemaker).

scamp -n- a person, esp. a child, who is mischievous in a likable or amusing way.

scapegoat -n- one blamed for another's sins; In the 2nd act of Yom Kipper (Day of Atonement), a goat was the recipient of the people's "sins", having them ceremoniously heaped on his head; he was then allowed to escape into the wilderness, taking the sins with him. (A lamb was sacrificed as the 1st act of YK.)

scat -n/v- droppings/secretions of animals//secretions; meaningless runs in jazz music; slang for scram/get out of here.

---

scatology/oligical -n- the study of excrement as in paleontology; cp. scat (secretions).

scepter -n- an ornamental staff held by a sovereign (ruler); cp. trident (a three-pronged spear, esp. held by Poseidon or Neptune (gods of the sea).

scion -n- a shoot or twig of a plant; also one who descends from a noble or wealthy family.

schism -n- a split or division, esp. of a religion; a disagreement, breach, parting.

schizophrenia/ic/oid -n/a- psychotic (disordered mentally) reactions causing *withdrawal from reality*; *split personality*; multiple personalities; cp. bi-polar; manic depressive (alternately happy/sad). Prevalence is roughly 1% worldwide.

sciata -n- back pain, esp. lower back.

scintillate -v- to *sparkle* with wit or humor; coruscating (sparkling); refulgent (shining brightly).

sclerotic/osis -a/n- a thickened or hardened body part (artery, bone); Lat. harden.

score -n- *a record of numbers*; also a group of **twenty** ("Four ___ and seven...", from Lincoln's Gettysburg Address = 87; i.e. 1776+87=1863, the year of the Battle of Gettysburg.

Scourge -n/v- a person or thing that causes great harm; Lat. whip.

scree -n- an accumulation of loose stones, usually at the foot of a hill; Scan.

scrim -n- a transparent or translucent screen, *theater drop*; root unknown; also, a strong course fabric used mainly to line upholstery or a gauze, opaque; cp. scud.

scruff -n- the back of the neck; source unknown; syn. nape.

scud/ding -n- anything moving in a straight line, esp. thin, vapory clouds; *a vapory mist of rain*; a gust of snow; Fr.; cp. scrim. VERB: to move in straight line, as clouds often do.

scup/per -n/v- *an opening in the side of a ship to let water run off; also to extract;* a type of fish.

scurrilous -a- *vulgar,* esp. insulting one's reputation; near syns. lewd// ribald**;** cp. lascivious; profane.

sear or sere -a/v- withered//dry//wizened//atrophied/y (withering); or to do so, as in "seer meat on the grill"; cp. ossify (turn to bone) and petrify (turn to stone); mortify (deathly afraid); Ger.

sect -n- a group adhering to specific beliefs, usually religious.

secular -a- **_not_** belonging to a religious order (areligious); *worldly,* not spiritual; root: present world; not catholic//ecumenical// worldwide, esp. a church); cp. ecclesiastical (assembled group) evangelical (relating to gospels).

secrete/tions -v- conceal or hide; biological = discharge of animals; syn: "scat"; cp. excrete (human discharge).

sedate/sedative -v/n- to *make sleepy*; that which does so; cp. bromide; soporific; somnambulistic.

sedentary -a- sitting much (as in a chair).

sedition/ious -n/a- rebellion/ious, mutinous, esp. against a government; cp. secede (withdraw).

seduce -n- to lead a person into improper conduct; cp. suborn (seduce perjury).

sedulous -a- *diligent*; industrious; assiduous.

seer [see-er] -n- one that sees the future; a clairvoyant; prophet; cp. sere (wizened).

seismic/seizmology -a- something subject to, related to, or caused by, an earthquake; the study of same; Gr. earthquake.

semantics -n- the branch of linguistics concerned with the meaning of words and phrases; study and science *of language forms* / words, esp. grammar; syn. etymology; cp. lexicography (dictionaries), linguistics (languages), philology (love of learning); syntax (sentence structure, grammar).

Semite/ic -n/a- generally refers only to Jews, but actually includes Arabs and Jews; Heb. & Lat. root.

seminal -n/a- of or pertaining to semen or seed; *creative; an event that gives birth.*

senesce/nt/titude -n/v/a- aging; growing old; *final stage of life*; cp. sere/withered/atrophied). **senile/ity** -n- old age; at the end of an erosion.

sententious -a- (1) given to moralizing and (2) *succinct or laconic* in *speech* / terse / pithy / concise; cp. sentient (sensitive in feeling).

sentient -a- capable of feeling or thinking.

sepulchral/sepulcher -n- a burial vault; tomb; receptacle for ancient relics; mausoleum (stately tomb or bldg).

sequestered -v- retired; secluded; *set apart*; esp. a jury.

seraglio -n- the women's quarters in a Muslim palace; syn. harem; aka a Turkish palace; Lat.

seraph -n- a celestial being having *three pair of wings*; Lat.

serrate/ation -v/n- the *jagged edge* of a cutting blade; to cut so; L. to saw.

servile -a- *slavish* in demeanor; obeisant / obsequious; subservient; cp: sycophant / toady (parasite / flatterer); unctuous (oily).

servitor -n- attendant; servant; varlet/valet; cp. acolyte (priest's attendant); a knight's page/squire.

Sexton -n- a caretaker of a church and graveyard; a bell ringer and gravedigger.

shanty -n- a low cost dwelling; often tied to the Irish as "shanty Irish".

shards -n- pieces/slivers of broken glass, metal or ceramic; orig. to shear.

Shibboleth -n- a language or term that distinguishes one *group* or class from another; Heb. ; see parlance for related terms.

shrew -n- a mammal with a pointed nose and close set eyes; a violent/ nagging woman; see Shakespeare's *Taming of The Shrew;* cp. virago/ aginous [veer-ah-go] (a large, domineering woman; Lat. vir = man); amazon; cp. termagant (overbearing woman); circe (a woman who destroys men); shrew (ill-tempered woman or mouselike mammal with a long pointed snout); vixen (ill-tempered woman).

shrift -n- a *confession* to a priest; *absolution* given by a priest; he gave short ___; origin unknown.

sibilant -n- producing a *hissing sound;* cp. **sibyl** (Gr. and Lat. female prophet).

Sibyl -name- a female prophet; fortune teller.

Sikh -n- a Punjab word meaning "disciple", from Sanscrit; a monotheistic religion found in Punjab, India; founded in 15-16th Centuries; believers in constant meditation, aspiring to selflessness and equality among humans; there are an estimated 25M, but growing as Middle Eastern non-terrorists gravitate it to it; it's the ninth largest world-religion; their God had no gender; no alcohol, tobacco, non-medicinal drugs and no red meat.

silicoN -n- one of 112 "elements" (types of atom); a slightly shiny, brown-grey substance that is a *semi-conductor*, which can be sliced into wafer/chips; when microscopic electrical devices are put on these "___ chips", they become "*microchips*" (integrated circuits) which are used in myriad things (planes, computers, satellites, music systems) to carry information. "_____ Valley" in CA., where many tech firms are located.

silicone -n- any of myriad polymeric organic silicon compounds as in oils or plastics; used in breast implants, varnishes, binders, electric insulators, etc.

simian -n- an ape or monkey; Lat.; cp. primate; cp. arboreal (those living in trees).

simile -n- figure of speech *comparing unlike* things ("the speedy turtle"), often using "as" or "like"; he's "strong as a bull", "smart as fox"; cp. **metaphor** = figure of speech *transferring* meaning by *analogy*; e.g., the evening of life.

sin cera -Latin term- without wax, *flawless*, refers to Renaissance sculptures so perfect as to not need wax to cover imperfections, hence, **today**, means "*true*" or "*without flaws*", perfection.

sinecure -n- an ecclesiastical benefice (office with fixed income) with no duties; *a job with little or no work.*

sine qua non [see-nay-qwa-non] -Lat. phrase- without-which-not; hence, condition precedent.

singularity -n- the only one of its kind/unique; physicists' term for things very rare; eg black hole.

siren -n- a woman who tempts men; in mythology, they were evil women who lived on a rocky island, singing in beautiful voices and luring sailors to shipwreck and death.

slake -v- to quench/relieve/satisfy thirst; cp. sate, satiate (satisfy until full). **slag** -n/v- stony, waste matter; to produced deposits of slag; cp. scree (rocks at hill-bottom).

slattern -a- an untidy, slovenly woman; aka a slut / prostitute.

Slave/ic [slah-ve] -n/a- an ethnonym for *people from central and eastern Europe*; the term originated from the fact that those peoples were so often conquered ***and enslaved*** by others, hence "slavs"; cp. spic, wetback, nigger, kike, etc.

slipstream -a- a current of air driven by a moving object, creating a vacuum, often used by those behind it to assist them in passing; any assisting force that draws something along behind it.

sluice/slucing [slewce] -v/n- a method of raising or lowering the flow of water, esp. via a gate.

smith/y -n- a worker in metals; e.g., a blacksmith; Gr. wood carving.

sobriquet -n- an affectionate or ***humorous nickname***; cp. moniker (nickname); appellation (title: Lord, Sir); rubric (heading).

---

sociopath -n- one with asocial or ***antisocial*** behavior; cp. psychopath (violent mental disorders).

sodomy/ize -n/v- to injure by inserting something in one's anus; root Sodom & Gomorra where homosexuality and sex with animals was prevalent; *a source of a long list of diseases*: for example, AIDS, cholera, dysentery, typhoid fever, syphilis, some cancers (colon, larynx) and virtually any disease that is triggered by excessive bacteria; in short, logic makes clear that it is not "normal"; it is a death wish.

soffit -n- the underside of a structure, such as a beam, arch, staircase; cp. balustrade.

sojourn -n/v- a temporary stay or visit; to do so.

soliloquy/ist -n- *a literary or dramatic performance* in which a character gives a *monologue to himself*, i.e., w/o addressing anyone else; he thinks out loud.

solecism [sole-sih-zem] -n- a grammatical error OR a *breach of good manners; a. solecistic.*

solipsism/tic -n- the belief that *self* is the *only reality*; extreme egoism, Lat. only + self + belief (ism cp. narcissism (self-love; eroticism aroused by one's own body).

solstice -n- a *highest point* or culmination; one of two times a year *when the sun has no apparent motion*; winter s./summer s. are 21 June/Dec. which are also the longest/shortest days of the year; cp. **equinox** or "equal night" (22 March (vernal)/22Sept(autumnal), when sun crosses equator and days/nights equal length); cp. apogee (most distant); acme//apex//capstone//pinnacle//summit//vertex//zenith (highest point).

somatic -a- relating to the body as perceived from within; soma = body; cp. psychosomatic (an imagined illness).

somnolence/lent -n- a state of drowsiness; *sleepiness;* cp. sedative// soporific (causing sleep); bromide (relaxing drug).

somnambulistic/ism -a- in a sleeplike condition; **sleep walking.**

sonata -n- an instrumental musical composition usually of 3 or 4 parts; syn. opus; cp. symphony (long opus).

sonnet -n- "little song"; a 14-line form (with 10 syllables/line) first popularized in the 1500's in Italy invented by Petrarch in the 1300's; elevated to its zenith by Shakespeare.

sonorous -a- having or producing *a full, rich or deep sound;* esp. musically pleasing; syn. orotund.

Sophia/Sophie -name- a Greek name for "wisdom"; cp. ken (perception/understanding).

sophists -n- a pursuer of wisdom; a member of a pre-Socratic school of philosophy in ancient Greece; *questioners;* looked within themselves; traveling teachers; scholars, thinkers, usually agnostics; *today*, one skillful in devious arguments or *fallacious reasoners* – often thought so because they were agnostics or atheists (which, of course, makes them "fallacious"); Gr. expert/knowledge; sophisticated; see casuistry.

sophistry -n- a *plausible but misleading* or fallacious argument; specious (seeming truth); cp. spurious (false/forgery).

soporific -a- *causing* sleep (esp. by drugs); syn. sedative; CP. bromide (sedative to relax); cp. somnolent (sleepy); somnambulistic, sleep walker.

sortie -n- an *armed attack*, esp. made when surrounded by enemies; cp. foray (sudden military advance); fray (scuffle, brawl); maelstrom (widespread conflict); melee (hand-to-hand combat).

soubrette [soo-**bret**] -n- a saucy, flirtatious *maid*, esp. in a comic play; cp. coquette / minx (flirtatious *girl*).

spa -n- a word from the Italian phrase: "solomente per aqua"/only for water; "soul-ah-ment-ay".

spangle -n- something that sparkles or glitters; cp. coruscating (flashing/sparkling); refulgent/fulgent (shining brightly).

spate -n- *sudden* flood/rush/*overflow*; ME. rainfall; cp. plentitude// profusion (abundance); glut/**plethora**/superfluity/surfeit (excess); effluent (something that flows out).

spatial -a- that which pertains to space.

spatulate [spat-tu-lut] -a- shaped like a spatula.

specious -a- ***seeming truth*** / *verisimilitude*; cp. hoax/hokum (impressive but untrue / insincere); humbuggery (nonsense); sophistry (*plausible but fallacious*); spurious (false / forgery).

spect -root- Lat. to look at; e.g., respect; prospect; prospectus; spectator.

spectral -a- of or like a ghost; also related to spectrum.

spelt -v- Brit. past tense of spell.

Spencer -n- a closely fitting waist-length jacket/vest worn by women (after an Earl).

Sphinx -n- *Egyptian* myth for *a figure having a lion's body with the head of a human, ram or hawk. Greek* myth for a *winged monster with a*

---

lion's body and a woman's head, which ate whoever couldn't answer her riddle; feline: the name for a breed of hairless cats.

spider web -n- a web of *silk* that is made by a spider; silk used in fabric comes from silkworms who make silk in their cocoons; the Chinese are the primary suppliers.

spirit -n- the *animating force* within living beings; also, the essence / karm.

spiritual -a- *not tangible or material;* most define it as supernatural.

splay -v- spread clumsily; e.g. his hand _____ over his cheek.

sporadic -a- irregular; *intermittent;* cp. desultory (flitting from one thing to another).

spurious -a- lacking authenticity; a forgery; Lat. false; cp. specious (seeming truth).

squire -n- a man of high social ranking esp. one living on a royal estate; cp. esquire (a title of respect esp. accorded to attorneys; origin: a young nobleman who is apprenticed to a knight before becoming a knight.

stagflation -n- economist's word meaning when the *inflation* rate *exceeds* the economy's *growth* rate; since the U.S. Government has learned how to manipulate the numbers, the masses can never know the real rate of inflation; although U.S. government has claimed inflation rates around 2% for many years (as of 2016), but some economists estimate it between 5 and 15%; stagflation has been and remains a way of life in the U.S.

stalwart -a- *strong, unwavering,* vigorous, M.E.; cp. stout (fat/corpulent/portly/rotund).

stanchion -n- an upright bar, post or frame forming a barrier, esp. used in streets to block access.

stealthy -a- cautious/doing something in secrete/clandestine/covert/furtive/secret/surreptitious.

Stella/stellar -name/n- Lat. for star; syn. Astra/astral; see Phoebe (Gr. goddess, moon, shining).

stentor -n- a person with a loud voice; Gk. herald (a messenger).

stentorian -a- extremely loud; a ____ voice (Greek herald).

stevedore -n- one who loads and unloads ships; Lat. to pack; origin of name **Steve/Stevenson.**

stigma/ata -n- mark of disdain or discredit; Gr. **tattoo.**

stipple -v/n- to engrave or *paint by making a series of dots*; to *speckle* or fleck; Fr. pointillere = to stipple; "Pointillism" (Impressionistic paintings filled with dots); e.g. sun-____ ground.

stipulate -v- agree or accept as true; postulate (assume/stipulate); cp. posit (state as fact); propound (suggest).

stoicism/stoic -n- *indifference to pain or pleasure*; cp. ascetic (inflexible self-control); historically, stoics were much more. They began with ancient Greeks, and Epictetus (55BC-135AD), the Roman slave, who lived during Christ's lifetime, developed a philosophy that is followed today by many (e.g., Epictetis' stoicism emphasized a virtuous, loving life *based on reason*, and the acceptance of things that one can't change, i.e., today's "**Serenity Prayer**": Grant me the *serenity* to accept the things I cannot change, the *courage* to change the things that I can, and the *wisdom* to know the difference."

stolid -a- having or showing *no emotion*; *impassive*; dependable Lat. stupid; cp. torpid (numb); torpor (inactive); vapid (dull); diffident (shy); taciturn (silent).

stout -a- *fat*/corpulent/portly/rotund; cp. stalwart (strong, unswerving).

stratum corneum -n- the horny outer layer of the epidermis (skin); Lat. horny layer.

strictures -n- restrictions on a person/activity; also a critical, censorious remark; reproof; reproach.

strident -a- loud, harsh, ***grating***, or shrill; discordant; cp. trenchant (biting); caustic / vitriolic (acidic, scathing); staccato (cut short, discordant).

stubborn -a- contumacious / obdurate / *obstinate* / pertinacious; cp. implacable (won't change); intractable / intransigent (inflexible); refractory / restive (resists control); recalcitrant (disobedient).

sua sponte -Lat. phrase- "of his/her own accord"; an action taken *without prompting;* voluntary.

suave -a- *polished* manners/urbane, *smooth*, able to change others' opinions.

subcutaneous -a- something beneath the skin; Lat. cutis = skin.

subjoin/der -v/n- to add supplemental comments at the end of a speech or text; a postscrip/epilogue.

sublimate -v- refine; *elevate*; sublime/a.; cp. subrogate (substitute); subsume (take up fm below); ant. subordinate (lower); see suffuse (spread through); subvert (destroy).

subliminal -a- existing below the threshold of the conscious mind / subconscious.

subordinate [sub-board-in-**ate**] -v- to *lower rank.*

subordinate [sub-**board**-in-ut] -n- someone or thing of lesser importance or rank; **ant.** sublimate.

suborn -v- to *bribe* or incite/seduce a wrongful act, *esp. to incite perjury*; cp. subvert (undermine/destroy).

subrogate -v- to substitute; surrogate (a noun also meaning a substitute).

sub rosa -Lat. term- *private; secret*; root: rosa = clean/clear; and rose is associated with secrecy; Lat. below + secret.

subservient -a- below servitude; slavish; servile / obsequious / cp. / unctuous; sycophant / toady.

subsist/ance -v/n- to remain; to *support oneself at **survival** level*; persist; Lat. stand up.

substantiate -v- prove to be true.

substrate -n- the base on which an organism lives, such as bacteria; Lat.

subsume -v- to reclassify by *taking up from below*; Lat. to take up; cp. presume; exhume (disinter).

subvert/sive -v/a- to *turn from beneath*; *to undermine the morals; to overthrow*; L. below + turn; cp. suborn. Ex. An attempt to subvert democratic government.

succor/our [**soo**-kor] -v/n- ***assist** in time of distress*; one who does so; Lat. to be useful.

---

suffix -n- an affix (attachment) *added to the end* of word (like "ing" or "ness"); cp. appendix; ant. prefix (a syllable at the beginning of a word, e.g., "meta" in metaphysics); root (origin of dominant syllable but can include prefixes and suffixes, e.g. "ordin" in subordinate).

suffuse -n- to *spread through or over*, as with *liquid, color, light or emotions*; cp. diffuse (spread freely/dilute).

sully/sullied -v- to soil or stain; that which is.

sultry -a- hot and humid; when referring to a woman, means a passionate nature.

summit -n- top / highest point / acme / apex / apogee (in orbit) / capstone / pinnacle / solstice (sun) / vertex /zenith.

sundry(ies) -n- miscellaneous items; items not important enough to mention individually.

super -root- Lat. above, over, beyond; e.g., supersede (go before); ant. Sub (below).

superannuate -v- retire with a pension; super + anno/year; OR cause to become obsolete; Lat. over + year.

superate -v- form puss; fester.

supercilious -a- feeling or showing *haughty disdain;* cp. hubris (excessive pride); imperious (w/o peers); egoistic (self-centered); solipsistic (self as the only reality).

superficial -a- *on the surface;* not genuine, *artificial.*

superfluous -a- *unnecessary; irrelevant;* glut / superfluity / surfeit.

Taoism [**D**ow-ism/Tao-ism] A belief system founded by Lao Tzu, a mentor of Confucius; a **b**elief that Tao (Nature) and tao (man's nature) are basically good; gave birth to trigrams/hexagrams as used to track and predict events, cycles, etc. Males are shown as unbroken lines, females as broken; some are both or are double or even triple lines. One of China's three main belief systems:

Buddhism, Confucianism and ___; they believe that *all things overlap in an infinite circle;* that *all life is one;* the ___ *circle of black and white with the inverted "S"* symbolizes this. Opposites.

tautology/tautological -n- *needless **repetition**,* redundancy; Gr. same + knowledge.

tawdry -a/n- cheap and gaudy in appearance or quality; tacky; root unknown.

tawny -a- of the color *tan,* a warm-sandy shade; Fr. tanner of leather.

tax -root- Lat. to handle.

taxidermy/ist -n- stuffing and mounting animal heads and skins; one who does so.

taxonomy/ic -n/a- the *science of classification of species;* Biol;. *Cladistics* (classifying organisms); cp. phylum (a division of species).

tectonic -a- pertaining to construction or architecture; Geol. re *shift in the earth's crust; having a major impact;* cp. seismic (earthquake, major impact).

teem/ing -v/a- to become pregnant; to *overflow* / spate; to be overflowing; O.E.; ___ masses; cp. plethora / surfeit / superfluity (excess).

teleology -n- something that explains (gives knowledge about) the purpose (tells about) something else; Ex. The teleology of a fork explains its purpose.

telepathy -n- *communication by other than the senses*; a mystical power; cp. clairvoyance.

temerarious -a- reckless; rash; cp. timorous / timid (fearful).

temerity -n- excessive confidence; cp. audacious (bold); effrontery (insolent).

temperance/temperate -n- self-control, esp re alcohol; ant. intemperate.

template -n- a *pattern* or gauge; something that supports or distributes pressure.

temporal -a- concerned with *worldly* affairs; short-lived; related to the mind/temples.

temporize -v- to avoid making a decision or to equivocate to gain time; Ex. She temporized her answer. Near syns. equivocate; procrastinate; stall.

ten -root- Lat. "to hold"; e.g., tenure, tenacious; tendril; tenable.

tenable -a- capable of being maintained or defended.

tendentious -a- *prejudiced*; *promoting a cause*, proselytize, not impartial, one's *tendency*; a protagonist; cp. ad hominine (to the man-appealing); e.g., Politicians are _____.

tendril -n- a *stem*; an *extension*; ____ of reason; cp. bine (flexible stem).

tenet -n- a doctrine or principle (*rule*) held as true, esp. *by an organization*; other words meaning a short *RULE*: adage, aphorism, apothegm, maxim, tenet (of an org), e.g. "Neither a lender nor a borrower be." Cp. a **TRUTH**: axiom; epigram; proverb; ("A stitch in time saves nine."); cp. epigram (short, witty and often *paradoxical truth*, "Too soon old, too late smart"); cp. trope (figure of speech or cliché).

tenuous -a- insecure; *flimsy*; slender; tentative (uncertain); untenable (can't be defended).

termagant -n- a harsh-tempered or overbearing woman; Lat.

terpsichore [turp-**sick**-kor-ee] -n- related to *song and dance*; the Greek of muse of same.

terra firma -idiom- dry land; solid ground; Lat. earth + firm.

tertiary -a- *third* in order/place/degree/rank; _____ Period (65M-2M BC, post-dinosaurs (150-65MYA), when modern flora, apes and other large mammals first appeared); Lat. terza/3rd; now called "Cenozoic Period"; see earth.

"Tess" -n- moniker for "Teresa or Theresa", as in Hardy's classic novel, _____ *of the D'Ubervilles;* From Gk. meaning "reaper" or "harvester".

testament -n- law; written document; *tangible proof;* Lat. to make + proof.

testimony -n- *proof* given *orally;* Lat. to make & state.

tetrapod -n- creatures with *four limbs*, each with *five fingers or toes* (e.g., humans, lizards, monkeys); Gr. 4 + foot; see trilobite (beetle-like bug, the longest living species, about 2 Billion years).

theism/ist -n- a belief in a *god as creator and overseer* of the universe; Gr. God + belief system); cp. agnosticism (not knowing); atheism (without god); deism (belief in a creator who abandoned his creation); monotheism; polytheism.

therapeutic -a- having or exhibiting *healing* powers; cp. catharsis (purge undesirable emotions by means of art); purgative/colonic (cleanse, esp. bowels).

theosophy/theosophist -n- any of a number of philosophies maintaining that knowledge of God may be achieved through spiritual ecstasy, direct intuition or special individual relations; Gk. theo-God + sophos - knowledge.

thesis -n- *proposition*; *dissertation* on a subject; tractate (treatise, essay); cp. syllogism.

thrall/enthrall -n/v- n. one who *captivates by charm* (physically, *intellectually*, morally); to do so.

throes [throws] -n- an intense struggle or pain; e.g. in the ___ of battle.

throng -n- a large group crowded together; cp. teem (overflow).

tilak/tika/pottu/bindi -n- an India-Indian word for the dot on the forehead which priests administer as a sign that you have *received a diety's blessing*. Red signifies from a Goddess, black from a God.

timorous/timid -a- apprehensive / fearful / nervous; Lat. fear; trepidation; cp. craven / pusillanimous (cowardly).

tincture -v/n- to stain with color; taint.

tintinnabulation -n- tinkling, ringing (as of bells, e.g. Poe's *The Bells*.

tip -n- acronym for "to improve performance".

titan -n- Gk. mythology (a race of giants); a person of colossal *size, strength, achievement*; Gr. mythology-a family of giants; behemoth; elephantine; gargantuan (after the huge circus gorilla, Gargantua); Gothic (12th-16th centuries) elaborate, large architecture.

TMS -n- scientific term for *transcranial magnetic stimulation*; where *magnets* are applied to the brain to impose activity; cp. **PET** (Position Emission Topography, using MRI's to scan *blood* flow).

toady -n- an obsequious ***flatterer***; blandish / inveigle / wheedle (persuade by flattery) fawning; sycophant; cp. obeisant / obsequious (bowing); servile (slavish); unctuous (oily, gushing).

togs/toggery -n- clothes/clothing store; vestments; cp. sartorial (tailoring).

tomography -n- a technique for displaying a cross section through the human body (or other matter) using *X-rays or ultrasound.*

tome [toam] -n- one of several books in a series, esp. a *scholarly* (and often long) one.

top -root- Gk. topos = place; e.g. utopia (no + place).

tomography -n- a technique for *displaying a cross section* of a human body or other object using X-rays or ultrasound; see topography below.

topography -n- graphing *locations* and *elevations* on a map; Gr. place + graph; cartography (study / love of maps).

topology -n- study of the location of things.

torpid -a- *numbed, hence motionless;* cp. stasis (motionless); stolid (no emotion); turgid (muddy).

torpor -n- *mental or physical **inactivity***; languor; quiescent; cp. apathy (indifference); *enervated (weakened); lassitude (exhaustion); lethargic / phlegmatic* (sluggish).

tour de force -phrase- a *feat of strength* or virtuosity.

tract -root- Lat. "to drag or pull"; e.g. traction, retract; protract (prolong); intractable (inflexible).

tractable -a- capable of being molded or changed; see malleable.

tractate -n- a treatise, essay, thesis; cp. tome (scholarly book or series of books).

traduce -v- to speak *falsely* or maliciously; to dishonor; cp.asperse / denigrate / derogate / malign.

traipse -n- to walk or move wearily; origin unknown.

transcendental -a- Philos: that which *transcends experience / supernatural*; cp. a priori (w/o experience).

tranche [trawn-che] -n/v- Fr. a slice or cut; an *installment*; to cut.

transient -a- *passing quickly*; ephemeral (short lived); trans = between.

translucent -a- transmitting light but diffusing images; shining through; syn. pellucid; cp. diaphanous (transparent).

Transducer -n- a device that converts variations in physical quantity (such as pressure or brightness) into electrical current or vice versa; Lat. trans – across + ducere – lead.

transmogrify [trans-mog-rif-fy] -v- to *transform humorously*; e.g. a Halloween costume transforms a child into a monster.

traverse -v- to travel across.

trawl/er -n/v- a large fishing net to catch fish; a boat that does so; cp. troll.

treacle/ly [**tree**-cul] -n/a- an antidote for poison.

trek -n/v- a hike; a slow or arduous journey; to do so.

tremulous -a- *trembling//palsied*, caused by weakness or disease; cp. tremor (shaking).

trenchant -a- caustic; biting; cp. acerbic (acidic); choleric; strident (harsh); vitriolic (scathing).

trepid/ation -a/n- fearful / apprehensive / timorous; cp. cowardly / craven / pusillanimous (same in adj. form); Lat. anxious.

triage [tree-ahge] -n- a place/system dispensing help to the injured or disadvantaged; from Fr. trier or to sort; cp. hospice (a shelter for travelers, providing physical and emotional needs, *now* a place for those expecting to die within a few weeks), where the strongest painkillers are given.

tribune -n- an official chosen by the people to be their protector; cp. sentry.

trident -n- a three-pronged spear carried by Neptune and Poseidon, Roma and Greek gods of the sea; Lat. 3 + teeth; cp. scepter (an ornamental staff held by a sovereign / ruler).

trilobite -n- a *beatle-like bug* that is believed to have avoided extinction longer than any other species (about *2 billion yrs*); cp. tetrapod (4 limbs with 5 digits (fingers or toes) on each, eg, humans, lizards, monkeys).

tripe -n- literally stomach tissue; general usage: *something worthless*; M.E. the contents of the 2nd stomach of a cow.

Trojan horse -metaphor- something that works from within to defeat another. See Homer's Odyssey.

troll -v/n- to fish by *trailing a line*; also a *supernatural* creature of Scandinavian folklore, often portrayed as a mischievous or friendly dwarf.

tromp l'oeil [trump loy] -n- A painting looking like another, e.g., a wall painted to look like stairway; Fr. *trick the eye.*

trope [troap] -n- a *figure of speech*; sometimes a cliché; Gr. turn, a style.

troth -n- good faith; *fidelity*; betrothal; M.E. truth.

trove -n- a discovery, a *find*, a treasure; Fr. to find; ex. a treasure ____.

truant -n- a student who skips school.

truckle -v- to behave obsequiously / fawning / cringing; Lat.; cp. sycophant (a parasite; *flatterer* / toady; unctuous (oily, too polite); obeisant / obsequious / servile / subservient (slavish); adj. blandish/ inveigle / wheedle (entice by flattery).

truculent -a- *quick to argue or fight; combative*; destructive; harsh; cp. pugilist/ic (a fighter); lethal / pernicious / bane; Lat. fierce, cp. virulent / venomous (poisonous).

trump -n/v- a card in a suit that will win over a card of another suit; to get the better of.

truncate -v- abbreviate / abridge / apostrophize / shorten.

truncheon -n- a short, thick stick/club carried as a weapon by a cop; aka a cudgel.

trundle -n/v- a small wheel or *roller*; moving via same; a ____ bed.

"U"

uber -a/n- German word for hyper, *mega, super, best,* often hyphenated. Source: Nietzsche.

ubiquitous -n- omnipresent.

ulterior -a- something intentionally hidden; Ex. an ulterior motive.

umbra -n- *any dark area*; the eclipsed area of the earth where sun is blocked; a sunspot (dark spots on the sun caused by magnetic fields).

umbrage -n- to feel offended; resentment; to take _____ at something; affronted, piqued, indignant.

unanimous -a- of one mind; not + animosity; cp. consensus (group opinion).

Uncertainty Principle -n- Physics. it is impossible to measure the *location and the speed or path* of an *electron or particle* simultaneously; see electron; quantum mechanics.

unconscionable -a- unreasonable; unethical; not + conscionable.

unction/ous -n- act of *anointing*; act of *gushing*; oily; obeisant; cp. sycophantic; servile; a toady.

ungainly -a- awkward, clumsy; not + straight.

umbr -root- Lat. from noun meaning "shadow"; e.g. penumbra (the edges of a shadow); umbrage (a feeling of being insulted).

unswerving -a- committed; devoted; not + swerving.

untenable -a- can't be defended; tenuous (flimsy).

urbane/urbanity -a/n- *polished*; courteous; Lat. city; ant. churlish (peasant-like).

urchin -n- a poor, raggedly clothed youngster; root is not helpful.

uxorious [uhk-sor-ee-us] -a- having or showing an *excessive or submissive fondness for one's wife;* Lat. uxor = wife.

vacillate [vas-sil-ate] -v- to sway or swing from one side to other; Lat.

vainglorious -a- *boastful*; **excessive vanity** / conceit; to *glorify one's vanity*; cp. egotism (conceit); egoism (selfishness); imperious (w/o peers); supercilious (haughty disdain); solipsistic (self as only reality).

vagarious [vay-gar-e-us] -a- capricious / *erratic* / *unpredictable* / mercurial behavior; cp. bipolar (extreme highs and lows, manic depressive); mutable (changeable).

valediction/valedictorian -n- the act of saying farewell; one who does so; Lat. farewell + to say.

valedictorian -n- the top student who gives the farewell address at graduation.

Valhalla -n- a Norse or Scandanavian *heaven for heroes*, a place of glory; see Utopia.

valor/ous -n- *bravery*; strength of mind or spirit; ant. craven / pusillanimous (cowardly); timorous (fearful).

vanguard -n- a group *leading* the way with new ideas.

vapid -a- flat; dull; insipid; cp. stolid (no emotion); torpid (numbed).

variegate/ed -v- to diversify or vary appearance, as with varied colors; to dapple.

varlet -n- an attendant or servant//servitor; a knight's page / squire / valet; M.E.; cp. servitor; acolyte.

vatic -a- predicting the future; prescience; clairvoyance; Lat. prophet; cp. Vatican ; Lat.

vaunt/ed -v- to boast or praise to excess; Lat. vain/empty; e.g. our much ___ leader.

vector -n/v- a *one* dimensional *force or influence; to guide;* Fr. carrier, to carry.

Veda -n- Sanskrit for "**word**" or "The Word" or "view" or "truth"; refers to the most basic Hindu bible. Includes Mahabharata, Upanishads & Baghavad Gita are others; a veritable sea of literature. "Vedantism" denotes contemporary Hinduism.

venal -a- open to corrupt influence or bribery; cp. depraved (corrupt).

venereal -a- relating to sex or the genitals; Lat. Venus, love goddess.

venerable -a- worthy of great respect (due to age or reputation).

venerate/tion -v- to give great respect; *honor; revere.*

ver -root- Lat. from word for "truth"; e.g. verify; aver (to assert, often under oath); verisimilitude (appearing to be true).

veracity -n- truthfulness; cp. verify (to prove to be true); Lat. veritas (truth); Harvard's motto is "ve ri tas".

verbose/ity -a/n- wordy / prolix; near syn. garrulous (too talkative); cp. bloviate (to be verbose); voluble (fluent); loquacious (talkative).

verisimilitude -n- something having the appearance of truth; truth + similar; syn. specious (seeming true but not, intentionally misleading); cp. spurious (false).

vernacular -n- the *native language* of a *country or region*; syn. dialect; cp. parlance (of a trade); shibboleth (language peculiar to a group); jargon (incoherent or hybrid).

vernal -a- the spring; cp. equinox (when sun crosses celestial equator, 22 Mar (vernal) & Sept (Autumnal) and ght/day of = length; Vernal Equinox and the Autumnal Equinox).

vert -root- Lat. from verb "to turn"; e.g., revert; invert; convert; pervert; vertigo; convert; advertise.

vertebrate -n- a creature with *a spine*; Lat. jointed; includes mammals, amphibians, birds, fish and reptiles.

vertex -n- the highest point; acme; apex; apogee; pinnacle; solstice; summit; zenith; Horeb height; cp. vertical (at right angle to horizon); vortex (core or center).

vertical -a- at right angles to the horizon; n. to s.; *perpendicular*; ant. horizontal; see meridian.

vertiginous -a- *dizzy;* turning about an axis; affected by **vertigo** (loss of sense of direction); Lat. to turn.

vestal -a- *chaste, pure*; _____ virgins; relating to Vesta, mythological virgins who tended the temple fires.

vested -v- Law: *settled*; without contingency; e.g., His rights had ____.

vestibule/bular -n/a- *front room* / foyer / lobby; something functioning as that.

vestments -n- a garment or clothes; esp. indicating an office or state.

vespers -n- the time set aside for prayer (esp. in late afternoon); an RCC *late Sun. service.*

vet -v/n- to critically *examine*; one who does so.

vex/vexation/atious -v/n/a- to *irritate* / annoy / harrow.

viands -n- food; Lat. to live.

vicarious/ly -a- something done or *felt through another*; e.g. the audience _____ feels the emotions of the actor in a play; a "virtual" experience is a vicarious one.

vicissitude -n- the quality/state of being changeable, mutable; Fr. change; cp. capricious (impetuous).

victual(s) [vih-tals] -n- nourishment; provisions; L./Fr. vivere – to live.

vignette -n- a *short literary work or scene*; a *picture/drawing* with softened edges; Fr. from vine; cp. pastiche (an artistic work that imitates another one).

vilify -v- to *censure/chasten/chastise scathingly;* excoriate/vituperate; cp. asperse; abase; calumniate (slander); debase; defame; denigrate; deride; derogate; malign; eviscerate (gut); reprimand; revile; vitiate (make false, debase).

virago/aginous [veer-ah-go] -n/a- a large, domineering woman; Lat. vir = man; amazon; cp. termagant (overbearing woman); circe (a woman who destroys men); shrew (ill-tempered woman or mouselike mammal with a long pointed snout).

virga(s) -n- wisps of *rain evaporating before* they reach the ground; L. streaks; ___ of ice.

virulent -a- *poisonous*// venomous; deadly; *full of hate*; cp. lethal / pernicious / truculent (deadly).

vis -v- to see; e.g., vision; vista / view; vis-à-vis (compared to). Lat.

viscid/cous -a- sticking or adhering; syrupy or gelatinous; that which sticks.

visage -n- the face, *countenance or look* of a person; cp. karma (essence/ aura), ethos (character of a place).

visceral -a- felt in the viscera (intestine); *deep; instinctive*; unreasoning; cp. eviscerate (disembowel).

viscose [vis-coss] -n- a thick solution used to make rayon.

viscous [vis-cus] -a- having high resistance to flow; cp. viscid (sticky).

visitation -n- an official visit; sometimes refers to an affliction.

vitriol/ic -n/a- Chem. sulfuric acid; acerbic; acidic; bitingly critical; caustic; trenchant.

vituperate/ation -v/n- censure scathingly in words; excoriate; fulminate; inveigh; vitiate; revile; vilification; (nouns: cp. obloquy/ calumny/slander).

vivify/ification -v/n- to bring to life; to enliven or *animate*; Lat. to live.

vivisect -v- dissection of animals; cp. eviscerate (disembowel).

"VIX" -n- Chicago Board of **Options** Exchange (CBOE) **Volatility Index**; high (50) = fear / oversold; low (under 30) = comfort zone/ overbought. In Spring 2012—14; 2011—30's, 20's, 50's, teens; 2010—teens, 20's, teens; 2009—20's, 30's, 40's, 50's; 2008-40's 50's, 60's, 30's, 20's.

vixen -n- an ill-tempered woman; shrew; cp. termagant (overbearing woman); virago (domineering woman); circe.

viz -Lat. term- in other words; cp. i.e. (that is), e.g. (for example).

---

voc -root- Lat. speak / voice; e.g., vocal; vocab; equivocate (equal on both sides).

vociferous [voh-**siff**-er-us] -a- loud; cp. stentorian (extremely loud voice of a Greek herald).

volatile -a- prone to change / capricious / impetuous / mercurial / precipitous / unstable; mutable / unpredictable / vagarious / whimsical / willy nilly; cp. bipolar (extreme highs and lows, manic depressive); mutable (changeable).

volition [voh-**lih**-tion] -n- *a willing act*; e.g. He did it of his own _____. Syn. voluntary.

voluble -a- an easy flow of speech; *fluent*; cp. prolix/verbose (wordy), loquacious (talkative); garrulous (too talkactive).

vor -root- Lat. from verb "to eat"; exs: voracious (excessive consumption); carnivorous (eats meat).

voracious/acity -n/a- excessive, immoderate, *insatiable*, esp. in eating or drinking; _____ appetite.

vortex -n- *core*; that which *draws things to the center*; often used in chemistry; cp. whirlpool; eddy (a current moving contrary to the primary water flow); cp. vertex (highest point).

votary [**voh**-tary] -n- one *bound to religious vows*; e.g., priest; a staunch supporter of anything.

votive -a- expressing a *wish, vow or pledge* or vote; a _____ candle in church to seal a prayer; cp. vote (as in an election).

vouch -v- to supply evidence in *support*; recommend; validate; affirm.

vouchsafe -v- to grant a privilege; cp. remise (release a claim); deign (condescend); fain (happily); feign (pretend).

Vulcan/ize -n/v- the Roman god of fire; to strengthen.

Vulcanize -v- to make rubber hard with chemicals; hence, *to strengthen anything.*

vulgar/ian -a/n- crude//*common*; one who is; syn. ribald(sexually explicit); scurrilous (morally defamatory); cp. vile (morally despicable).

vulpine -a- cunning, sly; Lat. fox; cp. lupine (wolf).

"W"

wanton -a- *immoral* or unchaste; base//dissolute// licentious; a libertine; also, *maliciously cruel*; see lascivious.

warren -n- an area where rabbits live; a colony of rabbits; an *overcrowded habitat.*

water -n- H2O (2 atoms hydrogen + one atom oxygen); 60% of earth's surface; 97% saline in oceans; 3% fresh in lakes, rivers, streams, clouds; see oceans.

weal -n- *prosperity or happiness*, esp. of the community/*the common good*; also, a welt.

welter -n/v- a confused mass of items; ex. a welter of conflicting rules; to move in a turbulent manner; ex. the stream foams and welters.

wheedle/ing -n/a- to persuade by flattery or guile; *syns. blandish / inveigle*; root: unknown; see toady.

whisk -v- to take away.

whist -v- hush; be silent; used as an explicative: Whist! Scot./Irish.

whit -n- the least bit; iota//modicum (small amount); ex. I don't care a ___; paucity / dearth (fewness).

wine gods -n- Bacchus (Italian); Dionysius/Liber (Greek).

winnow [win-no] -v- to *separate the chaff/bad from grain/good* (by airflow); to blow away.

winsome -a- *winning, a youthful, innocent charm*; cp. blithe (carefree joy); eupeptic (healthy good spirits); ME.

---

wistful -a- full of *yearning / longing*, often *melancholy*; a ____ smile; cp. pensive (thinking).

wizen/ed/ing -n- to *wither or dry up*; shriveled; seared; atrophied; e.g., The flowers are _ ; Ger.

wont -n- *custom*; *habit*; inclination (as "he is ___ to..."); disposition/ *predilection*; prone; e.g., it is his ___.

(The) Word -n- Christian's term for the Bible. Loosely means "truth". In Sanskrit, "Veda" means "word" and refers to the voluminous texts that comprise the Hindu scriptures.

wool -n- a soft, wavy, curly, thick fabric made from the undercoat of heavy mammals, e.g., sheep and goats.

wraith -n- a ghost or ghostlike image; esp. as seen shortly before or after death; syns. apparition / poltergeist; wraith also often used to describe a pale, think, sickly person; also a faint trace or image of something.

wreak [reek] -v- to *inflict* (vengeance); to ____ havoc upon.

wretch -n- *one profoundly unhappy, miserable*; a *despicable* or vile / horrid / obnoxious person; Ger., vile.

wry -a/v- having a *twisted* shape; usually means *grimly humorous,* humorous in a strange way.

"X"

xenophobe / zenophobe -n- a person unduly *fearful of strangers* or foreigners (or of those with very foreign beliefs); Lat. strangers + fear/aversion.

"Y"

yeoman -n- a naval officer who works as a clerk; *any assistant.* M.E. a household servant; *one who man's the laboring (yeoman) oar.* George Yeoman Pocock, the 20th Century most renowned builder of racing shells was well-named; see best-seller, *Boys in the Boat,* about racing shells.

Yiddish -n- a Ger. word for Jewish; refers to a type of German language (or slang) borrowing from Hebrew and Slavic (Central and Eastern European) tongues.

yoga -n- *hypnotic **meditation*** (key Hindu & Buddhist technique) the Hindus have four primary.

Yom Kipper -n- the most important Jewish holiday (*Day of Atonement*) *in **September***; see scapegoat cp. **Hanukkah** -n- Jewish celebration usually a week in ***December***, heralding the return of the light of God to the temple.

yore -n- long ago; yesteryear; O.E., ex. "days of ___".

zealot/zeal/ous -n/a- one *obsessively in pursuit of something*; *over-devoted*; orig. the Jewish *guerillas* who roamed the hills of Galilee, outside Rome, who attacked the Romans.

zeitgeist -n- the intellectual, moral and cultural *climate of an era*; Ger. spirit.

zenophobe -n- see "xenophobe" = a person *unduly fearful* of strangers/foreigners.

"zero sum game" -term- an activity where *one man's gain roughly equals another man's loss*; and/or *any game where no one wins, where all efforts total "zero"*; see Pyrric victory (where losses exceed gains).

z/Zhivago -a- Russian word meaning "lively"- also, the name Boris Pasternak facetiously gave his tragic, lead character in his Pulitzer Prize-winning novel of the same name, *Dr. Zhivago;* in fact, Zhivago was pensive, taciturn and diffident.

Zion/ist -n- refers to *the Jewish people and/or to Israel*; a place devoted to the worship of God.

Part II

FACTS
YOU'RE EMBARRASSED
NOT TO KNOW

There are an infinite number of Facts You're Embarrassed Not to Know. Those that follow are simply a handful that the reader should enjoy reading and learning, if needed, and they can make an entertaining "after dinner quiz" or party game.

Abraham/Abram, who was he? c. 1850BC. He was successor to **Adam** and **Noah** and allegedly lived to be 175 and is said to have lived "10 generations after Noah and 20 after Adam"; the Bible seems to state that a generation is 100 years (Gen. 15:16) or 40 years (Gen. 21:5) or 70 years (Psalm 90:10); as calendars and time-marking were not then precise, they may have assumed that one life spanned 100 years, not really attempting to define "year"; paleontologists, however, estimate lifespans between 15 and 40 years in Biblical times; however, based on Biblical scholars (ignoring scientific evidence indicating primate life going back 2 million years) estimate Creation c. 4,000+/- years **BC**); so, if Moses was 20 generations after Adam, the Bible is asserting that **Moses** was 800 to 2000 years after Creation (20 x 40= 800 and 20 x 100 = 2000); we know, however, that hominids go back some 2M years and homo sapiens 50,000 to 200,000, depending on the level of "sapiens". Regardless, Biblical scholars seem to variously place Abraham as c. 1900 or 1800 BC (one guess being as good as the next). **Moses,** when putatively 80, allegedly discovered "the Promise Land" c. 1180. Abram had children by two wives and two maids. He and his wife, **Sarah**, "the parents" of the Jewish people; had **Isaac** who had **Jacob** (aka "**Israel**"), the father of the 12 sons who fathered the **12 tribes of Israel** (including Levi who spawned the Levites-Moses-Aaron (the priests); Jacob also had Judah, who led to Kings David and Solomon, Kings of Judah and Jesus); Abraham & **Hagar** (a slave) had **Ishmael** (the *father of the 12 tribes of Arabs*. So, **Abraham spawned the Jewish, Islamic and Christian faiths**. So, while they fight like dogs and cats, they have putatively common ancestry.

Achilles, who was he and what did his heels signify? He was the hero of Homer's epic *Illiad*, whose only weakness was in his heel.

A.D., what does it stand for? "anno domini" or year of our lord; today, scholars now prefer **C.E.** (common era) and B.C.E. (before common era) in lieu of BC (before Christ) -- as scholars move away from Christianity.

Adam and Eve, when did they live? *Only "4,004" years ago and date Noah and the arc 2900 years ago*, but geologists, archeologists and paleontologists have found no evidence of any such worldwide floods. Modern Christian Bibles no longer attempt to date these events. DNA evidence demonstrates that the DNA of humans is 99% identical to chimps, 98% identical to gorillas & 65% identical to fruit flies. Quoting the renowned, Harvard-paleontologist, Stephen Jay Gould, in his magnum opus, *Wonderful Life* (1989), "All life forms are interrelated and interdependent...*Humans are related not only to apes but to cabbages*...Evolution is not a tale of steadily increase...**Evolution is a lottery...All life is one**". Rational Creationists now accept evolution and simply attribute it to the Creator, but this makes "literal" acceptance of Adam, Noah, etc. possible only as allegorical stories or parables, anachronisms suitable for the less educated minds of 2,000 years ago. Also, the only genealogies of Jesus are in Matt. 1:1 and Luke 3:23, which trace Jesus' lineage **through Joseph** (back to Abraham & Adam, respectively) but they don't name enough ancestors (only 72 generations), to reach Adam (in 4004BC); in reality, it would take roughly 120 generations (4004/100=40 centuries x 2.5 generations *minimum* per 100 yrs = 100 generations). None of these chronologies are within the realm of feasibility, nor is the assertion that all earthly life forms were created in a single week, as fossil evidence demonstrates that hundreds of millions of years were required. Tracing Jesus' genealogy thru Joseph indicates that the concept of his virgin birth was an afterthought. Only Matt. & Luke discuss Jesus' genealogy, and some biblical scholars state that earlier Aramaic manuscripts appear to contradict the virgin birth and other aspects of Jesus' life, as stated in the New Testatment. Biblical writings describing Jesus' siblings, wife and progeny have been ignored (as written in the now discredited "Apocrapha", which is still part of the author's 1886 Family Bible and in the records at Nag Hammadi, which contains Biblical books antedating the Dead Sea Scrolls. See Nag Hammadi.

Adam Smith, who was he? He was the Author of *Wealth of Nations (1776)* – Considered to be the Founder of Modern Economics, his book is characterized as the bible of capitalism; argues that *free competition is* the best way to optimize the wealth of nations and results in a positive *division and specialization of labor*; WoN also advanced the value of ***private property rights*** as the backbone of a strong economy. Some 200 years later (1960's), in the classic *Dr. Zhivago*, author-Pasternak made the timeless observation about communism's elimination of private property rights: "When everything belongs to everyone, no one takes care of anything."

Adonai, who does he refer to? It is the most common name for God (in the first five books of the Bible, aka the Torah) was Adonai; Elohim or El is 2nd(which literally meant "the mountain"); Yahweh/Jehovah is 3rd, and was YHWH originally, as Aramaic and Ancient Hebrew (the two dominant languages used in the early versions of the O.T., had no vowels; some modern languages follow that pattern: do a Google test for Sanskrit, Hindi, Japanese, Chinese and Arabic for comparisons; the terms "Lord" and "Lord God" were introduced later; the origin of the word God is believed to the Anglos-Saxon word "good"; the older the Bible, the higher the incidence of the use of the earlier words for God.

Age of Enlightenment, what was it? An era, c. 1700's-1800's, followed the **Age of Reason** (late 1600's, Spinoza et al) and was a part of the **Renaissance** (14th-18th Centuries), a time when "enlightened" philosophy, science and culture made major advances, *when questioning supplanted the urge to prove things* and create dogma (Middle Ages); book publishing became widespread; leading figures included Descartes, Voltaire, Diderot, Newton, Kant, Adam Smith, Darwin; The Church and State stopped burning books & suppressing all thinking that contravened their religious and political dogmas; the fear of knowledge, sadly, has plagued religions from time-to-time.

Ajax, who was this character? -n- a hero of the Trojan war, renowned for immense size and strength; cp. Achilles; Trojan War.

al-Queda, what is it? [al-kah-**aa**-da] -n- "the base", an anti-Western terrorist group; formed by Osama Bin Laden, who was recruited by the CIA to lead the Afgan-Arabs against Soviet forces in Afganistan in the 1980's; Bin Laden later converted his CIA weapons and CIA-terrorist training against the U.S. by orchestrating the "9/11" 2001 World Trade Center destruction by suicide aircraft crashes; **Taliban** (means student) an Afghanistan-religious terrorist group; **Hezbollah** (means party of God) a similar group in Lebanon. *See ISIS* (means Islamic State of Iran and Syria); **Boko Haram** -n- term meaning "Western education is forbidden"; refers to a Nigerian-based group of 1-K to 10K killers, who claim to control 20K sq. miles of Nigeria, and who pledge alliance to ISIS.

America, where did it get its name? From **Amerigo Vespuci.** He was the Italian after whom America was named (an obscure *cartographer*) came to America in 1499, did a map of America and signed his name, which was adopted as the country's name; it should have been named "Columbia" after Columbus, who arrived 7 years earlier (1492); or even "Ericka" for Leif Erickson, the Norseman (Norwegian) who lived in Greenland and *allegedly* discovered No. America 500 years earlier and who may have started a small colony either in New England or Canada.

Amon, who was he? [a-mon] -n- *Egyptian* **god** of *fertility*; **Why did Leonardo name his masterpiece painting, "Mona Lisa"?** Some believe, because L'Isa was the Egyptian female goddess. (Aphrodite was the Gr. love goddess). Leonardo's "Mona" seems to be an anagram of Amon and Lisa of L'Isa, whose smile may symbolize her "secret" possibly that she is a hermaphrodite); see *Da Vinci Code* by Dan Brown. Lisa remains a popular girl's name in the Western World.

Animism, what is it? -n- a belief that *observable events w/o visible causes have invisible causes*; common to many religions; also an ancient belief that animate and inanimate things have a "soul"; advanced by Pythagoras (570-490BC) and Plato (478-348BC) & Hindus (who maintain that their faith pre-dates Moses by 1,000 years).

Aphrodite, who was she? [aff-fro-**die**-tee] -n- Gr. God**dess** of love/fertility. Compare **Astarte**/Phoenican; **Ishtar.** (Babylonian); **(L')** **Isa** (Egyptian); **Lalita** (Hindu); **Venus** (Roman); cp. **God** of same: **Amon**/Egyptian; **Eros/Cupid**/Gr.

Aopcrapha, what is it? -n- refers to the first 13 books of early Christian Bibles which originally preceded Genesis in the Old Testament, which were removed, in the 20th Century, from most Christian Bibles as they included books by Mary Magdalene, Thomas, Phillip and others that seemed to contradict parts of the New Testament, relating to Jesus' birth, miracles', resurrection, etc., and discussed Jesus' siblings and his relationship with Mary Magdalene, and the graves in which Jesus and his family are believed by some to be buried. The 1876 Lovett Family Bible (which was Grandmother Lovett's, Laura Gilson Lovett) includes the Aopcrapha, which I read with some interest. As the Apocrapha was discredited by The Roman Catholic Church, the word "apocraphal" has come to mean things of questionable veracity.

Apollo, who was he? The Greek God of the sun, light, truth; cp. Adonis (handsome Gr god).

Apostles, who were they? They were TWELVE followers of Jesus; according to **Matthew 10:2-4**, they were: *Andrew, Bartholomew, James, James, John, Judas (Iscariot), Matthew, Phillip, Simon, Simon* *called Peter, Thaddeus and Thomas.* Mathias or Paul supposedly replaced Judas, but some scholars maintain that Paul never met Jesus. In **Mark 3:16-19**, Mark (not an Apostle) gives a somewhat different list, but *Matthew's list is the list preferred by most Biblical scholars.* The many conflicts in the OT indicate that the authors did not compare their texts and/or simply relied on hearsay or creative writing.

Aquinas, St. Thos., who was he? [ack-**quine**-us] He was the 13th Century theologian who sought to reconcile faith and reason as mutually dependent; **contrast:**. Kant, Hume, Locke (all 1700's), the Humanists, et al who, in the Age of Reason, repudiated Aquinas, who held that good conduct can stem from reason alone; see St, Augustine (400AD, argued that man has a duty to accept/ have faith where he can't understand).

Arabs, what are their religions? Islam (major **sects**: Shite, Sikh, Sufi, Sunni), Hindu, Shi, And Buddhist.

Aramaic, what is it? It is the ancient language of the Sinai Peninsula and of the early Hebrew Bible, on which the Old Testament is based. It was used by Jews before Hebrew became common; is the dominant language of the OT; *no vowels* or punctuation (like Ancient Hebrew); cp Coptic (a latter day Aramaic, used mainly 100BC-100AD); hieroglyphics (Egyptian writing in pix); Chinese/Japanese. Devoid of vowels and punctuation, it was an earlier outgrowth of hieroglyphics (writing by symbols, vis a vis ancient Egyptian).

Artificial Intelligence, what is it? Intelligence demonstrated by machines, in contrast to the natural intelligence displayed by humans and other animals. AI research is defined as the study of "intelligent agents": any device that perceives its environment and takes actions that maximize its chance of successfully achieving its goals. Colloquially, the term "artificial intelligence" is applied when a machine mimics "cognitive" functions that humans associate with other human minds, such as learning and problem solving.

Asia Minor, what is it? What is "Lesser Asia"? *Roughly modern-day Turkey*; cp. Eurasia (Europe & Asia).

Asteroid, what is it? They are smaller, rocky, celestial bodies (dust particle to600 miles wide), mostly between Mars & Jupiter; Gk. "star-like; some enter earth's atmosphere as meteors; cp. meteor (from specs of dust to asteroid, a term sometimes used synonymously with comet, which is an elongated, gaseous body; there are an estimated 1 billion comets in our solar system and some 100M of them regularly cross through the earth's orbital path; statistically, scientists believe that one will hit the earth within the next million years, as did the KT Meteor, which is believed to extinguished the dinosaurs; dictionaries make few distinctions among these words; see comet.

Atom, what is it? -n- *anything irreducible*; Science: 00.99999% energy and .00001 physical substance; the *smallest BASIC component of ALL matter*. Root: Gr. indivisible; (in 2010), *about 112* known *kinds* of atoms (often called "elements"); in stable groups, they are "molecules" about one millionth of a meter wide; cp. "**ions**" (molecules with an electric charge); atoms have 3 subatomic particles: protons (containing positive charges), electrons (negative), & neutrons (no charge). Each atom *looks a bit like a solar system* with the protons and neutrons in the center/

nucleus, and the electrons orbiting around the nucleus and forming a cloudlike shell of sorts. An atom is congealed energy. Atoms are not solid stuff, as once thought; they are 99.99999% energy/space and 0.0000!% particlkes/matter. The are more "no thing" than "some thing". Quantum physics demonstrates that the person observing atoms affects the behavior of the energy and the particles. See atomic bombs. *The no. of protons give the atom its identity.* With *one* proton, an atom is **hydrogen** (comprises 80% of earth's air (oxygen 20%), while **nitrogen** (7 protons) comprises 70% of the universe's air); helium (2); lithium (3), and so on. Protons are always balanced by an *equal no. of electrons.* The no. of neutrons add to the mass but don't change the character or "personality" of the atom. **500M atoms** could hide behind a single human hair. (**500T protons** could fit within the dot in this "i".) *In every cubic inch of air, there are 45 billion-billion molecules.* When we die, our atoms disassemble and move on to find new uses (in a leaf, a drop of dew, in another human, etc.) Probably one billion or so of the atoms in each of us once belonged to a famous predecessor; a de facto form of the Hindu's reincarnation. The more that our scientists learn, the more they seem to conclude, as Lucretius (1BC-99AD, the author of the amazingly prescient *In the Nature of* Things) said, *"All things are full of emptiness."* See animism (the belief that animate & inanimate things can have souls, as Pythagoras, Plato and Hindus asserted). See isotope (an atom with an unusual number of neutrons); see Patterson, Claire.

St. Augustine, who was he? 354-430AD. He was "the formulator of Christian (Catholic) theology", a professor of rhetoric who was renowned sermonizer, a master manipulator of crowd-emotion even making them cry; integrated opposing Hebriac and Greek ideals; embraced Aristotle (not Plato); introduced concept of "Free Will"; debated "Will and Reason"; implausibly argued that God made man perfect, and man (Adam) sinned; and **man has a duty to believe what he can't understand**; he also believed that most will burn in Hell; see Aquinas (13ᵗʰ Century).

Aurelius, Marcus, who was he? He was putatively the most loved of all Roman Emperors. Marcus Aurelius Antonius Caesar (121-180 AD) the last of the "Five Good Roman Emperors"; next to Epictetus, the most important of the Stoic philosophers; his *Meditations,* essays on finding peace and harmony through nature, are still widely read. "Our life is what our thoughts make it." See stoic/Serenity Prayer.

Baccus, who was he? He is the Roman god of wine; Dionysus/Liber (Greek god of wine).

Bacon, Francis, who was he? (1561-1626) He was the first great philosopher since the ancient Greeks; argued that theory w/o practice/action or vice versa is useless; England's greatest philosopher, a *Lord Chancellor* of England, *Ambassador* to France, *Attorney General,* a *judge,* Member of *Parliament, knighted; convicted of bribery and disgraced* but still revered; his sentence was commuted after three days by King James (of King James Bible fame); a prolific writer, best known for his *Essays* and his novel, **New Atlantis** (in which slavery, debtor's prisons and restrictions on free speech were abolished and church was separated from state and wealth were more evenly distributed to avoid revolutions); he *inspired the Age of Enlightenment* and, *some say, democracy's rebirth; Jefferson heralded "Bacon, Lock and Newton" as the greatest men who ever lived.* Some of his quotes include, "Knowledge is power...Begin in certainty, end in doubt; begin in doubt, end in certainty...Chance is the name of a thing that does not exist." Died bankrupt, owing 2000 equivalent of $3M.

Baird, John, who was he? (1888-1946) He was the first and greatest contributor to the invention of the **first TV** in **1925** and color TV later but no commercial use until 1940's. **Marconi, Guglielmo** (1874-1937), a non-scientist and confessed layman but, nonetheless, the recipient of the Nobel Prize for Physics (1909) and the *inventor of long range **wireless telegraphy and radiotelegraphy*** (which led to AM and FM radio and, later, all wireless technologies). See book "Thunderstruck" by Larson. See Edison, his contemporary.

The 8 Beatitudes, what are they? [Bee-at-ti-tudes] They are the 8 statements in the Sermon on the Mt. which begin "Blessed are..."See Matthew 5:3-12; blessed are *meek, merciful, mourners, peacemakers, persecuted, poor; pure and those who hunger after righteousness (3M's, 4 P's & hunger)*.

Bhagavad Gita, what is it? [bah-gah-vahd gee-tah] It is likely the most universally loved of all the world's scriptures, the BG (Song of God) is a part of the Hindu scriptures (the Veda or Word); it is comprised largely of a dialogue between Krisha (the Supreme Being) and Arjuna (every man); it preaches non-violence of seeing life as a seamless whole, of finding the ultimate goodness within ourselves and others; it was Mahatma Gandhi's favorite scripture, which he summarized in two words: selfless action; it is a Must Read.

Bible, what is the origin of this word? In Greek, "biblos" means *book*; ancient Phoenician *town of **Byblos***, a port thru which papyrus then came; documents of many pages became known as "bibles" (from Byblos); The Bible, of course, was the most popular. Phoenicia now comprises part of Lebanon and Israel; see DSS; earliest Bible-versions c. 1100BC written c. Moses' time in Aramaic, as Hebrew not popular then; in 350BC, Egyptian Emperor-Ptolmey II's *Septuagint* (70 *Rabbinical* scholars) re-did it in Greek; translated into Latin by Romans. **When was the first English version of the Bible? 700AD**, then again c. 1200AD. **What is the most commonly used version of the Christian Bible?** *The King James Version.* **When was it first published? 1625**; **How many books are in the Christian Bible?** 66 books of Judeo-Christian bible includes Torah/Pentateuch (books 1-5 of OT), Tanach includes all 39 books of OT); Talmud (all of Tanach plus 25 other Rabbinical writings); Torah (teaching), aka Pentateuch (5 scrolls, one for each of the first five books of the OT). The author's Sunday School teachers expected all of us to be able to recite these books in the order in which they appear in the Christian Bible. They are listed in Appendix 1.

Big Bang, what was it? According to the consensus of scientists today (e.g., Stephen Hawking, Edwin Hubble et al), the universe was likely created about 14.5 billion years ago, when the density of matter was infinitely dense/small, which led to "the Big Bang"; the observed Red Shift of distant galaxies indicates that they are moving away from the earth ("the open universe theory"), which process will lead to a reversal of direction as the distant galaxies exhaust their momentum, and gravitational pull will gradually bring them into dense, small mass (the "Big Crunch") and another Big Bang later. Before Hubble, the term "Big Bang" came from Georges Lemaitre's "Expanding Universe", calling it "the hypothesis of the primeval atom, which he published in 1927, two years before Hubble's article re same. Einstein disagreed but later reversed his position. See Einstein; black hole; universe.

"Big Data", what is it? Refers to data sets that are so voluminous and complex that traditional data-processing application software are inadequate to deal with them. Big data challenges include but are not limited to: capturing data, data storage, data analysis, search, sharing, transfer, visualization, querying, updating, information privacy, and data source. Big Data also refers to the use of predictive analytics, user behavior analytics, or certain other advanced data analytics methods that extract value from data, and seldom to a particular size of data set. Analysis of data sets can find new correlations to spot business trends, prevent diseases, combat crime, and so on.

Black hole, what is it? An outgrowth of Einstein's 1915 Theory of Relativity (TOR), which shows how gravity bends light, slows time and distorts space; *scientists conjured the black hole (BH) theory in the 1930's* and added exploding/simultaneously collapsing stars (supernovas) in the 1960's. *Gravity bends light and won't let it escape, hence blackness.* Most galaxies are believed to have at least one BH; they may begin small and gobble smaller ones up. Sizes range *from millions to billions of times the size of the sun* ; the sun is 100 x size of earth. By some estimates, in 200M years, the suns fries our earth; in 600M, the earth is sucked into the sun. In *4B years*, our Milky Way galaxy (MWG) may collide with the equally large Andromeda galaxy, destroying both. Or, our solar system might be pitched out of the MWG before then. *BH's eat stars or create new ones (by exploding when they become too dense) and lead* *to the death and birth of new galaxies.* So, **why are black holes called "black"?** Because no light can escape.

Black Market, what is it? It refers to wherever goods are sold illegally (above or below fixed prices or goods that are simply illegal).

Black Plague, what is it? It refers to a period of time (late 1340s) where a disease carried by fleas on rats that eradicated almost *half* the population of England and *30%* of Europe (75M) in a two-year span. It was believed to be caused by the massive killing of cats, which some religions then believed were devils, which caused an explosion of the rat-population. Lesser outbreaks of The Plague occurred *every few years for centuries.* The **Bubonic Plague**, a less virulent but similar disease, occurred in the late 19th and early 20th centuries. "Bubonic" emanates from Gr. "the groin" which swells.

Blue chip stock, what is it? It's a term used to describe stocks of the highest quality, i.e., from the most financially sound companies.

Boats, what are some different types? brig (a twin-masted sailboat); **catamaran** (sailboat on twin hulls supporting a cabin with large net in front of cabin); **corsair** (pirate ship); **dinghy** (small boat, lifeboat); **frigate** (a light boat, a small warship); **punt** (a narrow, flat-bottomed boat with square ends) ; **skiff/punt** (small, flat bottomed, square at both ends); **schooner** (a twin masted vessel or large glass for drinking beer); **tender** (a smaller boat carried on a larger one); **yacht** (luxury boat).

Boccaccio, who was he? [beau-catch –eeo] 1313-1375. He was an Italian poet who wrote the Decameron. It included original and updated classic stories and became *possibly the most plagiarized group of stories (100 in all) ever writte*n; similar to his contemporary,

Cervantes, who was he? He was the author of *Don Quixote* (1605) and considered among the most influential and entertaining novels ever written, and it contains more commonly quoted lines than any other author, save Shakespeare; see *Don Quixote*.

Charlemagne, who was he? He was a ruler of parts of Germany, France, Rome, c. 800AD. Also referred to as "Charles the Great."

Chaucer, who was he? He was a renowned poet (1343-1400), known as "the father of English literature", a philosopher, wrote *Canterbury Tales, a* Contemporary of Petrarch (who invented the sonnet) and Boccacio (who wrote *Decameron*).

"Christ", from where did this name originate? It means "the anointed one"; From Christos (Gr) to Christ, later to "Lord" Jesus Christ; Heb. Messiach/*messiah*; Lat. Unctus/oily, all meaning "anointed as with oil" for exceptional performance, or "*anointed*", hence, a "chosen one".

Christianity, what is its history (in a nutshell)? *The Roman Catholic Church ("The Church") was the only **Christian** faith from roughly 100 AD until Luther broke from it in 1525.* (Hindus claim 2000 BC; Judaism dates from Moses c. 1200 BC; Islamic faith from Mohamed c. 625 AD). During the Reformation, in which Christianity was "reformed" into many churches or sects (1525-1750 or so), those who left Catholicism (all known as protestors of the Pope's authority, hence as "Protestants") formed their own churches (e.g. Episcopalian, Methodist, Baptist, etc.). This splintering continued through the 1800's, as many more churches emerged (e.g., Church of Christ, Christian Science). In the 1900's, the schisms continued as it became very easy and very profitable for any "divinely inspired" ("charismatic") good talker to form his own church (and keep the change). The "Religion Business" continues to flourish today on radio and TV, as many thousands of "inspired evangelists" (e.g., Jimmy Swaggart, Jim Bakker, Anglesey and thousands more), have formed their own independent churches, many virtually self-ordained, form their own "churches" or even by dubious online organizations, calling their separate churches by varied names. Titles like "Reverend", "Pastor", "Minister" may now be purchased online for as little as $25. Jesse Jackson was allegedly "ordained" by a black church in the south without taking any formal religious training, to give him a title to help him advance the Civil Rights Movement, and, of course, his own fame, hence wealth and legacy. Al Sharpton was "licensed and ordained a Pentecostal minister at age nine or ten", according to Google.

Christian Science, what is it? It is a religion based on Jesus' teachings but which aspires to overcome illness by prayer and understanding; at their personal option, Christian Scientists do not consult doctors; in effect, C.S. is a distant cousin of other forms of mind-control. C.S. may well be a harbinger of "neuroplasticity", which seems likely to presage mindtraining and mindcontrol as cornerstones of 21st Century medicines and the use of the mind, rather than pills (The Pill Epidemic) to control moods and even pain.

Churchill, Winston, who was he? He was generally conceded to have been the *greatest orator and world leader in the 20th Century*, a brilliant *war correspondent and journalist* who participated in WWI and multiple other Colonial wars; famous by his prose alone (and a plethora of *best selling books*), a *capitalist* who saw the *need to create the welfare state*, reform the prisons, build the

Navy pre-WWI; served as Chancellor and Prime Minister; *during WWII he served as PM and as Minister of Defense*, single-handedly *prevented the Brits from caving-in to Hitler* and signing a treaty what would made put GB under rule by a Hitler-puppet; Not a Christian, as he couldn't believe the Bible's stories/myths, but he had a Christian ethic. He earned the adulation of the masses and the devotion of those closest to him, a rare feat for such icons. Churchill *made YOU think YOU could do anything*, while Hitler made you think that HE could do anything. WC enjoyed a long and happy marriage to Clementine, a bright beauty who defended him with the ferocity of a tigress. See *The Churchill Factor*, Boris Johnson.

Cities and States, in U.S., how configured? (1) the names of the American Indian tribes who then lived in the territory, (2) the names of countries (or the leaders of same) from which the immigrants emanated, or (3) the names of U.S. Presidents or founders.

Civil War, in America, the dates and key facts: America's most costly war, 1861-65; 600,000 (400L-No., 200K-So.) died versus 400K in WWII and 200K in WWI. The North had 3 x the Army, but still took 4 years to prevail; less than 2% of Southerners owned slaves; the rest fought to defend their homeland. Read Margaret Mitchell's *Gone with the Wind*, viewed as America's greatest work of literary fiction (and even of fiction) by some.

Clouds, what are some different types? *cirrus* (feathery); *cumulous* (billowy); *nimbus* (rain); *strata* (layered).

Columbus, Cristopher, who was he? -n- a Genovese explorer (1451-1506) whose crossings of the Atlantic led to general Awareness of

---

America. Although not the first to reach America, he was credited with discovering America in **1492**, although the country was named after **Amerigo Vespuci**, an obscure Italian cartographer who is believed to have come to America in 1499. The Norseman, Leif Erikson, is said to have discovered the Americas some 500 years earlier.

Comet, why does it have a tail? When a comet enters our Solar System, as the sun's heat burns the material of the comet, the characteristic tail is formed; comets either pas through our SS and leave forever or slip into an elliptical pattern orbiting the sun; the best known comet, Haley's Comet, passes close to the earth every 76 years, as it famously did on the days of Mark Twain's birth and death.

Commandments (Ten) what are they? Also referred to as *Decalogue*. Here are condensed **paraphrases** of the versions appearing in **Exodus 19:20** by Moses from Mt. Sinai (aka Mt. Horeb) c 1280 BCE: Any self-respecting Christian should know these by number, period:

Thou shalt . . .

FIRST: have **no other Gods before me**... (Ex 20:2-3);

SECOND: have **no graven images** (Ex 20:4);

THIRD: **not take my name in vain**... (Ex 20:7);

FOURTH: **honor the Sabbath** and keep it holy (Ex 20:8);

FIFTH: **honor thy [worldly] father and mother** (Ex 20:12);

SIXTH: not kill (Ex 20:13);

SEVENTH: not commit adultery (Ex 20:14);

EIGHTH: not steal (Ex 20:15);

NINTH: not lie (Ex20:16);

TENTH: not covet anything that is thy neighbors (Ex 20:17).

In Deuteronomy (second law), Moses repeated the foregoing in a substantially different manner; *turn other cheek*; *love neighbors*; *love enemies*; be perfect; *give alms/charity in private;* no earthly treasures; no thought of food or clothing; seek kingdom of God – presaging Buddha's tenets c. 450 BC. See also the **Beatitudes** in Sermon on Mount.; Matt. 5:3-12.

Common denominator, what is it? A common denominator (such as, 12) is a number that will allow fractions with different denominations (1/3 and 1/2) to converted into mini fractions of 3/12 and 4/12; the expression "common denominator" also means a common factor in different events; e.g. a common denominator in medicine is a knowledge of anatomy.

Confucius (aka "Master Kong") who was he? (c. 550-479B.C.). Like Socrates (c.455-399 B.C.), considered the *prince of philosophers*, the wisest of sages, most quoted statesman, historian; translations of his sayings are few and poorly recorded; criticized today for his dearth of references to a supreme being (which is very Asian); discredited by Communists but still popular. Expanded Taoism [Dow-ism] into ethical, social and political philosophy. Like Lao Tzu (circa Confucius), his mentor (the founder of Taoism), believed death to be final; *indifferent to deities*; an approximate contemporary of Buddha, altho' they never met.

Constantine, who was he? 306-327AD. The original ruler of Rome, who *converted to Christianity* (some scholars believe to curry favor with the emerging view of the masses and to please his Christian mother); he was *the first to legalize Christianity*, to appoint Christians to high posts, and to encouraged the Christian leaders to *resolve their differences and conflicts regarding Biblical texts* (via his Council of Nicea in 325AD); *he also allowed idolatry to continue*, as many still worshipped many gods; he was possibly the *most revered of Roman emperors after Marcus Aurelius and Augustus Caesar.*

Continental Divide, what and where is it? It's an imaginary geographic line which marks the line at which water poured on one side would eventually flow into the ocean on that side, while water poured on the other side would flow into the ocean on the other side; the CD is located in the Rocky Mountains, west of Aspen, CO.

Continental Shelf, what is it and how formed? It's an area along the coastline that is elevated, similar to a shelf, generally less than a few hundred feet deep; it was created by sediments washed into the ocean by rivers and is generally rich with minerals.

Copernicus, who was he? He was a scientist; in 1543, days before his death (to avoid punishment by The Church), he finally published his treatise placing the sun at the center of our solar system, which lead to a rejection of Ptolemy's (1BC) long held view of the earth as its center.

Coral reef, what is it? It is a rock-like formation at or near the surface of the water, which was formed by deposits of corals (sea polyps that cling together); scientists consider them "animals" however immobile; they provide habitat and vegetation for other sea life; the world's largest is the Great Barrier Reef in Australia.

Croesus, who was he? c. 500BC. He was the King of Lydia, known for his great wealth; conquered parts of Greece before losing to the Persians.

Cupid, who is he? Gr. god of love, usually depicted as an angel with a bow and arrow; see Aphrodite; Lat. to desire; cp. cherub(angel) seraph (3-winged angel).

Currency, paper, from what is it made? Cotton and linen.

Currie, Marie, who was she? She was the only person to ever win the Nobel Prize in two different sciences. A circa 1900 scientist, who, with her husband, won Nobel Prize for physics in 1903 for discovering the element radium and coining the term "radioactivity"; she later won another NP for chemistry. She also consulted with Einstein.

Darwin, Charles, who was he? 1802-1882. Author of *Origin of The Species (1859)*, the scientists' "bible" of creation: Thesis: Species survive through *adaptation & evolution* His theses have been *accepted by 90+% of the scientific community*. Paleontologists and geologists have traced all primary life forms and dated them in rock formation, a Tree of Life Forms, from single cells (4BYA) to multi-cells (3.5BYA) to the splitting of life forms into plant and animal (3BYA), to the Cambrian Explosion (c. 600MYA) after which *soft-bodied sea-forms* emerged and evolved *to fish* to *amphibians* to *reptiles* and *mammals* to the predecessors of apes and hominids from which man stems; *to chimps/primates* 8MYA; *hominids* **3MYA;** *homo erectus* c. **200KYA** and *homo sapiens* c.

100KYA. Mankind is believed to have emigrated from African c. 50KYA. See DNA.

Days in a week, why 7? It's an arbitrary designation dating back to the Babylonians (c. 2300-1700 BCE – well predating Moses c. 1200 BCE), and re-affirmed in Moses' Genesis, now used worldwide; in other words, when Moses wrote (or spoke) Genesis and described the six days of God's creation and the seventh day of "rest", he was using the Babylonian's week, about which he surely knew, due to the closeness of Egypt and Babylonia.

Days in a month, how many and why? The moon takes an average 29.5 days to complete its rotation around the earth. The fractional days are adjusted via 28. 29, 30 and 31 day-months (and the fractional years are adjusted every four years in "Leap Year", where February has 29 days).

Days in a year, 365, why? The earth takes 365.25 days to orbit the sun once; every fourth year (Leap Year) one full day is added to compensate for the four quarter-days missed in our calendar.

The Dead Sea Scrolls, what are they? They are a collection of **972 books**, of which **220 were biblical** and **all but one were OT**, containing at least *fragments* of texts from the **Hebrew** Bible (**Old** Testament) found initially by Bedouin shepherds in 11 caves in **1947-56** on the Dead Sea at Qumran, near "the West Bank". (Some Jesuits argue that tiny portions of the **New** Testament were also found.) Written on scrolls in **Aramaic, Ancient Hebrew** (both devoid of vowels or punctuation, thus reading much like effectively unintelligible Egyptian hieroglyphics) and **Ancient Greek** on parchment (animal skins) or papyrus, they are believed to date to circa **200 BC** (antedating the NT). *These are **copies***

of texts that may have existed as long ago as 1000 BC. The texts provide fragments of *all books of the OT except Ester* and many other Rabbinical writings and of some books excluded from the Christian Bible (the writings of Apostle Philip, Mary Magdalene, et al), due to apparent conflicts with included books. Some of DSS were sold and shown in exhibits at the Rockefeller Museum; some were allegedly stolen, and most surviving books were returned to the Jews and are *now closely guarded by Jewish clergy* mostly in Israel, many in the Qumran Library and were shown only to "approved scholars" until 1991, when the Jews began to allow public viewings of *photographs* of the DSS. Unfortunately, once the scrolls were removed from their linen coverings, the ink rapidly faded, and *many can no longer be read.* The originals of these DSS-copies have likely been "restored" by the Jewish clergy. Copies of some of the DSS have been published and widely sold and Google made some available Online in 2011 (http://dss. collections.imj.org.il/). *Questions by scholars as to authenticity and editing continue to plague all of same.* The DSS discovery has not altered the Christian Bible, as developed, edited and selectively preserved by The Church (R.C.C.) from c. 200AD until the King James version (in 1625AD), which supplanted earlier, dominant versions (e.g., the Guttenberg Bible in 1452 and the Latin-only Vulgate Bible c. 4th Century AD). In the past 100 years, various Christian churches (many directed by a self-anointed "pastor" or "reverend") have published their own "Bibles" replete with result-oriented commentary and undisclosed editing. The 25-pound Lovett Family Bible (as given to my grandmother, Laura Gilson (Lovett) on her 16th birthday on Sept. 16, 1886) contains the Apocrypha (the first 13 books of the Bible), but these 13 books are now excluded from almost all Christian Bibles; so, endless editing of "The Word" continues unabated, rendering assertions of literal accuracy ludicrous. See "**Nag Hammadi**", a similar library with some conflicting texts that were discovered in *1945, prior to DSS (1947)*.

The Delphi, who was he? He was the *Ancient Gr. oracle*; Delphic Oracle: Gk. Mythology, the oracle of Delphi, a priestess, *delivered messages from Apollo which were usually obscure.*

Democritus, who was he? He was a Gr. philosopher, c. 400BC, developed the atomic theory as expostulated by Epicurus, a contemporary, and, later, by **Lucretius** (Roman philosopher-poet, *The Nature of Things;* don't confuse with **Epictetus** (a Buddha-like existentialist-philosopher). The word "democracy" comes from Greek (demos/the people and kratia/rule).

Demosthenes, who was he? [De-moss-thuh-neez] Gr. said to be "the standard of oratory", taught himself to overcome stuttering by speaking with pebbles in his mouth.

Descartes, Rene, who was he? He was a mathmetician and a committed Catholic (1596-1650). Challenged skeptics claiming that our very existence was "proof" sufficient of a creator, *but he rejected biblical myths* (Adam, Noah, miracles, etc.) Since Descartes, scientists have traced the origins of first life to bacteria c. 4 billion years ago (4BYA), multi-cell organisms about 3.5BYA; all of today's life forms to organisms from the Cambrian Explosion 600MYA; and primates c. 2MYA; hominids 200-300KYA; homo sapiens (us) 100KYA, all denuding a host of myths, e.g., of Adam & Eve (which old Christian Bibles date as 4004 BC, i.e. only 6100YA), Noah & the Arc (dated 2905 in old Bibles), the sharply conflicting patently fanciful genealogies of Jesus (Matt. 1:1-17 and Luke 3:23-38); current Bibles have removed the dates for Adam etc. to decrease exposure of the strained credulity of Biblical chronologies. The 1886 Lovett Family (KJV) Bible has a Chronology of Events as an appendix that dates all major events in the Bible. The consensus among scholars (not necessarily by will of the wisp, independent preachers), the King James Version (1625) is by consensus the most reliable of all Christian Bibles.

Dew, morning (and mist) what causes it? Dew is water in the form of droplets that appear on thin, exposed objects in the morning or evening due to condensation. As the sun projects heat on vegetation that has cooled during the night or is cooling as the sun fades, the atmospheric moisture condenses at a rate greater than that at which it can evaporate, resulting in the formation of *water droplets or dew*; the droplets then evaporate forming a *mist*; when temperatures are low enough, dew takes the form of *ice*, which is called *frost*.

Dickens, Charles, who was he? (1812-1870). The Victorian era's greatest novelist, his plots and prose are viewed by many as the greatest in the English language; like Cervantes & Hugo, Dickens' social commentary led to dramatic reforms in society's treatment of orphans; also penned incredible historical fiction of his own era and of the French Revolution (*Tale of Two Cities*).

Dionysus, who was he? The Greek God of wind. **"Liber"** was another Greek name for wine. **Baccus** was the Roman god of wine.

DNA, what is it? (deoxyribose nucleic acid) It is **the *molecule of life*;** *genes are comprised of ___; instructs all cells*) all living organisms; these instructions are known as the *genetic code; a genome* (an organism's *complete* set of genetic code) is comprised of 3 billion base pairs org'd. into 50-80K *genes. A DNA molecule is shaped like a spiral staircase*; the DNA is 99.9% identical in humans; a human's DNA is 98% the same as a chimpanzee's and 60% the same as a fruit fly – which prompted paleontologist S. J. Gould to conclude "All life is one". *Discovered by James Watson and Francis Crick in 1953* (same year as Clair Patterson dated the earth's age as 4.5B years by counting the isotopes in igneous rocks). See gene.

Don Juan, who was he? He was a ladies' man; refers to the 1600's Spanish literature's many tales of this womanizer, who is best remembered from works of Mozart, Byron and Shaw; cp. Casanova.

Don Quixote, who was this character? [Don Kee-hoat-tay] He is a chivalrous man who aids ladies in distress; from Cervantes' epic c. 1600 hilarious novel about a 1500's knight-errant (whose name is based on the word "quixotic" (too idealistic); *Cervantes' hero* loses his wits and believes he is a knight; he falls into many *comical* adventures. His Squire, Sancho *Panza,* and horse, *Rocinante,* are also literary legends. Cervantes' classic prose in DQ is more quoted than anyone save WS. His saying "God doesn't play dice" was plagiarized by Einstein.

E=mc2, can you explain this equation? *Einstein's famous formula* means that energy=mass times velocity/speed, and "speed" here refers to the speed of light squared; that is, *energy and mass are interchangeable* and the exchange rate is the speed of light squared. (The "c" probability refers to the Latin word "celer", meaning speed.) It leads us to the conclusion that **gravity** *is actually a force created by curving space* and that the earth is actually "falling in a straight line around the sun". Since the speed of light is the multiplier, this explains how such a small amount of matter can release a huge amount of energy (atom or hydrogen bonb). It also tells us that ***space and time do not actually exist independently***, but, rather, only a blend of the two ("***spacetime***", the 4th dimension) and that everything exists in space-time. In outer space, there is no air to slow motion & objects are beyond each other's gravitational pull.

Earth, when was it formed (in a nutshell)? The Universe was formed by a Big Bang about 14.6 **billion** years ago; **earth** was formed from molten 4.6B years ago; is about 8,500 miles in diameter (vs. Sun's 850K mile-diameter and the moon's 2,100, making the moon about 25% the size of earth), 22K miles in circumfrence; is about 88M from the sun and 225,000 miles from the moon). Earth is comprised of 1) upper crust, 2) lower mantle, 3) outer core or "magma" (hot) and 4) inner Core (molten). Scientists expect the earth to be destroyed by errant meteors within 1-3M years. If not, he earth will be fried in 200M yrs., and sucked into the sun in 600M years. See Patterson.

Earth's Key Geological Periods, what are some? Precambrian (4.57Bya—600Mya); Cambrian explosion—600Mya (enter mammals); Paleozoic (550-250Mya); Mesozoic (250-65Mya, roughly the era of dinosaurs); Cenozoic aka Tertiary (65-0Mya). Each of the foregoing major periods is divided into many epochs (e.g., Cenozoic is divided into Paleogene, Neogene, & Quaternary, the latter being 2.6-0Mya, the most recent, being when apes and humans developed).

Easter, what is it and what is its significance? It is the *first* Sunday following the full *moon* after March 21; commemorates the alleged resurrection of Christ; cp. vernal Equinox (when sun crosses equator) is 3/22; autumnal 9/22 (when day = night); cp. solstice (sun's most distant and closest points from earth, occurs twice year (6/21 the longest day and 12/21 the shortest day); see Pentecost.

Edict of Expulsion, what was it? (1492) The same year that Columbus was credited with discovering America), Ferdinand and Isabella of Spain *expelled the Jews & Muslims* by giving them the option of baptism or deportation; but those converted were generally subjected to Inquisition and often death. Many of Europe's countries followed Spain 's lead in 1400's, Holland an exception (see Spinoza).

Edison, Thomas, who was he? (1847-1931) America's greatest inventor was home-schooled. He eventually employed an army for R&D "assistants" and invented: the cylinder phonograph; the disc phonograph; a practical incandescent light; the electric light bulb; the kinescope; *film projector*; he received over 1,000 patents and founded the Edison Company. His most famous quote is, "Success is 99% perspiration and 1% inspiration."

Einstein, Albert, who was he? World's greatest scientist (1879-1955) Born in Germany; raised mostly in Milan; schooled in Switzerland; didn't speak until age three; brilliant but not outstanding student; *failed college entrance exams on first try.* (Giving some comfort to the rest of us.) Worked in Swiss Patent Office when, at **26**, he wrote **Theory of Relativity (1905)**; See his famous formula: **E=mc2** (squared) means energy = mass times velocity (the speed of light), squared; in essence, this says that *mass and energy are two forms of the same thing*; i.e., mass is energy and vice versa. So, there is a huge amount of energy in every material thing (mass times

186K mpsecond x 186K). "C" probably refers to the first letter of the Latin word for swiftness (celer) but some now define "c" as "physical constant"; either way it means "the speed of light". While releasing revolutionary papers on physics annually, *he was turned down for two teaching jobs.* (How stupid can we be?) **ToR explained** things including (1) **how radiation works** – e.g., why a rock could burn seemingly forever w/o exhausting its fuel. (2) Then, what happens when a thing in motion encounters gravity? (3) ToR says that ***space and time** are not absolute but are **relative** to the observer and to the thing being observed.* (4) **Time** is variable and (5) **space and time** actually exists only together, as "**spacetime**" (the 4th dimension). (6) Spacetime is *three parts space and one part time.* (7) **Gravity**, then, is not so much a force or cause as it is a by-product or effect of the warping of spacetime. (8) ToR suggests that the **universe** must be expanding **(open)** or contracting (**closed**) but not static (**closed**). For a while, he held that it was "balanced" or **static** (flat), i.e., his "cosmological constant", which he later repudiated as "the biggest blunder of my life", but, of late, this has regained some support. 2016's consensus favors an open/expanding universe.

El Dorado, what is it? A *mythical* place in Peru, a place of kindness, wealth and peace, a utopia, as written by Voltaire in his classic, *Candide.*(the optimist); cp., near syns. Arcadia; Elysium; Utopia; Valhalla.

Electricity, how is it generated? Electricity is generated in power plants by converting resources such as water, sun, coal, oil, natural gas and wind into electrical power; it is generated by a large magnet that spins inside coils of wire; moving magnets generate currents; electric currents make magnetic fields ("electro- magnetic Induction"), which is the basis for the world's electrical power stations & all electric motors; high pressure steam or water is used to turn a large fan, which is attached to a generator to get the magnet spinning; as the magnet rotates inside the loops of wire, electric current is produced, which is sent through a vast power grid of high-voltage transmission lines to substations, where the voltage is reduced and distributed to destinations, like homes. It was first demonstrated by David Faraday in London in 1802 and made into practical light bulb by Edison in 1878.

Elements, what are they? Science: the *term for different kinds of atoms*; a *substance or chemical* that has the *same number* of electrons, neutrons and protons; so far (2014), we know **112** elements/types of atoms: eg, calcium, coal, diamonds, gases, metals, silicon; the no. of protons determines the identity of the element; one proton is *hydrogen which comprises about 80% of the **EARTH's** atmospherel* air (oxygen being 20%); *nitrogen* (7 protons) comprises 75% of air in universe; see matter.

Elon Musk, who is he? A South-African born American business magnate, investor and engineer. He is the founder, CEO and leade designer of SpaceX; co-founder, CEO and product architect of **Tesla**, Inc.; and co-founder and CEO of Neuralink. "Tesla" (symbol T) is a derived unit of magnetic flux density (or magnetic field strength) in the International System of Units. One tesla is equal to one weber per square meter.

Enlightenment (Age) what was it? re epoch of 1650-1800- the *zenith of the Renaissance's (1300-1800) celebration of reason, man's individual rights, and rejection of doma and tyranny.* Enlightment

---

promoted scientific thought, skepticism and intellectual exchange, a revolution in human thought; Enlightenment thinkers substituted logic-based conclusions for superstition and based morality on logic; its way-showers included Francis Bacon (1562-1626), Spinoza (1632-77), Locke (1632-1704), Newton (1643-1727), Voltaire (1694-1778), Hume (1711-1776), Adam Smith (1723-90). These inspired Jefferson, Franklin et al in writing the Declaration of Independence, the U.S. Constitution, the Bill of Rights, and the foundation of a capitalist democracy and a separation of church and state.

Epictetus, who was he? Gr. slave (55-135AD), stoic-existentialist-philosopher, very loving; his teachings recorded by his pupils in *Discourses*; most likely authored *Serenity Prayer*; crippled by his enemies, exiled, later taught in Rome; *developed a code of morality based entirely on REASON*; a Buddha-like disinterest in personal possessions; *the essence of the gods is goodness, soul and reason*; influenced Marcus Aurelius (the most loved Roman Emperor, an important Stoic philosopher as well).

Epicurus, who was he? Gr. philosopher, c. 341-270BC, *father of Epicureanism* (the philosophy that life's purpose is to *achieve tranquility* and freedom from fear; that the *interaction of atoms in empty space determines events*; that *gods do not affect man*; that *death ends all*); his views are in resurgence; his physics were based on Democritus' theory that the universe is comprised of indestructible atoms moving in a void, unregulated by Divine Providence; he is erroneously attributed with the saying "Eat, drink and be merry, for tomorrow we may die." The goal of **Stoics** is not achieving tranquility but, rather, *not feeling at all*, the indifference to pleasure and pain. **Buddhism** is the only modern philosophy that seems to combine Stoic philosophy and Epicureanism. **Lucretius** (50BC), a Roman philosopher/poet/scientist, in his 7000-line poem, *The Nature of Things,* extols Epicurus, had amazing incite as to the workings of atoms and denounced the supernatural. **Socrates/ Plato** (c. 400BC) earlier introduced introspection, questioning and the blending of reason and morality. The power of thought (the greatest force in the universe) over the body and external events is only now beginning to gain momentum.

Etiquette & Table Manners: Good manners are matter of *courtesy and respect* for others, but there are certain basics that we should not ignore: (1) when you are seated, maintain good posture and keep your elbows off the table at all times; (2) immediately remove the napkin and put it in your lap; (3) do not begin eating anything until the hostess has eaten; (4) use the bread plate ON YOUR LEFT; (5) as each course is served, use the outside utensil (e.g., if there are three forks, use the one farthest away from you); (6) never reach across another person for anything; ask them to please pass it; (7) never chew with your mouth open, and do not make noises as you eat; (8) eat with the utensils; do not pick up food with your hands (other than bread), unless the hostess does so first; (9) to butter bread, use the butter knife if there is one; (10) once you start using a utensil, do not put it back on the table, as it will soil the table cloth; keep it on the plate (and never lean it against the plate, as it may fall or give the waiter a problem); (11) eat slowly; you are "dining"; it is a social experience, not "a feed"; (12) engage in non-combative conversation; ask questions; try to learn something; (13) if you are a guest, make a 1-minute or so toast to the hostess and host for their kindness and the lovely meal.

Euclid, who was he? (325-265 BC), Egyptian; a student of Plato; father of *geometry*; antiquity's greatest mathmetician.

Evolution, can you give a brief history? Evolutionists (95% of scientists, including *geologists, paleontologists, archeologists, physicists, genealogists, gerontologists, astronomers and others*) now maintain that the Big Bang created the universe's galaxies c. 14.6 billion years ago (BYA); thereafter, based on fossil discovery, DNA data, imprints in stone, etc., the consensus re the chronology of evolution is now held to have been:

14+/- BYA Big Bang

4.5BYA: our solar system born in a supernova; earth molten mass, slowly cooling

4 BYA: first life in form of single cells (see Patterson)

3.5 BYA: first two-celled life forms

3 BYA: cells split into animal and plant forms

600 MYA: Cambrian Explosion gave first birth to larger life forms. This was a period in which the continuing cooling of the earth, the availability of nutrients and climate, gradually allowed the emergence of most life forms, as documented in ever emerging fossil-records

530 MYA: first vertebrates

400 MYA: first tetrapods (creatures with four limbs and five finger-strutures)

220 MYA: first mammals (those with hair and who nurse their young)

150 MYA: dinosaurs

125 MYA: first mammals that birthed young alive (not from eggs)

100 MYA: first wet-nosed primates

65 MYA: dinosaurs extinguished (due to KT Meteor +/or minimization of swamp areas)

40 MYA: first dry-nosed primates (a major precursor to human forms)

20 MYA: some scholars assert hominids first appear but no consensus yet

8 MYA: chimps and others that began to resemble mankind

3 MYA: *first truly ape-like bipedal men*

2 MYA: *first human-like forms, walking on two feet (homo erectus)*

500-100: *KYA: first homo sapiens (us)*

50 KYA: *first elementary human languages*

4KYA: first recorded human history is traced by the first written records, which date to 3500BCE to the Summarians of Mesopotamia and the Ancient Egyptians, and, then, c. 2000BCE to the Ancient Chinese; followed by Moses and the Jews, c. 1200BCE.

Exodus, what is it? It literally means "departure"; Gr. "road out"; 2nd book of O.T./Torah; c. 1280BC, Moses, at age 80, took 600K Jews (who had been in Egypt 430 years, 210 as slaves, long after Abraham/Israel/Jacob's fame had been forgotten) and wandered for 40 years in the wilderness before finding the Promise Land, which the Jews then took by force from the Arabs (likely being the genesis of 3K years of wars). All of this, including Moses existence, is disputed by various historians, archeologists, Egyptologists and others.

believers in "the *fundamentals of faith*", commonly defined as **"the five dogmas of FC's"**: acceptance of 1) *infallibility* of Bible, 2) *virgin* birth, 3) Christ's *atonement* for our sins, 4) the validity of Christ's *miracles*, 5) resurrection/ascension; those who inexplicably believe *only faith (not good deeds) can lead to salvation*; see Calvinists and R.C.C.

Fundamentalists, Muslim, what do they believe? They take their Bible (Koran) literally; the madrassas schools, where the Koran and terrorism are taught, spring from this group of radicals. The Koran does repeatedly admonish the faithful to "kill the infidels", noting that no guilt should be felt as "You didn't do it; Allah did." Christian Fundamentalists read the Bible literally, accepting contradictions.

Galileo, who was he? He was the Italian physicist, mathematician & astronomer (1565-1642), called **"the father of modern science"** who proved that *objects with different masses fall at the same velocity* (**gravitational** pull); among the first to use a telescope to study the stars; forced to *renounce his acceptance of Copernicus'* (1543) Solar System, i.e., that the earth moves, repudiating Ptolmey's earth-center theory (c. 120AD); declared a heretic and rendered an outcast by The Church; spent the last 9 years of his life under house arrest; not absolved by R.C.C. till 1992, when his body was dug up (from a graveyard for criminals and moved to the largest R.C. Church in Florence, Italy).

Shakespeare was also born in 1564; Newton was born in the year that Galileo died, 1642.

Gene, what is it? It is a *functional hereditary unit that occupies a fixed location in a chromosome (a linear body of* cell nuclei); an *instruction* *to make protein*; each gene, like a piano key, plays the same note every time; all of the genes = the genome. Our 50-80K genes support our 15-100T cells (consensus 37T). Genes, which are comprised of DNA, in humans, are 99.9 identical and 98% the same as chimpanzees' and 60% the same as those in fruit flies. "All life is one," said paleontologist S.J. Gould. *It's the way that our genes work together that makes us different*...Humans are not only similar to apes, they are similar to cabages." Scientific consensus holds: **Thinking influences GENE behavior**; e.g., the man who thinks more about sex will eventually grow more of a beard. This explains the power of mind over matter, e.g., hypnosis, yoga, meditation & C.S. In time, to varying degrees, we become what we think, believe and do. See genome, DNA, chromosome & atom.

Geography, do you know the basics? What are the three countries north of America (Canada, Greenland, Iceland). **Ten countries in South America?** (Argentina, Brazil, Bolivia, Columbia, Ecudar, Paraguay, Peru, Uruguay, Venuzuala) **Eight countries in Central America?** (Beleize, Costa Rica, El Honduras, Guatamala, Salvador, Nicaragua, Costa Rica, Panama) **How many of the 19 in Western Europe can you name?** (Norway, Denmark, Netherlands, Belgium, France, Spain, Germany, Austria, Switzerland, Italy, Czech Republic, Croatia, Poland, Slovakia, Hungary, Serbia, Romania, Bulgaria, Greece, Estonia, Latvia, Lithuania, Belarus, Ukraine, Moldova) How many of the *16 counties considered to be in "the Middle East"* can you name? Those loosely considered to be there are: Bahrain, Israel, Iran, Iraq, Jordan, Kuwait, Lebanon, Palestine, Saudi Arabia, Syria, UAE, Turkey, Yemen). **How many of the *10 in Eastern Europe* can you name?** (Egypt, Iran, Turkey, Iraq, Saudi Arabia, Yemen, Syria, UAE, Israel, Jordon, Palestine,

Guttenberg, who was he? He was a German who invented the printing press in c. 1452, which some say was the most important invention since the wheel; he used "movable type", i.e., each letter could be reused; his first book: The Gutenberg Bible.

Hades, who was this character? The Greek and Roman god of the underworld; today, another word for Hell.

Halley, Edmund, who was he? (1656-1742) Identified *Halley's Comet*, was a *sea captain, cartographer, prof. of geometry* at Oxford, and the *inventor of the deep sea diving bell*, and the *weather map*. A friend of idiosyncratic Isaac Newton's and an opium user (before its evils were known), he wrote authoritatively on magnetism, tides and the motions of the planets. It can be seen on earth every 75 years. Mark Twain born on the day of one such appearance and died upon its reappearance.

Happiness in Seven Steps (book) what does it teach? One answer can be found book of same name by Lovett, with these steps: (1) **LOVE** -- "One word frees us of all the weight and pain of life and grants us happiness; that word is love." Sophocles *OedipusRex* "God is love." I John 4:8; "I've never met a man I didn't like" (Will Rogers); (2) **LAUGHTER** – "Laughter saves us from insanity...Laugh and make laugh", Voltaire; (3) **LABOR** – "To be self-reliant is our first duty," Emerson's *Essay on Self Reliance*; (4) **LEARNING** – "Knowledge is power," Francis Bacon, (5) **LOGIC** (reason) -- "The most formidable weapon against errors of every kind is Reason. I have never used any other." Thomas Paine, *Age of Reason*. (6) **DAILY DECISION** – In the end, *happiness is a decision* that we make for ourselves, every single day. (7) **DAILY PROCLAMATION** – Happiness needs to be proclaimed ("Today,

I shall make a happy day") every single day. Each of these produces happiness. Collectively, they overwhelm unhappiness. See Kant.

Hegel, G.W.F., who was he? He was the *dominant philosopher of the 19ᵗʰ Century* (1770-1830); runner-up was the renowned Immanuel Kant (1724-1804); heavily influenced Emerson and his Transcendentalists, Mary Baker Eddy (1821-1910, founder of Christian Science) and similar healing-based faiths such as Church of Divine Science, Joseph Murphy (1898-1981)) and countless others. Hegel's idealism = solipsism (self, the only reality); "*The only thing real is the mind*"; i.e., *consciousness or thought creates the reality of all matter.* Hence, *life is perception.* Like the Hindus, Buddhists and Jains, Hegel had little interest in material things. Some of Einstein's and Hawking's' writings support Hegle's views. The crushingly negative Schopenhauer, Hegel's contemporary, loathed Hegel and obsessed over his fame, criticizing but plagiarizing him at every opportunity.

Helen of Troy, who was she? According to Gk. mythology (or, as some say, history), the daughter of Zeus, whose abduction by Paris led to the Trojan War; Helen had "the face that launched a thousand ships", as the entire Greek army sailed to reclaim her.

Henry VIII, who was he? King of England (1491-1547) the 2ⁿᵈ monarch of the House of Tudor, infamous for his 6 wives (two of whom he had beheaded; brutally suppressed Luther's Reformation (1525), but later renounced the Pope to free himself from the anti-divorce Laws of the R.C.C. *and formed the Church of England* (the Anglican Church), which aided The Reformation.

"Heroes", who are some significant ones to know? (some of whom are summarized in this book: Allen (James); Aristotle, Bach, Bacon,

Buffett, Augustus Caesar, Dale Carnegie, Churchill, Confucius, Emile Coué, Copernicus, Darwin, Dickens, Will Durant, Edison, Emerson, Epictetus, Mary Baker Eddy, Einstein, Emerson, Freud, Franklin, Gandhi, Galileo; Stephen Jay Gould, Guttenberg, Stephen Hawking, Hegel, Hippocrates, Hume, Jefferson, Jesus, Kant, Lao Tzu, Lincoln, Lock, Mandela, Marconi, Michelangelo, Moses, Mozart, Newton, Boris Pasternak, Clair Paterson; Norman Vincent Peale, Plato, Alexander Pope, Puccini, Pythagoras; Ayn Rand, Will Rogers, the Romantic Poets, Shakespeare, Adam Smith, Socrates, Spinoza, Saint Teresa, Leonardo da Vinci, Voltaire, plus many teachers and all the great writers of historical fiction who teach us history and the poets who teach us to see, feel and search for the essence of things.

Hinduism, what is it? It is the world's oldest religion, believed by many to predate Moses by 1,000 years; (1) apodictically pacifistic, Hinduism offers a complex *belief in the union of Mother Nature, creatures and life forms*, from which modern humanism likely sprung; (2) involves *meditation-Yoga*; (3) emphasizes *conduct and thought* not deities; (4) thousands of "saints"; (5) defines *god as many faceted*; (6) people *mistakenly viewed as pagan,* because they pray to statues/icons, but these are like the Christian's cross and icons of Mary, Jesus, and the RCC Saints; (7) Hindu scriptures comprise tens of thousands of pages, including The Mahabharata, Veda (Word) and Upanishads being the most dominant; these scriptures include, perhaps, the most beloved of all the world's scriptures, see Bhagavad Gita (Song of God), which was Mahatma Gandhi's favorite scripture. As admirable as Hinduism is, Hindus, in business, seem to conduct themselves much like everyone else.

Hippocrates, who was he? The "Father of Modern Medicine". He was a Greek (460-370 BCE); all medical doctors take the Hippocratic Oath, swearing to uphold his goals and ideals of medicine.

Holy Grail, what is it? A cup or bowl that was the subject of many legends in the Middle Ages; it was said to have been the cup/chalice used by Jesus at the Last Supper; it became a quest for the Knights of the Round Table; *it symbolizes the ultimate goal of any pursuit or perfection.*

Holy See, what is it? Lat. Santa-Sedes or "holy chair" generally refers to the See of Rome, i.e., the seat of power or central government of the RCC. The word "see" comes from Latin "sedes" meaning "seat". See RCC.

Homer, who was he? (consensus c. 850BC) *Greek epic poet* (all in *hexameter*) of the *oldest works in Western literature*; his name likely a *pseudonym meaning "hostage"*; the works attributed to him may have had multiple authors; the *Iliad* and the *Odyssey* ; these epic 1,000-page poems, aggregating 15,000 lines, deal with *the alleged Greek-Trojan Wars* (putatively c. 1200 BC); composed as primarily a series of speeches which were memorized and passed down over centuries, with and without support from written texts in those illiterate times. These works comprise about half of the Greek writings on papyrus. As with other ancient figures, nothing demonstrable is really known about Homer or even if Troy ever existed; there is only hearsay and what remains of his poetic triumphs.

Hominid, what is it? *the family of primates* from which homo erectus and homo sapiens emerged. Homo sapiens is the only extant survivor; **hominids** first existed circa 3-4 million years ago (MYA); **homo erectus** (the first human to live in a hunter-gather society c. 2 MYA and now extinct, as is **ancient** homo sapiens-Neanderthals who lived in Europe 300-400KYA); the consensus now is that *modern* **homo sapiens** (like homo erectus) first evolved in Africa, c. 50-100KYA. While homo sapiens, homo erectus and others were hominids (who broke off from **chimps** about 5-7MYA), they likely evolved as *different branches on the same tree of life.* Christian Bibles, until well into the 1900's, routinely dated Adam as 4009 B.C. (or 6,019YA) and Noah as 2905 B.C. (or 4,915YA). **Creationists** rely on the genealogy of Jesus through Joseph, as given in Matthew (from Abraham) and Luke (from Adam), although these genealogies have only two names in common and, mathematically, both fail to name as many generations as would be needed to reach Jesus. See Matt. 1:1 and Luke 3:23, which *trace Jesus lineage through Joseph* (back to Abraham and Adam, respectively), and name only 72 generations, when it would take at least 120 generations to span 4004 years to Jesus (4004/100=40 centuries x 3 generations *minimum* per 100 yrs = 120, and, as life spans were shorter, perhaps twice 120 generations. The NT ignores Mary's genealogy, suggesting that her "virginity" (which is only mentioned twice and quite casually) was a thought added long after Joseph's genealogy was provided in such detail.

Mt. Horeb, what is it? From Exodus 33:6; The Bible says that Moses received the Ten Commandments from this location. Yet, no one has ever located it. Horeb is a Hebrew for mountain; Syns: acme; apex; capstone; pinnacle; solstice; summit; vertex; zenith; cp. seminal (an event that gives birth to something). The term "Horeb height" is often used to refer to the highest point.

Hormone, what is it? Gr. "arise to action"; a biomedical *messenger which enables our 60T cells to communicate.* E.g. CO-Q10, DHEA, estrogen, HGH, melatonin, pregnenolone, testosterone, etc.. Hormones regulate cell-functions, controlling extremes, like a thermostat or axis. The immune system is enhanced mostly by DHEA, melatonin and HGH. Three types: endocrine, autocrine and parocrine; most are endocrine (released by the brain by the hypothalamus) and travel the bloodstream throughout the body; autocrine and parocrine are released by cells and travel short distances.

Hours in a day, why 24? Ancient Egyptians were the first to use 24 hours for one day, using sun dial-shadow clocks. They called it "equinoctial hours", meaning *equal hours of day and night* (12 hours each). Why **60 minutes per hour?** Believed to have been an arbitrary round number that lent itself to division and the expression of fractions and numbers like 10 (the core number of fingers and toes), 12, 15, 20 and 30, which is known as the "sexagesimal" (scientists' term for using 60 as basis) system, which survives in geometry. Minutes and seconds were not used for daily timekeeping until many centuries later. Why **60 seconds per minute?** Also, apparently was arbitrary but followed the 60-pattern.

http, what does this acronym stand for? hypertext transfer protocol, created by Tim Berners Lee in 1989 (at CERN in Switzerland); is the basis for links that took one ot other computers and protocols for servers, allowing networks, hence the Internet, which included servers and became the worldwide web (www).

Hubble, Edwin, who was he? Edwin Hubble, an *astronomer* (1889-1953) observer, contemporary of Einstein's (1879-1955); he and his human "computers" (observers) *demonstrated that there is not one galaxy (our Milky Way) but billions* (140B by current estimate). **How do we know that distant galaxies are moving away from us?** He also observed that *the farther away the galaxy, the faster that it is moving away from us* (the "open universe" theory), disproving earlier beliefs in a static universe (Einstein's "Cosmological Constant" or "closed or flat universe"); due to changes in the light emitted by distant galaxies, it is indisputable that those galaxies are moving away from the earth. **What is "the Big Crunch"?** Today, consensus holds this implies that the universe started from some fixed central point and had a beginning, *supporting the Big Bang* theories – and, therefore, likely will have an end – i.e., when it exhausts its momentum and slowly reverses its direction, ultimately descending and imploding into its own Black Hole (the Big Crunch); see Big Bang, universe, and Einstein.

Hugo, Victor, who was he? French novelist, poet and essayist, wrote *Les Misserables* in 1862, providing some of the most elevated, philosophically profound, entertaining, gripping historical fiction ever written; it resulted in almost immediate reforms of French laws to help women, children and the poor.

Huguenots, who were they? [Hoog-eh-nots] *French* followers of Calvinism; see Calvin.

Hume, David, who was he? He was a Scot (1711-76), among the most prominent philosophers and essayists in history; a leader of the Age of Enlightenment/Reason with Voltaire, Diderot, Kant, Locke et al; a humanist (morality driven by reason), empiricist (experience determines conduct) and skeptic (agnostic); most remembered for his *Treatise on Human Nature* and many essays.

HVAC" (heating and ventilation) how does it work? It sucks in the hot air from the room and passes it over some chiller pipes through which a coolant fluid is circulating (very similar to a refrigerator); it cools down the air and a dehumidifier removes excess moisture; the hot air is sent to the unit outside the building (the compressor), where an electric fan blows it into the atmosphere. For heat, the process works similarly; there is a heating element, which heats the air in cold weather and sends the cold air to the unit outside.

Icarus, who was this character? Gr. myth: Icarus was imprisoned by **King Minos**, with his father, **Daedalus**, who made wings coated in wax to escape; Icarus flew too close to the sun; his wings melted and he fell into the Aegean Sea – *a warning to those with vaunting ambition.* From **Ovid's *Metamorphoses.***

"Illiad", what is its significance? It's the oldest "literature" in recorded history. Homer's 15,000-line epic poem (c. 800 B.C.) called "Illiad" re a Greek ("Trojan") war between King Agamemnon and warrior-Achilles; usually read with his sequel, **Odyssey** (Achilles trip home); the word "Illiad" refers to the city-capital of Troy.

Inquisition, what was it? Another name for "The Christian Crusades" or "The Crusades", The Inquisitions began in the 1100's and lasted through the mid-1800's. Until **Luther** gave rise to Protestantism (1525), the R.C.C. was the only Christian Church. Before the 1100's, throughout the Dark Ages (c. 300-1000), The Church (operated like a government) *routinely* punished heretics with prison, torture and death. Pope Gregory (reigned 1227-1241) instituted formal and widespread inquiries ("Inquisitions") to stamp out heresy; these practices *began in Rome but spread rapidly throughout Europe,* with Spain's rulers (Ferdinand and Isabella) leading the way with their Edict of Expulsion, exiling all Jews and Muslims who would not convert, and, in reality, torturing and/or killing those who stayed behind and claimed to convert. **Joan d'Arc** (1431 AD) was among its victims. While no one knows the actual numbers, likely hundreds of thousands were tried (as their assets were seized); many were tortured and many less were executed. The free thinking of the Renaissance (c.1400-1800) and the Age of Enlightenment (c.. 1600-1800), and the Protestant movement, finally ended the Inquisition.. The Muslim Faith was born in the greatest atrocities; e.g., Muhammed and his band of marauders (eventually 10,000 strong) spread Islamic faith offering "conversion or death"; his successors did the same and on a much wider geographic scale. Pushing far into Europe.

Jainism, what is it? It is the ancient, nontheistic Indian religion?

The cornerstone of which is *self-denial (a Indian tenant);* near syns. abnegation / abstinence; abstemious (temperate eater); similar to: asceticism (self-*control*); stoicism (indifference to pain or pleasure). Among the most admirable of all belief systems; *founded in **India*** in 6th Century B.C., a bit before Taoism (Lao Tzu, Confucius and Buddha, circa 500+, 450 and 450, respectively B.C.). The word "Jainism" comes from Sanskrit and means "conqueror" referring to conquering self – focusing on conquering desire (for possessions), anger, pride, deceitfulness and greed ("the four passions of the mind"). Teaches salvation is achieved by reaching perfection through successive lives, stressing self-control / asceticism, non-violence (non-violence to the hierarchy of life: humans, animals, insects and even minimizing injury to plants/environment. (*Hinduism is similar, as is Buddhism* which emerged from Hinduism, but Jainism may be the most pure form of this kind of philosophy.) The emphasis is placed on conduct, with relatively little reference to deities/gods. *The Five Vows of Jains"* (1) Cause no harm to humans by actions, speech or thought: actions spring from speech, and speech from thoughts, and we control our thoughts. (2) Always speak the truth; if doing so will lead to violence, one may be silent. (3) Never steal. (4) Be chaste. (5) Do not become attached to possessions; once you have enough to survive, share. *Thought Control:* Most important, as thought leads to speech and actions. Uses *mediation,* as do all Eastern philosophies. Over the centuries, many Jains were killed by Muslims; only 5 million or so survive today; many are in Japan.

Jehosophat, what is the significance of this place? According to the bible, this is where the Last Judgment will be held. Jehosophat [Geh-hose-o-fat], which is a valley in Palenstein; see Joel 3:2. Religions, thus, have been the pretense for conquest, pillage & murder throughout recorded history.

Jewish Friends, what are some good questions to ask them? Lovett enjoys asking his Jewish friends various questions about their heritage: For example: Can they define or explain: Torah, Tanach, Talmed? The meaning of the words Genesis, Exodus, Leviticus, Numbers & Deuteronomy? The word Yiddish? Zion? Yom Kipper? Hanukkah? What determines the dates of those holidays? Do they know in which two books Moses gave us The Commandments? How many Jews joined Moses to leave Egypt? Who (other than Adam and Eve) was the common ancestor of the Jews, Arabs and Christians (according to the Christian Bible)?

Mohammed (aka Muhammad, Mohamed, and myriad other spellings) who was he? Mohammed means "*prophet*"; founder of Islamic faith (570CA, like Christ, he "ascended" 632 CA). Claimed to receive his "divine revelation" from the angel, St. Gabriel, (as did John Smith, founder of the Mormon faith) at age 40 (**610 AD**) and began preaching; his band of followers grew into an army of 10,000 *which spread Islamic faith by force* throughout the Middle East: conversion or death (akin to the Christian's Inquisition, except the Muslims are still doing it). After his death, his successors continued the conquests and religious purgings throughout Eastern Europe – an excuse for pillaging, conquering or murdering others. A classic example of a group using religion to seize power and rule. The **Ottoman [Islamic] Empire** (c. 1300-1900, at peak in 16-17th centuries, covering three continents and dominating Southern Europe), which began in **Turkey**, was its largest extension. His name is spelled a variety of ways, as is Muslim/Moslem for his group, "the believers in Islam". **Islam** comes from the Arabic verb islama, meaning "surrender"; "Koran" means recitation and borrows liberally from and distorts from the Christian Bible, although filled with many more admonitions to "kill", such as "the infidels".. See *Christ (anointed as with oil); Buddha (awakened one); Confucius (Master Kong)*.

Months in a year, 12, why? The Babylonians had determined that the seasons were best divided into 12 periods/months; the Romans re-calculated and added two months, naming them after their revered Emperors, Julius and Augustus. **Why 7 Days in a Week:** An arbitrary designation dating back to the Babylonians (c. 2300-1700 BCE – well predating Moses c. 1200 BCE), and re-affirmed in Moses' Genesis, now used worldwide. **Why 24 hours in a day?**

The earth takes 23 hours and 56 minutes to rotate once (affecting the changing exposure of the sun to the earth's parts. Ancient Egyptians were the first to use 24 hours for one day, using sun dial-shadow clocks. They called it "equinoctial hours", meaning equal hours of day and night (12 hours each). **60 minutes per hour** is believed to have been an arbitrary round number that lent itself to division and the expression of fractions and numbers like 10 (the core number of fingers and toes), 12, 15, 20 and 30, which is known as the "sexagesimal" (scientists' term for using 60 as basis) system, which survives in geometry. Minutes and seconds were not used for daily timekeeping until many centuries later. **60 seconds per hour** apparently was arbitrary but followed the 60-pattern. **Why do we have years and 365 days/year?** *A year is the time that it takes the earth to orbit the sun (365.25 days).* Every four years, one day is added to February to catch up with the fractional days. The word "year" is Old English, relating to "a complete cycle".

Moon, what makes it shine? The earth's natural satellite that "*shines*" due to its reflection of the sun's light; it takes *27.322 days to circle the earth*. It does so in a slighted bent circle (an "elipse") and, as the earth blocks the sun's light from it, the moon's shape varies from full to a thin crescent. The moon's *diameter* is about 2160 miles (versus the earth's 8,000 and the sun's 800,000 mile-diameter). Origin of the word "moon" not clear; in German, "mond" means moon; muna in Arabic means "unreachable". It is about 25K miles from the earth. **Is the moon a planet?** It is a satellite that revolves around the planet-earth.

Moore's Law, what is it? It is a Rule that states: *Computer-processing speeds will double every 18 months.* This term was coined in 1965 by Gordon Moore, the founder of Intel. He has been correct through 2015, but physicists now predict it will end by, 2025 because computer chips can only get so small.

Morpheus, who was this character? The Roman god of sleep and dreams.

Moses, who was he? He who took an estimated 600,000 Jews from Egypt (speculated as c. 1260-1140 BC) in Hebrew means "to draw or take" as from the water, as did Pharaoh's daughter who, legend has it, found him floating in a basket in the Nile, where he was put to avoid execution of all first-born Jew's sons. Moses' very existence is disputed by some Rabbinical and other biblical scholars.

Mountains, what are tallest and most famous ones? *Mt. Everest* in Tibet is world's tallest at 29K feet above sea level. "K2" in Pakistan at 28K ft asl is second and considered the hardest mountain to climb; **Mt. McKinley** in Alaska at 20K feet asl is tallest in U.S. **Pikes Peak** in Colo. Springs, CO, at 14K+ feet is the best known of 14 similar height mountains, mostly in the Rockies, which are the tallest in the Continental U.S. **Mount Rushmore** is the national monument in **SOUTH Dakota**, featuring the faces of Presidents Washington, Jefferson, Teddy Roosevelt and Lincoln, as carved some 5K feet above sea level (named after NY City attorney, Charles Rushmore who searched the title). Carving began in 1927 and ended in 1939. **Mt Sinai/aka Mt. Horeb** is where Moses ostensibly received the Ten Commandments but scholars are not sure where it is/was located, but for tourists, the

Egyptian government has designated a "possible" mountain in the Sinai Peninsula as it; **Mt. Calvery** is near Jerusalem and is where Jesus was *crucified*; the **Sermon on the Mount**, the site of Jesus' most famous sermon (Matt. 5-7), did not identify the name of the mount; **Mt. Olympus** (highest mtn. in Greece 9500ft, widely known as the home of 12 mythological Greek gods.

Musketeers, The Three, what is it? A much-loved novel by Alexander Dumas (1844), the fabled story of a young man, D'Artagnan, who travels far to join his idols, the captioned musketeers, Aramis, Athos & Porthos. D'Artagnan coined the motto, "All for one and one for all." Popular trivial question.

Music history, when did first flute, violin, piano and guitar first appear? 33,000BC: first flute (made of bird's bones); 4000BC wooden flutes; 1352BC first trumpet found in King Tut's tomb; 1000BC a 7-stringed zither in China; *1558AD first **violin**; 1700AD: **first piano*** (the harpsichord was invented c. 1600); Bach, Beethoven and Mozart (circa 1700, 1750 and 1780, respectively, made the piano popular); **1931: electric guitar**; See Bible's dates of creation (Adam & Eve in 4909, according to early Bibles).

Murders, what percentage are committed by family members or friends? 98%.

Narcissism, from whom did the word originate? The word means eroticism *aroused by one's own body*; *self-love*; Gr. myth of youth **(Narcissus)** who used to admire his beauty in a lake but fell into the lake and drown; a new flower grew at the spot called the narcissus; Ovid wrote about him; cp. egoistic (self-centered) and solipsistic (self as only reality).

New Testament, when were the 27 books in such written (Matt. Thru. Rev.)? Consensus 50-100 years after Christ's death; while the authorship is not claimed and can't be proved, St. Paul is generally credited with 13 of the 27 books, Matthew to Matthew, Mark to Mark, etc., and the rest by unknown persons who may or may not have ever known Christ. Some scholars maintain that St. Paul never knew Christ. In 385 AD, Emperor **Constantine** legalized Christianity to keep the peace and to keep the Christian slaves working; he convened the **Council of Nicea**, and the members voted which (of the hundreds of books that Christians then used) to include or exclude. **Name the 27 books of the NT**: Matthew, Mark, Luke, John, Acts, Romans, 1 Corinthians, 2 Corinthians, Galatians, Ephesians, Philippians, Colossians, 1 Thessalonians, 2 Thessalonians, 1 Timothy, 2 Timothy, Titus, Philemon, Hebrews, James, 1 Peter, 2 Peter, 1 John, 2 John, 3 John, Jude, Revelations.

Newton, Isaac, who was he? (1642-1727). Possibly *the greatest mathematical mind in history*. Wrote the 3-volume *Principia* (1713) *expanding the laws of gravity*: (i) things move in the direction pushed; (ii) actions have opposite and equal reactions, showing gravitational tugs; (iii) *the pull of any object is proportional to its mass and varies inversely as the square of the distance between them*; (iv) the earth is not exactly round; it bulges slightly at the poles. A joyless, prickly man, an introvert, who was given to bizarre experiments on himself (jamming a needle in his eye socket, etc.). He invented *calculus* and dabbled in *alchemy* (medieval chemistry). Didn't speak of the bible (to avoid censure) but publicly claimed that the order of the universe was too perfect to have happened accidentally (thus averting exile or imprisonment), but he still rejected all biblical myths (e.g., Adam and Eve, the virgin birth, miracles, resurrection, etc.) Some scholars assert that without Galileo (1564-1642), no Newton; and without Newton, no Einstein.

New York, how did it get its name? When the English took over the territory, they changed its name from New Amsterdam (as the Dutch had named it) to New York, in honor of the Duke of York, who later became King James II of England (1633-1701).

Nietzsche, Friederich, who was he? (1844-1900) Like him or loathe him, we cannot ignore the genius, **Nietzsche.** In his *Will to Power*, took satanic negativism to another level. N's *Thus Spake Zarathustra"* revealed his Superhero (or Super-monster to us), suggesting *the strongest and most brutal prevail* – sadly, a historically irrefutable fact, which does not prove his conclusions that "Might is right!" This son of a minister had extreme contempt for democracy (as did Plato, Ayn Rand, et al), Christianity and women. Hitler induced a relative of N's to manipulate and distort his writings to support Hitler's theories of a Super Race of Arians. However much N has been maligned, the history of mankind (from ancient emperors to Genghis Khan, Attila the Hun, Mohammed, Machiavelli, the Russian Tsars, Hitler, Stalin, Hussein, et al.), tragically affirms N's beliefs; i.e., *Super-monsters continue to rule many societies to this day* (Castro, Chavez, Khadafy, Putin and many of the African countries), although democracy has greatly reduced the percentage of such rulers worldwide. For an analogous treatise on point, see **Machiavelli's classic, *The Prince* ("The end justifies the means,"** being his popular one-liner). N, like Machiavelli, wasn't so much praising his anti-hero as he was stating that "This is the way of the world." History and current events seem to support their observations as sad truths.

Noah's Arc, what is the myth behind it? Early KJR versions of the Christian Bible, including the multi-thousand page Lovett Family Bible (dated 1886) dates Noah's Arc as 2948BC. (Egypt was the world's first significant civilization, said to have begun c. 3000BCE.) According to **Genesis** 6-9, God decided to purge the earth of evil and wash it clean, and *he chose Noah to be the survivor in the new earth*; Noah allegedly gathered two of every species on earth onto the monster arc that he built; then came the flood; Noah and two of all the world's animals were ***aboard the arc for a year*** before the flood subsided. Noah is said to have lived 10 generations after Adam and 10 before Jesus – a mathematical impossibility. Paleontologists and other scientists have found **zero evidence** of any such world-wide flood. All, except Biblical literalists, long ago dismissed this entertaining tale as fantasy intended to convince the gullible and "prove" God's existence & involvement in our lives.

Nostradamus, who was he? Fr. physician (1503-1566) published his prophecies in 1555; he predicted thousands of things and, by law of averages, was sometimes correct.

Occam's razor (aka Occam's razor) what is it? It is *lex parsimoniae* in Latin, which means law of parsimony; a problem-solving principle attributed to William of Ockham (c. 1287–1347), who was an English Franciscan friar and scholastic philosopher and theologian. The principle can be interpreted as stating: *Among competing hypotheses, the one with the fewest assumptions should be selected.* Occam's razor is not considered an irrefutable principle of logic, but its precept is often advanced, as simpler theories are more testable, hence easier to prove or disprove than complex ones.

Oceans, what are the world's five? Arctic, Atlantic, Pacific, Southern, Indian; cp. **sea** (a substantially land-locked body of *salt* water; misused as a syn. for ocean; e.g. South China Sea; Caribbean Sea); **river** (a stream of water of considerable size); **lake** (an inland body of fresh water); *70% of earth's surface is water; 97% saline in oceans; 3% fresh* in lakes, rivers, streams, clouds.

Old Testament, how many books are there and can you name them in order? The 39 books, Genesis-Malachi; pre-Christ books of the Christian Bible, which were written, and re-written over many centuries, c. 1000-300 BC; in 285 BC, Pharaoh Ptolemy II organized the "**Septuagint**", a group of 70 Rabbis, to translate the OT into **Greek** for his library. The Rabbis voted on what to include and what not. Original was lost in a fire that burned Ptolemy's library. The RCC put it in Latin. *The first English translation was by Tyndale c. 1300.* Luther did an early translation from Latin to English in 1525; Guttenberg did one in c. 1542 and King James' clericstook25 years (1600-1625) to do **KJV**.

Know the 39 books of the OT: Genesis, Exodus, Leviticus, Numbers, Deuteronomy, Joshua, Judges, Ruth, 1 Samuel, 2 Samuel, 1 Kings, 2 Kings, 1Chronicles,2 Chronicles, Ezra, Nehemiah, Ester, Job, Psalms, Proverbs, Ecclesiastes, Song of Songs, Isaiah, Jeremiah, Lamentations, Ezekiel, Daniel, Hosea, Joel, Obadiah, Jonah, Micah, Nahum, Habakkuk, Zephaniah, Hagai, Zacheria, Malachi. First five books (Genisis-Deut) aka "Pentatuch" (5 scrolls)and"Torah" (teaching). See DSS and Nag Hamadi.

Olympic Symbol, what do its five rings represent? The world's five, primary continents (Africa, Asia, No. America, So. America, and Europe).

Mt. Olympus, what is it? A mountain in Greece, the home of its 12 mythological gods; see mountains.

The Ottoman Empire, can you describe it, give its dates, and general efficacy? A period of rule by the Ottomans/Turks/Muslims (which began c. 1300, thrived 1450-1700 and expired about 1800), and spread from Turkey through most of Europe, which became, in effect, one massive caliphate. The Ottomans combined love of plunder and religious zeal, as they enslaved or murdered thousands of Christians. The Muslim inroads into Europe actually began c. 1281, but Ottoman advanced and entrenched it. During its height in the 17th Century, its leader was Suleiman the Magnificant. Eventually, it lost wars with other European armies and its area of influence began to shrink back to its roots in Turkey (aka Asia Minor).

OPEC, what is it? An organization which stands for: Organization of Petroleum Exporting Countries; began with 7 Middle Eastern countries and has expanded to 13 or so today. These are not oil companies; they are countries. Controlled world energy prices in the early 1970's, they raised oil prices from $3 to $30 or so and cut supplies, causing long lines at the pumps everywhere. Now that the U.S. has become a major producer, OPEC is losing its death grip on oil prices; fracking is changing the dynamics of the oil industry.

Panama Canal, what is it? Opened in 1914, a 51-mile-long straight of water between *Central and South America* that connects the

Pacific and the *Caribbean Sea*, which is part of the *Atlantic* Ocean. It enables some 13,000 ships annually to avoid the 8,000-mile journey around the tip of So. America; cp. **Suez Canal** (opened in 1869, a 120 mile stretch of water that connects the *Mediterranean Sea* to the Red Sea, which feeds into the *Indian Ocean*, allowing ships to travel between *Europe and So. Asia* without going around Africa, a 4,300 mile detour).

"Pandora's Box," what is the origin and meaning behind it? Gr./ Rom. Myth: The god-Zeus gave Pandora a box and gave her strict instructions never to open the Box. *She did, unleashing all the misery and suffering in the world and leaving only "hope" in the box.* Hence, *Pandora's Box refers to unknown, extensive bad things*, as released by a woman, another Eve (of Adam & Eve) for men to use as scapegoats for male-failings; cp. Pollyanna (a congenital optimist).

Parts of Speech, can you name and define the eight parts? Noun, pronoun, adjective (modifies nouns), verb, adverb (modifies verbs or other adverbs), conjunction (words that join: and, but, or), preposition (words that show position: on, off, for, by, in, out, of, with, etc.), interjection (words of exclamation: Oh! Ouch! Wow!). See participle and gerund. Grammer is to written and verbal communications what anatomy is to medicine.

Pascal, Blaise, who was he and what is "Pascal's Wager"? (1623-62) Fr. mathematician, invented an early calculator, the barometer, hydraulic press etc., from a family of scientists and Jains (extreme ascetics, akin to Buddhism). Believed that *opting to believe in God was a win-wi*n, as one had nothing to lose and possibly something to gain. He *characterized God's existence as a "coin flip", now known as "Pascal's Wager".*

Patent, what is it? What does it mean to be patent? This classic homonym has one spelling, two pronunciations & two meanings. If pronounced "**pat**-ent" it means a government grant of exclusive rights; if pronounced "**pay**-tent" it means apparent / obvious / manifest / self-evident; cp. apodictic (irrefutable).

Paterson, Clair, who was he? One of the most important men of the 20th Century who is unknown; he lived from 1922-1995; he was the most accomplished GEOLOGIST in history. Incredibly, he was the *first to accurately date the age of the earth* (at 4.55 billion years). He did this in **1953** by counting the isotopes in igneous rocks (rocks created by heat rather than by laying down sediments). He also virtually single-handily and against all opposition, identified, *exposed and fought the dangers of lead poisoning* (in Ethyl gas, in refrigerator coolants, by the food-canning industry), which led to the *Clean Air Act of 1970.* He fought Standard Oil, DuPont, GM, etc. and won, but he was persecuted in various ways by Big Oil (which controlled Congress on such matters), and *he died in 1995 without reward or recognition* of any meaningful kind. Like Tucker, who created a better automobile but was crushed by Big Auto's lock on Congress), Patterson was blocked and discredited, although he succeeded in helping the world enormously.

Pegasus, who was this creature and what does it symbolize? It is the most common name for a horse with wings. Gr. Mythology, **"Pegasus,"** Hercules' horse, which is a symbol of great imagination (a cousin of the Zodiak sign, Acquarius, or visionary).

Pentacle, what is it? A *five-pointed star* formed by five straight lines connecting the verticals of a pentagon and enclosing another pentagon; *originally* a symbol of **Venus** which is called both the **Morning Star** and the **Evening Star,** because Venus is inside the orbit of the earth; so, it appears before sunrise and at night as the first star we see; symbol of the feminine ideal (see Aphrodite); converted into a *symbol of Satan* by Catholics to discredit women (by linking women with Satan); penta=five; **cp. Star of David**: a hexagram (SIX points) or combination of two equilateral triangles; worn as an amulet; putatively dates to 1000AD, provides the protection of King David, whose shield may have been so shaped. Make a pentacle by overlaying a triangle horizontally on top of a triangle.

Pentacle   Star of David

Petrarch, who was he? An Italian poet (1304-1374)- *created* the model for the *sonnet* (a lyric poem of 14 lines with 10 syllables per line) the form rendered divine by Shakespeare; Petrarch was also the *father of Italian Humanism* (a pantheistic form of religion that is on the rise today).

"The Phoenix", what is its significance? Mythical bird that periodically burned to death and rose from its own ashes every 500 years; there was never more than one phoenix alive; Gk mythology;

thus, it symbolizes renewal and rebirth and the resilience of the soul.

Plasma, what is it? Medical term sterilized blood; Physics term for *atoms without electrons*; electrons are forced out by excessive heat; *most of the matter in the universe is plasma*, because stars are generally so hot; so, plasma is an *electronically neutral highly ionized* (electrically charged) *gas*; **4 states of matter**: solid, liquid, gas & plasma; see matter and ion and covalent bond (atoms that share electrons and form stronger bonds or liquid glass shields); see atom, elements, matter & molecule.

Plato, who was he? The 2nd most famous Gr. philosopher (428-348BC); he preserved Socrates for us; his *Republic* is the most respected treatise ever written on the ideal form of government; he abhorred democracy, because it led to the execution of Socrates. "In democracy, fools rule."

"Power," in math, what does it mean? It refers to a number being multiplied by itself. 10 to the 1st power = 10; 10 to the 2nd power = 10x10 or 100; to the 3rd = 10x10x10 or 1,000; to 10th = 10B; to the minus 4 power = 0.0001. See Google (1 with 100 zeros or 1 to the 1000th power or 1 to the 100th which is 10 to the 100th).

Ptolmey, who was he? Gr. astrologer (c. 1 BC) whose solar system had the earth at its center; repudiated in 1543 by ***Copernicus***; don't confuse with Ptolmey II, the Pharoh who had the OT translated into Greek in 285 BC by the Septuagint (a committee of 70 Rabbinical clergymen that he organized).

Pythagoras, who was he? A Greek mathematician (570-490BC) credited with *"Triangulation"*; also, perhaps the most controversial of all Greek philosophers; like Socrates, he wrote nothing; he is said to have believed that *inanimate, as well as animate things*, have souls (as later did Plato). His **Pythagorian Theory**: the square of the hypotenuse = the sum of the squares of the other two sides ($x2 + y2 = z2$). Triangulation is a method of determining the distance/length of two legs of a triangle where the distance/length of only one side is known; i.e, since the sum of the interior angles of a triangle always equal 180 degrees, *if you know the length of one side AND the angles of two corners, you can compute the length of the other two sides, hence the distance to the object.* In 150 B.C., Greek astronomers computed the distance to the moon (250K miles) this way.

Quaker, what is it? A member of the Religious Society of Friends, a group that uses no scripture and believes in great simplicity in daily life (rejecting modern conveniences); their services consist mainly of silent mediation (reminiscent of Buddhism); they are resolute pacifists (refusing to fight); many of them reside in Pennsylvania; the **Mennonites** or **Amish** are similar but are distinct groups.

Quantum, what is it? A *specified quantity* of something; Physics: an *indivisible* unit of energy; e.g., a **quantum leap** occurs when something (e.g. an electron) *leaves one orbit and simultaneously appears in another* without occupying the space in between. This theory explains how electrons avoid falling into the nucleus of an atom. **Quantum mechanics**: Heisenburg's 1926 proposition *that electrons are* "at once everywhere and nowhere"; i.e., you can know their path OR their location at a given moment but not both. So, in essence, electrons don't exist until observed. QM deals with physical phenomena at nanoscopic levels; it provides mathematical description of the waver-like interaction of energy and matter. See Uncertainty Principle and atom.

Radio, how does it work? Broadcast radio, TV, cellular telephone and data transmissions work similarly; they convert sounds and pictures into radio waves (for broadcast and cellular) but convert them into digits (for Internet); transmitters make these conversions at the point of origination and receivers reverse the process at the point of reception; the concepts are simple; the mechanics require much explaining.

"Rapture," what is it? Prediction: Based on Paul's fanciful 1 Thessalonians 4: 15-17, Christian eschatologists maintain that the chosen Christians will be gathered together in the air to meet Christ at, or up to seven years prior to, his return to earth.

"Reformation", what was it and its significance? 16-17th cent. Religious movement when Protestants left the Catholic Church; Martin Luther began it in 1525. Wm. James said that Luther's urge to marry a nun was behind his break from The Church. For several hundred years, many churches splintered off his Lutheran Church (e.g., Episcopalian, Baptist, Methodist, Church of Christ, C.S., Scientology). During the last 200 years, many basically one-founder "Ministries" have sprung up (e.g., Swaggart, Baker, Angsley, Oral Roberts), some being charlatans of the highest order, and creating enormous tax-free cash flows. Religion has become a big and very profitable, *tax-free* business. Today, anyone can buy a license Online as an "ordained" "Minister" for $25, which is legally sufficient to perform weddings, etc. and begin proselytizing. Sadly, any smooth talking actor or charlatan can so become a "minister" or "reverend" and beguile the masses and achieve great fame and wealth. *"Rev." Jesse Jackson became ordained in two months by a Baptist Minister*, it takes three years to complete the courses in most religious seminaries. See Luther & Calvin.

Religions, what percentages do the varying ones comprise of the world? No two sources have the same allocations, as there are no reliable records anywhere. Consensus seems to approximate: Creationists, including **Christians-35%**; **Jews.**only **0.02%**; **Muslims-20%**; **Hindus-14%**; **Buddhists-6%**; Non-Creationists, including Chinese. Taoists, Confucians, Japanese Jainists-**10%**, plus a series of overlapping belief-systems, including pantheists, humanists, agnostics and atheists and others-**15%**.

Religions in China, what are they? (1) Taoism, (2) Confucianism and (3) Buddhism.

Renaissance, what occurred during this period? During this Epoch, there was a revival of art, culture, money, trade etc., circa **1300-1800**; Lat. for "rebirth"; cultural movement, a resurgence of learning based on classical sources, often credited to *Petrarch* (the 1300's poet who invented the sonnet); the term "**Renaissance Man**" has come to mean one widely educated and cultured; the Renaissance witnessed a flowering of literature, art, science and philosophy; polymaths like *Leonardo da Vinci, Bach, Shakespeare* led the way; in the R., the custom was *to observe and question*; in the **M.A (c.1000-1500).**, the custom was to *prove* things. See **Age of Reason (1600's)** and *Spinoza*, **Age of Enlightenment (1700's-1800's)** and *Voltaire* (1698-1778) were the culmination of the Renaissance.

Rivers, which are the largest (longest) in the U.S.? Missouri and Mississippi (over 2,000 miles each); the Colarado, Rio Grande and Yukon (over 1,500 miles each).

Robespierre, who was he? (1758-94) French revolutionary who led the mobs Reign of Terror, executing 17,000; he was finally executed by the mob that he fomented into action.

Roman Catholic Church (aka "The Church") what is it? Some scholars claim that it was formed on the "Pentecost" or 50th day after Christ's resurrection when the Holy Spirit allegedly visited the Disciples. I can find no date asserted as the founding day of The Church. The first Christian religion was given its *first government sanctions by Roman Emperor Constantine* c. 316AD to enhance his control over the masses who were increasingly gravitating to that faith. After the collapse of the **Roman Empire, in the Dark Ages c. 500-1300AD**, The Church was the strongest unified force throughout the Dark Ages in the West, offering *the only schools, libraries and order*, even having its own "army" of sorts in Rome, enforcing its faith when necessary (e.g., The Inquisitions, c. 1300-1600). As such, the RCC contributed greatly to the preservation of whatever civilization then existed. The Islamic Empire, birthed by **Mohammed** c. 610AD, was the faith in the Middle East during that time, and via the **Ottoman Empire (c. 1300-1600)** expanded into Eastern Europe. These two were *the imposed glue of the pre-Renaissance world*. The Greeks, Poles and many others renounced the Pope but retained the rest of the RCC, calling themselves "**Orthodox** Catholics"; the Brits did the same, via Henry VIII, and called themselves The **Anglican Church** (which became the High Episcopal Church in the US).

(Locals like to control their own turf; answering to a Pope in Room grew old; besides they wanted to control their own collection plates.) **Martin Luther** renounced the Pope and various Catholic Sacraments in **1516**, which *led to Protestantism* – another method of ceding control to the most local member of the cloth (priest, minister, etc.) Of the world's 7 billion people in 2016, the total Church Membership is unknown, but claims are (as of 2012): 1.18B Catholics; 2.1B Christians; 1.5B Muslims; 900M Hindus; 1.1B Secular/Agnostics/Atheists; 900M Buddhists; 15M Jewish; 200M Other. "*Evangelism*" (independent churches led by one "inspired", self-anointed pastor, is fast taking over Christianity, as it allows endless splintering of Christians into manageable groups controlled by an *individual* pastor, who established "the local, evangelical church". Many are well-meaning, of course; some are somewhat, and some are charlatans of the rankest order (Bakker, Swaggert), who pocket whatever portion of the donations that they like and beat the tax system with impunity. Evangelism is The Best Business of our times, as it is simply too easy and tempting for articulate hucksters to resist.

Roman Empire, when was it? (c. 300BC-200AD) It was preceded by the Greek Empire (c. 500BC-100AC) and followed by the Dark Ages c. 300-1000AD; Middle Ages c. 1000-1300; Reformation c. 1600's; Renaissance (1300-1800); Age of Enlightenment/Reason (18th Century); Industrial Age 1750-1950; Information Age 1980--___). These great epochs overlapped; opinions vary as to the dates.

Roman numeral systems, what do they do? It converts letters of the alphabet to digits; **I-1; V-5; X-10; L-50; C-100; D-500; M-1,000**; V (with a horizontal dash OVER the V) - 5,000. *Lesser* *digits placed before a larger digits are minus; e.g. IV=4*; conversely, VI=6. Super Bowl 44 is XLIV.; 60-70-80 are LX-LXX-LXXX; XC=90; CCCLXIX=369; CDXLVIII=448; MCMXCVIII=1998; and 2010= MMX; 2011-MMXI.

Roman Poets, can you same some famous ones? During the reign of the most beloved of all Roman Emperors (**Augustus**, who succeeded Julius Caesar (his great-uncle) as Emperor) art thrived, including great poets: **Virgil** (70-19BC, best known for his epic, "Aeneid"); **Horace** (65-8BC, lyric, satirical verse, best known for his "Odes"); **Ovid** (43BC-18AD, best known for "Metamorphoses"). Note that **Homer** was Greek, not Roman and antedated Virgil et al by 800 years).

Rome, where did this country get its name? Rome took its name from a legend concerning two, twin brothers, Romulus and Remus, who were raised by a she-wolf.

"Sagittarius A", what is it? First off, it should not be confused with the Constellation Sagittarius (the archer/November in the Zodiac), Sagittarius A is a bright and very compact radio source at the center of the Milky Way, which is believed to be *the border of a supermassive black hole within the Milky Way Galaxy*; more than 25K light years away; it is about *4 x size of sun or 400 x size of earth (i.e., 3.2M miles diameter)*; rotates at about *half the speed of light*; is about 10B years old; best seen in August; from No. America, it will be toward the south and not very high in the sky; cp. supernova.

Satan, the meaning and origin of the word? The name stems from a *Hebrew word meaning "Adversary"*; first introduced by the Zoroastrians (who had conquered Jews while they were in exile in Babylonia (where Babylonian King Nebuchadnezzar had taken them, c. 585 BCE, where they remained under Zoroastrian rule for 200 years to c.350BCE. The Apocrypha (which most Christians have now removed from their Bible, due to its conflicts with The OT and NT) mentions Satan, but Job and Revelation are the only books in the Bible where I have found Satan is mentioned. Loose synonyms include **Devil**, **Lucifer** (Milton's name for him); **Mephistopheles** (Dante's and Goethe's term). Devil has Greek root (diablos) Meaning *slanderer*. Lucifer is mentioned in Isaiah 14:12, referring to "Son of the Morning" or "fallen star"; it also referred to the Babylonian King who enslaved the Jews. The name Lucifer was equated with Satan by Milton in *Paradise Lost*; "Mephistopheles" is the term that Dante used for Satan in his *Inferno* and Goethe used in his *Faust*. Hindus do not recognize any central Evil force that is opposed to God. "Satanism" refers to religious worship of Satan. Rev. 13:17 asserts that the number "666" is "the sign of the beast", which many Christians equate with Satan. As such, 666 is a not a number we want to use. **"Beelzebub"** is another name for Satan, as it's Latin for Devil.

Scaramouche, who was he? The title of Rafael Sabatini's famous 1921-novel about a great swordsman and actor during the Fr. Revolution (late 1700's). In Medieval times, this word was popularly given to *comics, clowns and buffoons*; it is based on the Italian word "squirmish". Today, it also refers to anyone who fits Sabatini's definition, as stated in perhaps the most unforgettable first line in all of literature: "*Born with the gift of laughter and a sense that the world is mad*" – a worthy disposition to which Lovett aspires.

Science, what are the 4 branches? biology; chemistry; physics and mathematics; others substitute astronomy for math; still others include only chemistry, physics and astronomy.

Sea of Reeds, what is the story behind it? The sea in Egypt (aka Red Sea) which Moses' allegedly parted (Ex. 14:21) to escape Egyptian army; some refer to it as "the Red Sea", but most believe that Red is a mistranslation by the Septuagint of reeds; there is a Red Sea near India; no sea has been found on modern maps in the area, only a salt lake, causing geologists to ask, "Was it just another fantasy of the author, whoever he/she was?"

Sphinx Riddle, what is it? In Gr. Mythology, The Sphinx ate anyone who could not answer this riddle: "What moves on four legs in the morning, two legs at Noon and three legs at night?" Answer: A baby first crawls; an adult walks on two legs; an old person uses a cane. **Oedipus** (who in Gr. mythology, desired to sexually possess his mother and kill his father) allegedly figured out the riddle, and the Sphinx then ate herself. **Freud's Oedipus Complex** relates to a son's or daughter's sexual desires for his/her mother. The philosophers (Seneca, 1 BC, and Sophocles 406BC) wrote famous plays about Oedipus. Cp. **Electra Complex** (daughter's attraction to father).

Spinoza, who was he? The greatest of all Jewish philosophers (1632-1677) **Spinoza's** *Ethics* is his greatest work. More of a proponent of pantheism than Judaism or Christianity, although he claimed to believe in immortality and something he called "God" (albeit with Jewish-Rabbi guns pointed at his head most of his days, as a *formally exiled* Jew to whom other Jews were barred from speaking, due to the anti-religious/pantheistic tone of his works).

Stalin, Joseph, who was he? The Dictator of Russia from 1928-1953; he used Communism as the pretense to murder an estimated 8M kulacs (property owners and Russian intelligencia) and guesstimated at 20M Russians in all, including whole villages of peasants to intimidate the masses; used mock-trials to attack his enemies and exiled another estimated 30M to Siberia (poets, writers, professors), where over half of them were killed, starved or died of various diseases. A monster larger than Hitler at his worst. (His real name was Dzhugashvili, which he changed to Stalin, the word for "strength").

Septuagint, what was it? -n- "The Greek Septuagint", in **285BC**, **Egyptian emperor Ptolmey II** formed a committee of 70 Rabbis to make a copy of OT in Gr. for his library; they were asked to work independently; when they produced very similar results, it was viewed as divine intervention; the library was later burned; don't confuse with Gr. astrologer-**Ptolmey** (who held that the earth was the center of our solar system, a view that survived until Copernicus (1543).

Serenity Prayer, what is it? Greek Stoics' Prayer: "Give me the **serenity** to accept the things that I cannot change, the **courage** to change those that I can, and the **wisdom** to know the difference."; see Epictetus.

Sermon on the Mount, what is it? -Matthew 5&6- Includes the 7 Beatitudes, the Lord's Prayer and The Golden Rule) in the *Sermon on Mt.*, Jesus gave some 20 Commandments (Matt. 5&6): no killing, adultery, lying; *turn other cheek; love neighbors; love enemies*; be perfect; *give alms/charity in private;* no earthly treasures; no thought of food or clothing; seek kingdom of God. See Beatitudes (which were given in Serm. On Mt.).

Seven Cardinal Sins, what are they? -RRC & *consensus*: envy, gluttony, greed, lust, pride, sloth, wrath (formalized by Pope Gregory in 6th Century; popularized in 1300's by Chaucer's *Canterbury Tales*; **The Church** reordered them in the 17th Century. The lesser discussed "Seven Cardinal Virtues" are: faith, hope, charity (love), fortitude, justice, prudence, temperance.

Seven Wonders of the World, what are they? This list changes constantly. Some of those included, now or once, are: Egyptian pyramids; Grand Canyon; Great Wall of China; Mt. Rushmore; Roman Coliseum; Golden Gate Bridge; Taj Mahal; some include Niagra Falls.

Shakespeare, William, who was he? He was the World's Most Heralded Poet (1564-1616) the author of **40 plays** (comedies, tragedies & histories) and **150+ sonnets**, the ageless spokesman of all people to all people, the mirror of mankind, with limitless humor, vast wisdom, amazing historical research, limpid grace, quiet pathos, unforgettable phrases, pervasive melodies, singing syllables, the most splendid verbal music ever heard, not of a time but for all time, a mirror of the soul of mankind, the greatest craftsman of words that the English language has ever known, influenced Voltaire, Hugo, Goethe and all lovers of poetry and literature.

"Shantaram", what does it mean? Hindi for "man of peace/god"; the name of David Gregory Roberts' great novel.

Sharia Law, what is it? An Arabic term; "sharia" means "way" or "path"; it is *another name for Islamic law*; which means the conduct *putatively* suggested in the Koran but as reformed and dictated at the caprice of the head/dictator (caliph) of the Islamic group in that region (caliphate, some of which are mobile, such as ISIS); SL covers everything imaginable (crime, politics, economics, hygiene, diet, sexual intercourse, fasting, etiquette, individual rights, etc. and invokes Draconian punishments (cutting off hands, stoning to death, beheadings, etc., a veritable throwback to prehistoric mankind. Sharia law treats women like private property or slaves. Believers in Islam generally seek to replace the local laws, constitutions, etc. with Sharia law. (I found nothing like today's barbaric Sharia rules in *The Koran;* I surmise that Sharia Law is not written anywhere and is purely and simply what the local caliph dictates.) As they reproduce at nearly twice the rate of most Western nations, they seem destined to someday have enough votes to overthrow democracies in countries which do nothing to stop it. (Muslims whom I have known cannot (or chose not to) explain SL with any clarity, nor have I known even one who would admit to the Koran's repeated admonitions to "kill the infidel" and "not to befriend Christians or Jews". Everyone needs to read *The Koran* and take defensive precautions. Forewarned is forearmed.

Shiites, Sufis, and Sunnis, what are they? The three principal Muslim sects. **SHIITES ...** believe that all caliphs (successors to Muhammed) should be his *direct descendants* and, hence, divinely inspired like the Pope. Disagreements over descendants have led to more splinter groups. One descendent, known as "the Divorcer" had 90 wives 'n 100 concubines. M. allowed himself eleven wives, altho' M's *Koran limits men to four each.* Each major country has a "caliph"; **SUNNIS** chooses the most learned to lead them. **SUFIS** are less literal interpreters of the Koran) and are viewed as pagans. Sufis also have the Order of Whirling Dirvishes, who perform a well known dance emulating the planet's movements towards heaven.

S.H.I.T, what does the acronym mean? It's an acronym for "Ship High In Transit"; the stamp put on bags of manure shipped in the hold where water got to it, *fermented it into methane gas* after which it exploded when the first ship's lantern came near it, sinking many ships, a mystery that took decades to understand. Thus the word "shit" is not a swearword per se; it has only become one through usage.

Sky, what makes it blue? Blue light is scattered in tiny molecules of air in the earth's atmosphere, and, because it travels in shorter, smaller waves than other colors, the sky is often blue; see sunset colors.

Slave, what is it and what does slavery generally refer to? One who forced to work for another on terms dictated by the oppressor; **black slavery:** While the term "slavery" commonly refers to the 250-year period (1525-1866) in which Africans found it profitable to sell their own people into slavery to all comers; Europeans and Americans bought many of same. An estimated 12.5 million blacks were sold into slavery, of which 10.7 million survived the ships but less than 500,000 were putatively enslaved in America, or 2% of U.S. then 30M pop and 5% of the Confederate States' 10 million population; less than 2% of all Southerners actually owned slaves; hence, 98% of the Confederate army was fighting simply to protect their own homeland; in 2015, blacks total 40M or 14% of

U.S. 325M pop; since 1860, the black population in the U.S. has increased by *80 times* (500K to 40M), the white population by 10 times (30M to 300M); hence, blacks have procreated at 8 times the rate of whites.

white slavery: Enslavement of whites has existed from time immemorial; that is, whichever peoples conquered another group, those conquered commonly became slaves. In the 16-17th Centuries, the Brits enslaved hundreds of thousands of the Irish. The Ottomans enslaved or murdered thousands of Christians (c. 1300-1650) as they spread the Islamic faith through most of Europe. The entire Feudal Era, which existed through much of the Dark Ages and through most of the Middle Ages (roughly 500-1500 AD) the "serfs" who worked the land were, in fact or practice, indentured servants of the Feudal Lords, and were whipped and treated like chattel by many. Egyptian civilization (roughly 3000 BCE to the time of Christ) witnessed the Egyptians' enslavement of many, esp. the Jews for over 200 years, until 600K Jews escaped with Moses). Enslaving those conquered has been commonplace throughout recorded history and before it. The blacks are the only group known to have sold their own people, like cattle, into slavery. Historically, Russians have enslaved those captured (almost exclusively whites). Slavery in Russia was not ended until 1723 but, in 2013, according to Wikipedia, there are still an estimated 500K slaves in Russia.

Smith, Adam, who was he? A Scottish economist (1723-1790), *the father of the free market economy* (capitalism); preached "specialization and division of labor ; published his classic treatise on capitalism, *Wealth of Nations* in **1776** (same yr. as Declaration of Independence – the antithesis of communism (where everyone owns "everything and no one takes care of anything", as Boris Pasternak observed in *Dr. Zhivago*).

Socrates, who was he? He was an infamous Greek philosopher (470-399BC) best remembered through the writings of his pupil, Plato. His **Socratic Method** was one of questioning, looking within ourselves, introspection; he focused on ethics, the study of the ideal form of conduct (good and evil); he sought solutions to problems by *defining them*; he began all discourse by seeking agreement on the definition of the key terms under discussion. *The best way to change people's minds is by questioning them.* It is impossible to know where Socrates left off and Plato began, or to whom we should give the most credit.

Solar Systems, can you describe them? It's comprised of the Sun (an average size star approximately 850K miles in diameter or vs. 8000 for earth and 2150 for moon) and 8 **planets** (non-luminous bodies that revolve around **stars**: 4 crusty/rocky ones; 4 gassy ones and 1 ice ball (Mercury, Venus, Earth, Mars, Jupiter, Saturn, Uranus, Neptune). The Moon is a satellite of Earth; Jupiter and Saturn (some 10 x Earth's size have many **satellites** (which revolve around planets)). Our SS also includes **asteroids** ("little stars" or smaller celestial bodies 1-300 miles wide), mainly between M&J and comets (small, gaseous elongated bodies/tails whose tails can be stretched for millions of miles as they approach the Sun and which can be seen only when they pass close to the Sun). *Our SS is in the SE corner of the Milky Way*, a galaxy of 200 **billion stars**. Universe has about 200 **billion galaxies**. See planet, comet; Big Bang. Planets are NON-luminous (like those in our Solar System) shine because they are reflecting the sun's rays, then coming from the opposite side of the earth.

Spacetime, what is it? Any mathematical model that combines space & time into a single continuum. *Usually considered a fourth dimension*: length, width, height and time/spacetime. Time cannot be separated from the three dimensions of space, because the observed rate at which time passes for any object depends upon that objects's *velocity* relative to the observer and also upon the gravitational fields which can slow or ben he passage of time, hence Einstein's theory that, ***if we could go faster than speed of light, we could go backwards in time***. To wit, *time does not pass at a fixed rate; the passage of time slows at higher speeds; time warps;* such slowing is called "time dilation", as explained in Einstein's "special relativity theory". Experiments have confirmed this via atomic clocks on space shuttles relative to earth-bound clocks. Therefore, the duration of time varies according to events and reference times (such as the observer's position and speed). The term "spacetime" is thus more simply the fourth dimension. It is the *combining* of space and time. Oddly, the idea of space and time as open was first propounded Edgar Allan Poe in his **1848** essay, "Eureka". In **1895**, in his novel "The Time Machine", H.G. Wells expanded on this theory. In 1898, in his never finished novel, "The Mysterious Stranger", Mark Twain speculated on point. Einstein brought spacetime to fruition in his **Theory of Relativity in 1905**. In 1913, Marcel Proust's novel, "Swan's Way", described the village church as being located in the fourth dimension: Time.

Stars, why do they shine? A start is a twinkling celestial object that is comprised of *hydrogen*; *gravity* (the bending of space, Einstein told

---

us) compresses it; the same gravitational pull that pulls smaller planets toward larger ones, *pulls smaller clusters of matter towards larger clusters, causing compression of matter* toward the center; *as these clusters contract, they heat until they ignite, creating light*; as it burns and shines, it is visible to us; eventually, gravity keeps contracting it until it implodes into a black hole, where it remains (for seconds or for some time) until the *gravitational pressure* makes it so small that it explodes, causing an enormous bright light, a supernova.

Statue of Liberty, what is it? This 151 foot-tall, copper statue, designed by French sculptor Bartholdi, was given to the U.S. by the French in 1886, shipped in sections and re-assembled on *Liberty Island;* Ellis Island, where immigrants first disembark, is one mile north of Liberty Island; the SOL is modeled after the Roman goddess, Libertas; she holds a torch to light the way and a tablet which contains the text of the Declaration of Independence, and a broken chain (of slavery) lies at her feet.

Stem cells, what are they? They are cells in all living organisms that *can divide into diverse types and **self-renew*** to replicate themselves; often called "embryonic ____", they can now be artificially grown as well; they can *repair and regenerate dying cells*; they can be extracted from myriad places, such as bone marrow, blood or fatty tissue; *one may now (2011) "bank" one's own stem cells* to be used to repair one's own body; in theory, they might enable re-growing human limbs; *first discovered by McCulloch and Till at Toronto U. in 1960's*; as of 2011, most research of same done only on mice; sight has been restored to a mouse's blind eye; repair of spinal cord injuries seems imminent; *embryonic stem cell engineering* currently entails: (1) *creation of embryos* at fertility clinics through in vitro fertilization (where a woman's egg is fertilized outside her body); (2) embryos *not used in fertility procedures* can be donated for research; scientists extract stem cells from these embryos and reproduce them; (3) *chemicals are added* to the SC's *to differentiate them into other (needed) cell types*; (4) the altered SC's are *then injected into the patient* to repair damaged tissue, eyes, spinal cords, etc.

Steve Jobs, who was he? (1955-2011) An American entrepreneur and business magnate. He was the chairman, chief executive officer, and a co-founder of Apple Inc., chairman and majority shareholder of Pixar, and a member of The Walt Disney Company's board of directors following its acquisition of Pixar, and the founder, chairman, and CEO of NeXt. Jobs and Apple co-founder Steve Wozniak are widely recognized as pioneers of the microcomputer revolution of the 1970s and 1980s.

"Stock exchange" what is it? A place where shares of public companies are traded; Can you name the largest stock exchanges in the U.S.? (New York Stock Exchange and American Stock Exchange and NASDAQ) Commodities (wheat, corn, gold, etc.) are traded on many exchanges, the CME (Commodity Mercantile Exchange in Chicago) being the best known.

Stomach acid, what is its function? The stomach produces a new layer of mucus every two weeks to prevent stomach acids from eating the stomach; chewing gum causes the mind to send acids to the stomach in anticipation of the need to eat; those acids attack the empty stomach; this can lead to dyspepsia an ulcers, in addition to making the seemingly mindless chewer appear to have the IQ of a chimpanzee.

"String theory" what is it? Maintains that all of nature (forces, atoms and particles) are comprised of *tiny strings wriggling in 10 dimensions*. Articulated in 1985, it is believed to hold the key to solving Einstein's "cosmological constant" conundrum. 400 scientists met in Toronto in 2005 and reaffirmed this and predicted a solution "within this century", unless "faith-based religions cut off their funding". See Bryson re Einstein.

Suez Canal, what is it? It is a body of water in the Middle East with a canal built in 1869, a 120 mile stretch of water that connects the Mediterranean Sea to the Red Sea, allowing ships to travel between Europe and So. Asia without going around Africa, a 4,300 mile detour; cp. **Panama Canal** - opened in 1914, a 51-mile-long straight of water between Central and South America that connects the Pacific and the Caribbean Sea, which is part of the Atlantic Ocean. It enables some 13,000 ships annually to avoid the 8,000-mile journey around the tip of So. America.

Sun, what is it? An average size star (gaseous, burning mass) which is 850K miles in diameter (vs. earth's 8,000-mile diameter and moon's 2100 width); sun is 88M miles from earth (vs. moon's 250K miles); light takes 8 minutes to reach the sun and less than 2 seconds to reach the moon; Sun's gravitational pull encompasses all planets and stellar objects in our solar system; see earth, solar system.

Sun-moon optical illusions, what are they? When the sun or moon are at the horizon, our eyes and brain have nothing to reference them to (the horizon) and, thus, see them larger than they are. Is this placed correctly?

Sunsets, why are they red and orange? The darker colors scatter less than the lighter blue, and sunset colors must travel farther to reach our eyes than does the sky directly overhead; by the time that it **When will the sun die?** In about 5 billion years, the sun will begin to die; as it grows old, it will expand. As its core exhausts all hydrogen and then helium, the core will contract, and the outer layers will expand, cool and become less bright, until it becomes a red giant star. Some scientists believe that, as gravitational pull takes the earth closer to the sun, the earth will be "fried" in about 200 million years and sucked into the sun in some 600 million years. If gravitational pull did not accomplish this, the earth would freeze in billions of years as the sun's heat diminished. arrives, we see only the darker colors.

Superstition, what is it? It is a belief held in spite of contrary evidence; see myth (vague or ill-defined belief). Also, Recall Twain's priceless comment: "Faith is what you believe that you know ain't so." Examples of some stunning long-accepted superstitions or myths include: The earth is the center of the Solar System; the earth is flat; the universe is static (doesn't change or expand); the earth is a few thousand years old, later a few million vs. 4.6 billion today; there is only one galaxy (the Milky Way) vs. 140 billion or so; Adam & Eve were 4009BC and Noah 2948 BC, as repeatedly dated in many Christian Bibles until 1950 or so, when the error became noticeable to most, as paleontologists can date human-like beings 8M or so years ago (so far and some say 20MYA) and homo erectus 150KYA, and homo sapiens 50-100KYA (some say 200KYA), but new discoveries keep pushing the dates farther into the past. Homo sapiens remain the only fully bi-pedal creatures.

Taj Mahal, what is it? It is a marble mausoleum in India, built in the 1600's by a king for his wife, is sometimes listed as "one of the seven wonders of the world".

Tartuffe, who was this character? A *pretender to excellence* in something; fm. Moliere's play of same name near syn: dilettante (a pretender to excellence, esp. in the arts).

Texas, where did this state get its name? It came from an American Indian word meaning "allies" or "friends", which identified the various Indian tribes in that area.

Thermopylae, what was significant about this battle? The Battle of Thermopylae [ther-mop-o-lee] was the biggest upset in wartime history. Circa 480BC when 300 Spartans famously prevented 20,000 Persians (under Xerses) from going through the narrow Thermopylae Pass, saving the Greek army.

Theological Virtues, can you name the most vital ones? The best known are **Faith, hope, charity**/love, *according to* St. Paul, are deemed "not natural to man and are conferred on man *only* by Baptism (if that makes sense to you).

Tides, why does oceans have them? Gravity. The gravitational pull on the earth alternates between the sun and the moon. The gravitational force of both cause a bulge in the oceans; as the earth turns, the bulge follows the sun and moon; where the bulge occurs, high tide results, and, where there is no bulge, low tide occurs; as the sun and moon do not remain in fixed positions (relative to the earth), the sizes of the bulges vary and, thus, some tides are higher or lower than others.

Time zones, how many are there? There are **24** time zones, of 15 degrees each worldwide (15x24=360); the **International Date Line** (where the day begins) is directly opposite the Prime Meridian (by agreement is in Greenwich, England), making it run just east of New Zealand. Cp. equator (great horizontal circle dividing the No. and Southern hemispheres; see meridian (great verticle circles passing thru No./So. Poles.

"Torah" what does it mean? In Hebrew, means *"teaching"*, includes first five *books* of the O.T., syn. *Pentateuch* (5 scrolls); some Rabbinical scholars claim Moses was author and received same at Mt. Sinai (including 10 Cmdmts); others say he wrote only Deuteronomy or that he was illiterate like 99% then; texts written in Aramaic or the then less popular Hebrew; scholars disagree as to the percentages of each; scholar-Rabbi Sharfstein says Aramiac; Hebrew/Aramaic had no vowels or punctuation when OT written. Torah is dated circa 1280; BCE (but some argue c. 700BCE); the rest of the O.T over the ensuing 1000 yrs.; O.T. translated into Greek by Ptolmey II's "the 70"(Septuagint) scholars c. 285 BCE; from 600-1000 AD, Torah was re-written by the Masoretes (Heb. Scholars) who *standardized* prior 1500+ years to enable each temple to have its own reasonably similar version. Scribe originally meant copier or secretary, a then prestigious title, as so many (even Kings) were often illiterate. Many scribes were illiterate too and simply reproduced the letters/marks that they saw, surely making mistakes; See **Tanuch/Tanakh** (OT including Torah) and **Talmud** (OT + 25 Rabinical writings). Today's Tanuch (compiled c. 1985) seems to simply replicate the 1625 KJV in more contemporary language.

"Triangulation" what is it? Trigonometry – the Pythagorean (570-490BC) method of determining the distance or length of two legs of a triangle where the distance-length of only one side is known; i.e, since the sum of the interior angles of a triangle always equal 180 degrees, *if you know the length of one side AND the angles of two corners, you can compute the length of the other two sides*, hence the distance to the object. In 150 B.C., Greek astronomers computed the distance to the moon this way (240,000 miles).

The Holy Trinity, what is it? The Father, Son and Holy Ghost (nee Spirit). ***Only John*** *claims that Jesus said that he was* **God** (hence **Father**); the other Gospels refer to him as referring to himself as "the ***son*** of God" and "the son of Man" (hence "Son"). **Ghost** stems from *Matt's & Luke's* claims that Mary was impregnated by a ghost (i.e., a *dove or the wind*, respectively, which The Church has dubbed "**Ghost**"). The word "ghost" was not used; "spirit" was, until the 1982 Revised KJV was released; see Matt 14:25-27. makes no other reference. Only two Gospels *trace Jesus lineage and both do so from* **Joseph's** side. If Mary was a virgin, Mary's lineage should have been traced. *Matthew* gives 42 and *Luke* names 56 ancestors to Abraham. Clearly, Matthew and Luke did not compare notes; both were guessing about the lineage. Also, if Mary was a virgin, why didn't they trace Jesus' lineage through Mary's side of the family? The Bible gives us no answer, which suggests that her virginity was creative writing added later. Its creative writers simply ignored the obvious inconsistencies (or, perhaps, never read the conflicting works of other authors).

Trojan War, what was it? Based on Homer's 800BC account of it in his *Illiad* and his *Odyssey;* the dates of the war antedate Homer's writings of course but are unknown; most scholars view it as Greek mythology, but it a long and fascinating tale including the famous Trojan horse, Helen of Troy, Achilles, Paris, Odysseus and many others.

Twelve Ulysses, who was this character? The Roman name of the Greek hero Odysseus, who devised the Trojan Horse that the Greeks used to conquer Troy (in **Homer's** *Iliad*, c. 750BC); in **Virgil's** *Aeneid*, c. 15AD, Odysseus is called Ulysses; the Irish author, James Joyce, adopted the name *Ulysses* for his 20th century heralded novel, which re-tells the tale in part. Tennyson wrote a famous poem by that name; See **Ovid** (*Metamorphes*). The *Iliad* is Greek mythology about the Greek wars between Troy and Mycenaean. Homer, Herodotus, Sophocles and Virgil wrote about it. Troy is believed to have been in Turkey. Some scholars dispute Troy's existence.

Twelve (12), what is significance of this number? It is the most frequently used number in the Bible and beyond.

Jacob's 12 *tribes* of Israel;

Ishmael's 12 *tribes* of Arabs;

12 *judges* in Judges;

12 *jurors* in American courts;

12 *stars* in the crown of Mary who bore the Jesus (Rev. 12);

12 *disciples who followed Jesus*;

12 *fruits* of the Holy Spirit (from Catholicism only);

12 *signs* of the Western and Chinese Zodiacs;

12 mythological gods at the Greek's Mount Olympus;

12 *months in a year*;

12 *days* of Christmas (Dec. 25-Jan 5, marking gifts to Christ, inspiring the family-tradition of gift-giving at Xmas);

12 hours, numbered 1-12, in a half-day;

12 is divisible by 1, 2, 3, 4, 6 and 12, and 12 is central to many forms of accounting

12 inches in a foot;

12 face cards in a deck of cards;

12 pairs of ribs in the human body;

12 is key throughout the arts (Virgil, Milton, Shakespeare and countless others since);

12 Federal Reserve Districts in the U.S.

Universe, what comprises it? All existing things in space; approx *200 billion galaxies, each containing 100's of billions of stars*; cp. cosmos (ordered); the universe seems deeply flawed at all levels and, like the earth, destined for self-destruction. As the stars constantly move farther away from us, scientists state the universe is expanding. It is as least as old the oldest objects in it, some of which have been dated as c. 14 BY. The U. is believed to be comprised of atoms (5%), dark matter (23%) and dark energy (72%); the latter drives expansion. By measuring the thermal radiation left over from the Big Bang, scientists determine the density, composition and expansion rate of the U. If dark energy is strong enough, the U. could expand indefinitely.

Is our universe open, closed or flat? Open means expanding; closed means contracting; flat means static. The consensus today is that it is open, because light emitted from distant planets changes in manner that proves those celestial bodies are moving away from us. Einstein held that it was flat but later repudiated that view as his biggest mistake. An expanding universe, most believe, will eventually exhaust its momentum and begin to contract, eventually returning to one point, a massive black hole, creating a "Big Crunch" that would lead to another supernova-type Big Bang.

u/Utopia, what is it? It is an ideal country (from Thos. Moore's 1516 book); root: Gr. "ou" = not; "topos" = place; hence, an ideal place which can never be; cp. **Arcadia** (a blissful place in Ancient Gr.); **Atlantis** (an imaginary island, first mentioned by Plato, where ancient civilizations were very advanced, which inspired Moore's *Utopia*); **El Dorado** (in Voltaire's *Candide,* a mythical place in Peru, where kindness, wealth and peace prevail; Milton discussed it, too, as did Poe); *Erewhon*, Samuel Butler's 1872 novel, an anonym for "Nowhere"; **Elysium** / elysian (Gr. Heaven for heroes); *New Atlantis* (Francis Bacon's c.1600 novel about a country where there was freedom of speech, child labor laws, no debtors' prisons, etc., which some say inspired democracy in America; **Valhalla** (a Norse or Scandinavian Heaven for heroes, a place of glory); **Nirvana** – a state of mind in which you want nothing is the primary goal of Hinduism and Buddhism; salvation, thus a heaven of sorts; **Shangri La,** a Tibetan word for mountain, popularized by James Hilton's 1933 book *Lost Horizon*, a mythical Himalayan utopia where people live long and age little and a great song made popular in 1957 by the Four Coins and the Four Letterman.

Valentines' Day, what is it? It is a holiday based on the tradition/ ancient belief that *birds choose their mates* on Feb 14th, which is also the birthday of St. Valentine.

Venus, who was she? A Greek goddess and the symbol of the feminine ideal; it is also planet since it can be seen AM and PM. It is sometimes called the **Morning Star** and/or the **Evening Star** (altho' it is only a planet) because it is inside the orbit of the earth and its gaseous cloud layer reflects the sun brilliantly; so, we can see it before sunrise and again at night, right after dark, the first star we see; Venus is the third brightest object in our solar system, behind the sun and the moon.

Victorian Era, what was it? The era during the reign of Queen Victoria (1837-1901); a time of great British. prosperity, world domination via its navy and colonies and of peace, Britain at its apogee; cp. Renaissance (14th-18th Centuries) and Age of Enlightenment/Age of Reason (both together in 1700's); The Era was known for unrelenting morality.

"Vitruvian Man," who was it? DaVinci's (1487AD) sketch of a nude man, spread eagle within a circle; it *represents the ideal proportions of man*; DaVinci's drawing was accompanied by his notes from Marcus Vitruvius Pollio (c.75-15BC), a writer/architect known as "the world's first engineer", hence its name.

Voltaire (Francois Marie de Arouet) who was he? (Francois Marie de Arouet) (1694-1778). He was mong the world's favorite philosophers and essayists. His nom de plume is *an anagram of a family home* which he used to avoid confusion with another writer of his day. Next to Shakespeare and Alexander Pope, possibly the most quoted human in history (e.g., "**Laugh** and make laugh"; "Laughter saves us from insanity"; "**Most men** lead lives of quiet desperation"; "**God** save me from my friends, I can take care of my enemies"), a philosopher, playwright, poet, author of volumes of essays (saying he "sent forth his ideas like soldiers, one at a time, rather than in armies"), and a successful investor, *possibly the most prolific writer who ever lived*, convicted of "felonies" (related to bond trading) by the King of France and of other transgressions by the Prussian King but his irrepressible wit and inspirational profundities always made him a hero in both of their Courts, a founder of the Encyclopedists with Diderot (both prime movers of The Age of Enlightment), ***an existentialist and humanist too, but didn't reject God, per se, as Voltaire saw "the absence of a belief in God as fatal to [human] virtue"***. "If **God** didn't exist, we would have had to invent him." (These statements provide more rational support for religion than anything that I have read or heard.) He still rejected religious dogma, biblical myths and abhorred the intolerance and bloodshed that religions historically spawned. "I view **death** as the great sleep, and I've never minded sleep." "**I die** loving my friends, not hating my enemies **and detesting superstition**," were among his last words, a final protest against all violence and judgmental attitudes that are attributable to emotional ideologies (e.g. religions, politics, bigotry and cliques of all stripes); Voltaire, in essence, was Aristotle's "Ideal Man".

www, what is this abbreviation? Stands for: **worldwide web; the Internet,** generally said to have been *"invented" by a host of contributors, but **Tim Berners-Lee**, a physicist in **1989**, created the first large node* (a central, originating point that interconnected URL's) *for it*; he did this at CERN (Central European Research of Neutrons), a multi-national group of scientists working on the border of France and Switzerland at the *world's largest particle physics lab, founded by 12 European countries.*

Wright, Wilbur & Orville, who were they? They were inventors of the airplane in **1903** in Kitty Hawk, N.C. By 1912, one of five flights still resulted in death.

Years, what are some words measuring them? annual (yearly); biennial (every 2 years); triennia (3); quadrennial (4); quinquennial [kwin-kwen-ee-al] (every 5 years); sexennial (6 years); septennial (7); octennial (8); novennial (9); decennial (10); vicennial (20); centennial (100); millennial (1,000); perennial (endless).

Yin and Yang, what is it? A Taoist (orig. Hindu) term - referring to *the positive, negative and overlapping traits of opposites*: i.e., Yang = the *initiation* of action (**male**), heaven, good (?). Yin = the completion of action (**female**), Mother Earth, held by some to be bad (the religious-historical, idiotic view espoused by males to maintain supremacy over females and to continue the tradition of treating them as slaves) In Physics, opposites attracts. Opposites are complimentary and follow one another in an overlapping, endlessly repetitive cycle; one becomes the other, the other becomes the one, and are thus the same, a part of one whole. (*The* **Taoist [Dowist] circle-symbol**, *with a flowing, inverted "S" inside that divides the colors black and white, joining all opposites* (good and bad, salvation and sin, God and man).

The Chinese use lines as symbols for Y&Y (*the unbroken line (—) for male and the broken line (- -) for female*). Y&Y are thus *simultaneously contradictory, complementary* and overlapping

– much like the particles of an atom and all of Nature and life itself. So, think of *Yin and Yang as an Eastern concept (supported by Physics) that is comprised of opposites that attract one another and become part of a homogenous whole.* The term is used loosely to refer to any opposites that attract.

Yoga, what are the different types? karma-yoga (the *aura or spirit* that flows from one's *actions* and thoughts); **raja**-yoga (*meditation*); **bhakti**-yoga (*worship* in endless unspecified forms – austerities, reading, chanting, pilgrimages); and **jnana**-yoga (*knowledge*-yoga, "If you know the truth, it will set you free", the truth being the ultimate reality of the unchanging eternal soul of all persons and things; whatever happens is temporal and has no real effect on our ultimate nature). See Zen.

Zodiac, what is it? In Gr., means "circle of life"; *a **portion** of the celestial sphere* that is divided into 12 bands of 30 degrees each, with constellations (representing 88 mythological figures), the names of which are the astrological "signs" of those born on certain dates. See constellation and time zones. *While the zodiac and its influence on human lives is purely mythical, many humans are superstitious and follow their "sign" and its daily readings religiously. As such, it's appropriate to know the basics* about it. The Twelve Signs of the Zodiac:

12 Signs of the Zodiak

Source: Universal Psychic Guide

www.psychicguild.com/horoscopes_zodiac.

SIGN:	DATES	CHARACTERISTIC--SIGN
Aquarius:	Jan20-Feb18	Visionary—Water carrier
Pisces	Feb19-Mar 20	Erratic Energy Levels--Fish
Aries:	Mar. 21- Ap19	Aggressive--Ram
Taurus;	Ap 20-May 20	Grounded--Bull
Gemini:	May 21-Jun 20	Talkative--Twins
Cancer	Jun 21-Jul 22	Nurturing--Crab
Leo;	Jul 23-Aug 22	Ego--Lion
Virgo;	Aug 23-Sep 22	Service--Virgin
Libra;	Sep 23-Oct 22	Peace Maker—Scales of Justice
Scorpio;	Oct 23-Nov 21	Passionate, Magnetic --Scorpio
Sagittarius;	Nov22-Dec21	Idealistic--Archer
Capricorn;	Dec 22-Jan19	Determined--Goat

World History of Mankind in a Nutshell

Can you summarize world history in several minutes? Sadly, too many college graduates can't list half the events below and can't organize same chronologically. The dates given below are approximate and rely on the consensus as of 2016.

Pre-Recorded History

Evolutionists (which now include 95% of scientists, including *geologists, paleontologists, archeologists, physicists, astronomers and others*) now maintain that the Big Bang created the universe's galaxies c. 14.6 billion years ago (BYA); thereafter, based on fossil discovery, DNA data, imprints in stone, etc., the consensus re the chronology of evolution is now held to have been:

14+/- BYA Big Bang

4.5BYA: our solar system born in a supernova; earth molten mass, slowly cooling

4 BYA: first life in form of single cells (see Patterson)

3.5 BYA: first two-celled life forms

3 BYA: cells split into animal and plant forms

600 MYA: Cambrian Explosion gave first birth to larger life forms

530 MYA: first vertebrates

400 MYA: first tetrapods (creatures with four limbs and five finger-structures)

220 MYA: first mammals (those with hair and who nurse their young)

150 MYA: dinosaurs

125 MYA: first mammals that birthed young alive (not from eggs)

100 MYA: first wet-nosed primates

65 MYA: dinosaurs extinguished (due to KT Meteor +/or minimization of swamp areas)

40 MYA: first dry-nosed primates

20 MYA: some scholars assert hominids first appear but no consensus yet

8 MYA: chimps and others that began to resemble mankind

3 MYA: first truly ape-like bipedal men

2 MYA: first human-like forms (homo erectus)

500-100: KYA: first homo sapiens (us)

50 KYA: first human languages

Recorded History

With emphasis on the fact that there are often no precise dates for many events and many epochs or periods of history overlap with their antecedents and successors, a layman's 300 word summary of mankind might be something like that which follows. In deference to "political correctness" (or simple acceptance of its momentum), BC (before Christ) is below called BCE (before Common Era) and the long-standing A.D. (Latin for year of our Lord) is dubbed "CE" for Common Era (that is, from Christ's birth forward).

1) **Earliest Civilizations (Age of Antiquity), 3000 BCE,** developed in **Egypt** (which gave us the pyramids), and, possibly, also in China, although records there are scant; **Babylon** (in center of what is now Iran) thrived **2300-500 BC.**

2) **Greek Era (500BCE-100BCE),** which gave us the world's first democracy, Socrates, Plato, Aristotle, Alexander the Great, Athenian culture (playwrights, poets), Euclid (geometry), early biology, botany, cladistics, astronomy, medicine, libraries; and **simultaneously in China**, Lao Tsu (?-531BCE and his Taoism), Confucius (551-470BCE) emerged, and Buddha, circa 500BCE, and his Buddhism emerged from Hinduism in India).

3) **Roman Empire (300BCE-200CE)** followed, giving us Julius and Augustus Caesar, Epictetus, Lucretius, Homer, Horace, Virgil, roads, aqueducts, huge edifices, Christ and Christianity; Pax Romana (or Roman peace) existed throughout the Roman

empire (effectively the then Western World) and to No. Africa and even Persia, c. 27BCE (August Caesar's reign – successor to Julius Caesar) through 180CE (the end of Marcus Aurelius' reign); Pax Romana, then, prevailed for some 200 years, an enormous achievement; August Caesar may have been the most loved leader in recorded history; his Essays are a Must Read.

4) **Dark Ages (300-900/1000 CE)** followed the fall of Rome, a period of little trade, the return of barter, humans reverting to very primitive lifestyles, living animal-like in the forests; walled cities, to keep marauders out, began to emerge (feudal cities); interestingly, this is the abysmal epoch that gave us Muhammad (600CE), the Islamic faith and Muslims as we now know them, which was spread largely by force by Muhammad and his 10K warriors and by his successors (califs) and larger armies later, including those of the Ottoman Empire (which began in Turkey in 1299 and spread throughout most of Europe, lasting until the 1920's); **Charlemagne,** a/k/a Charles the Great (742-814CE), a devout Catholic, King of Francs (parts of Germany and France) and Emperor of Rome (c. 768-814AD) brought unity in Western Europe and a precursor of Renaissance culture.

5) **Middle Ages (c. 1000-1500CE but some include the Dark Ages in the M.A.)** saw the Feudal System reach its peak of protecting (and enslaving) people, but commerce, coined-money, trade, culture re-emerged; Guttenberg's inventing of the printing press (1442) led to great progress and the next major epoch; the "Golden Age of Islam" (if you buy that metaphor) ran from 800 to 1258, when Genghis Kahn, the Great Mongol Chief, sacked Bagdad, conquered vast portions of northern China and southwestern Asia,

and became known for his cruelty; the Hundred Years War (1350-1450) between France and England, which Joan of Arc helped end and drive the English out; the Inquisition (in which the RCC tortured and murdered to convert infidels to Christianity) operated c. 1150-1500, but was most violent in Spain in the 1400's); the Middle Ages ended with Henry VIII's reign in England, his six wives (five of whom he divorced or murdered), and his replacement of the R.C.C. with his own Church of England, when the Pope declined to sanction his divorces.

6) **Martin Luther's *Reformation* (1517) accompanied and assisted the *Renaissance*** (rebirth of culture) **including the *Age of Reason/Enlightenment* (1450-1750)** gave history's greatest explosion to date of culture, reason, the arts, a curtailment of The [RC] Church's control over governments, thus leading to the French and American Revolutions, individual freedoms, and far too many luminaries to list (e.g., Luther, Voltaire, Diderot, Kant, Hegel, Hume, Thos. Paine; Leonardo da Vinci, Michelangelo, Jefferson, Franklin, Shakespeare, Marlow, the Romantic Poets, Bach, Beethoven, Mozart). In 1620, a group of English Puritans, who were persecuted in England, emigrated to America, arriving on the Mayflower in 1620 at Plymouth Rock, in what is now Massachusetts. William Bradford and Miles Standish were the noted leaders of what was then a British Colony, operated under rules as stated in a document the settlors signed, the Mayflower Compact. They did have authority as contracted with England, hence their colonial status. By 1750 or so, 13 Colonies had been formed along the East Coast of the U.S.

7) **Industrial Revolution (1750-1950)**, which brought us Adam Smith, capitalism and a rebirth of Greek democracy, its antipodes (socialism and communism), the end of eons of legalized slavery (which began with the Egyptians enslavement of the Jews and continued in Greek, Roman and Feudal societies, as *many conquerors have historically enslaved their vanquished victims*. The rulers of Nigeria sold their own people into slavery, some 13 million blacks, of which 500,000 were sold in the U.S.. Slavery in the U.S., of course, was terminated by the Civil War (1864) and simultaneously in Russian where there many more slaves (all white. The Industrial Revolution gave us endless inventions (spinning wheel, cotton gin, steam engine, railroads and trains, telegraph, telephone, phonograph, electricity, advanced science, heating, air-conditioning, radio, television, modern physics, chemistry, medicine, and astronomy, not to mention Einstein. Unfortunately, much of "history" is the history of wars: who conquered, raped, pillaged and often enslaved whom? (The blacks are but a tiny portion of the countless millions enslaved beginning as long ago as 2000BCE. This Industrial Revolution Era also suffered major wars, including the American Revolution (1776), the French Revolution (1788-1794), the War of 1812 (in which America again defeated the British over rights to the seaways), the Mexican War (1846-1848), the Civil War (1861-1864), the American Indian Wars (from the late 1700's into the 1900's), WWI (1914-1918), and WWII (1941-1945). Americans lost 25,000 in its Revolutionary War, 13,000 in the Mexican War (1846-1848), unknown numbers in the American Indian Wars, 625,000 in the Civil War, 115,000 in WWI and 405,000 in WWII.

The current age might be broken into the following three overlapping segments:

8) **Information Age (1950--)**, which has brought us even more, far too much to list (e.g., television, cable television, computers, the Internet, wireless communications and huge advances in medicine. This Era witnessed the Korean War (1950-1953) and the Viet Nam War (1955-1975) with 37,000 and 60,000 lives lost, respectively. The Civil War, then, resulted in by bar the most lives lost.

9) **Internet Age (1988-)** began when the Tim Berners Lee and other scientists at CERN in Switzerland established the first large node to interconnect URL's. This term may not define a major era. For now, most maintain that we live in "the Internet Age".

10) **Nanotechnology Age** became "the hot topic" in 1995, although it is still just beginning. It will likely revolutionize our worlds in ways beyond our imagination.

What is Zen? -n- *a major religion* in Japan ; an outgrowth of *Buddhism* (a Chinese & Japanese belief that enlightenment and Nirvana can be achieved thru **meditation**; Zen owes much to *Taoism [Dow-ism]* and *Confucianism*, too. *It sees life largely as "being" and acceptance of circumstance*s; see "**stoic**" and the Stoic's Serenity Prayer ("Grant me the serenity to accept what I cannot change; the courage to change what I can, and the wisdom to know the difference.") Zen is, thus, *a belief system that relies on logical contemplation rather than allegorical mysticism.*

POST SCRIPT

The original author of this Word book uses it as his *dictionary of first resort*, kept next to whatever book he is reading, *adding new words regularly*. Memories, like biceps, must be exercised daily or they atrophy, ossify or simply vaporize. We can improve our memories by memorizing. To really know and use our words, we should test ourselves by looking at the definitions and try to recall the word(s) that best fit the definition. Rejuvenating one's Word book or list is an excellent gymnastic to fight dementia. So, if we *review, say, a few pages a week*, we can cover all pages in a year. If we review on a regular basis, it should only take us 15 minutes or so per page or 30-60 minutes or so a week to keep the words reasonably fresh and, thus, enabling us to use them and making us ever more interesting communicators. A great time to do this is before going to sleep. Words can become one of the games of your life, always improving your ability to communicate and others' perception of you.

If you have words or facts that you believe should have been included in this book, or any comments that you'd like to make, PLEASE email the author: info@leeglovett.com.

If you'd like a gift copy of the Kindle version of this book, just email the author. While the author reserves the right to discontinue these gifts at any time, he has every intention of continuing this practice, as long as volume and time permit.

Appendix 1

BOOKS OF THE CHRISTIAN BIBLE

Old Testament: Genesis -- Zechariah (39 books)

New Testament: Matthew -- Revelations (27 books)

OLD TESTAMENT:

Genesis

Exodus

Leviticus

Numbers

Dueterononomy

Joshua

Judges

Ruth

1 Samuel

2 Samuel

1 Kings

2 Kings

1 Chronicals

2 Chronicals

Ezra

Nehemiah

Ester

Job

Psalms
Proverbs
Ecclesiastes
Song of Songs
Isaiah
Jeremiah
Lamentations
Ezekiel
Daniel
Hosea
Joel
Amos
Obadiah
Jonah
Micha
Nahum
Habakkuk
Zephania
Haggai
Zechariah
Malachi

NEW TESTAMENT:

Matthew
Mark
Luke
John
Acts
Romans

1 Corinthians

2 Corinthians

Galatians

Ephesians

Philippians

Colossians

1 Thessalonians

2 Thessalonians

1 Timothy

2 Timothy

Titus

Philemon

Hebrews

James

1 Peter

2 Peter

1 John

2 John

3 John

Jude

Revelation

About the Authors

Lee G. Lovett's father, Eliot C. Lovett, and aunt, Laura E. Lovett, were word-lovers of the highest order. Both graduated Magna Cum Laude as English Majors from Harvard and Radcliff (now part of Harvard) and made it a habit to carry small dictionaries on their persons much of the time. So, Lee G. Lovett (Lee) was raised in a home where words were a common topic of discussion; his father and aunt taught that words were like people; they had histories and told interesting stories. Lee and his brother, Bob, joined them as a lovers of English courses and the English language.

When Lee was battling a stuttering problem, mainly in his teens and twenties, he decided that massively expanding his vocabulary would give him a repository of synonyms to help him avert stuttering-incidents. So, word-memorization became a lifestyle. Then, after graduating from law school, Lee became a voracious reader, consuming, on average, a book a week for over fifty years, and, from each book, he faithfully added virtually all unknown words to his own word list. Lee began to add facts that he was embarrassed not to know.

Then, in Lee's 2016 1st Edition of "Stuttering & Anxiety Self-Cures", he wrote that vocabulary-expansion became one of the tools that he used to defeat stuttering. His readers urged him to publish his word list, which became "WORDS You Need to Know", which he released later in the same year.

In 2017, it became apparent that 1ˢᵗ Edition was in need of significant revisions, additions and more editing. Lee's grandson, Lee G. Lovett III (Lee III) volunteered to do this and thus became the co-author of this 2ⁿᵈ Edition. Lee III committed to publish later editions, as the need became apparent.

Lee (I) began his career as a door-to-door salesman for an electronics company. He later practiced law and authored several books on communications law, and co-founded something around 100 radio, cable TV and telephone-related companies. For more about Lee, see http://leeglovett.com/about/ and also see https://speechanxietyanonymous.org/ and https://www.youtube.com/LeeLovettSpeechWhisperer. He enjoys a long marriage to Lynda Barnes Lovett and four sons, 13 grandchildren (including Lee III) and one great grandchild. Readers are invited to contact Lee at info@leeglovett.com.

Lee III has embraced Clan Lovett's etymological affinities, becoming a devotee of words and this book. When it became apparent that the 1ˢᵗ Edition would not be revised and expanded except by another editor, Lee III volunteered to do it and, thus, became co-author of the 2ⁿᵈ Edition. Lee III graduated with honors from the University of Maryland, College Park, with a Bachelor of Arts in Psychology, and a minor in Entrepreneurship & Innovation. He is currently (2018) enrolled at the University of Maryland, Baltimore County, pursuing a Master's degree in Clinical Social Work. Within the next five years, he hopes to open a private practice, where he can assist individuals struggling with various mental illnesses. Lee also plans to attain further education in computer science and neuroplasticity, and potentially achieve a PhD in one of these evolving, dynamic fields.

You can reach to Lee III at info@lglovett3.com

Other Books
by LEE LOVETT

Happiness in Seven Steps

The Watergate Rhymes

Stuttering & Anxiety Self-Cures 1st Edition (2016)
Stuttering & Anxiety Self-Cures 2nd Edition (2017)
(available in English, French, Chinese and Hindi)
Stuttering & Anxiety Self-Cures 3rd Edition (2018)

All available on Amazon as Kindle. Paperback and Audio Books

Interpreting the Rules & Regulations
of The Federal Communications Commission
(1965, 1966 & 1968, Tab Books (McGraw Hill))
No longer in print